TABLE OF CONTENTS

Preface 9

Introduction 11

Chapter 1.   Economic Growth in the Twentieth Century 13
Chapter 2.   The International Economy in the Twentieth Century 25
Chapter 3.   Phases of Development 31
Chapter 4.   Performance and Policy in a Liberal World Order 1900-13 43
Chapter 5.   Wars, Depression and Autarky 1913-50 51
Chapter 6.   The Postwar Golden Age : 1900-73 65
Chapter 7.   The Slowdown in the World Economy Since 1973 85
Chapter 8.   Conclusions 105

Appendix A.   Estimates of GDP Level 111
Appendix B.   Estimates of GDP Growth 114
Appendix C.   Population, Employment and Education 127
Appendix D.   Exports and Related Items 137

LIST OF TABLES

Text

1.1   The "World" Economy and its Components 1900-87 14
1.2   Individual Country Growth Performance 1900-87 15
1.3   GDP Per Capita in International Dollars (1980 Prices) 19
1.4   Long term Changes in Structure of Employment and Output 20
1.5   Growth Accounts for 5 OECD Countries 1913-84 22

2.1   World Trade and its Components 1900-86 26
2.2   Export Performance of Individual Countries 1900-86 27
2.3   Ranking of Top 10 Countries in 1900 and 1987 29
2.4   Gross Value of Foreign Capital in Developing Countries 1870-1985 30

3.1   Quantitative Evidence of the Existence of Separate Phases 32
3.2   Per Capita Real GDP Growth 1900-87 35
3.3   Real GDP Growth 1900-87 36
3.4   Annual Indicators of Characteristics of Phases III and IV for 16 OECD Countries . 38
3.5   Annual Indicators of Characteristics of Phases III and IV for 6 Latin American
       Countries 39
3.6   Annual Indicators of Characteristics of Phases III and IV for 9 Asian Countries . 40

4.1   Exports Per Capita 1900-86 44
4.2   Foreign Capital (Portfolio and Direct) around 1913 45

4.3	Gold/Gold Exchange Standards 1821-1936	46
4.4	Average Tariff Levels 1913-25	47
4.5	Relative Density of Railway Infrastructure in 1913	48
5.1	Fiscal Outcomes : General Government Net Lending as a Proportion of GDP at Current Prices, 1929-38	54
5.2	Indicators of Recession and Recovery in Western Countries in the 1930s	55
5.3	Regional Impact of World Depression, 1929-38	57
5.4	Dimensions of Foreign Presence Under Colonialism	60
5.5	Per Capita Net Foreign Capital Stock (Portfolio and Direct) in 1938	61
6.1	Variations in Export Performance 1900-86	67
6.2	Experience of Inflation 1900-86	70
6.3	Total Government Expenditure as a Percentage of GDP at Current Prices, 1913-86	71
6.4	Inequality of Pre-Tax Income of Households Around 1970	71
6.5	Rates of Growth of Fixed Capital Stock	74
6.6	Ratio of Gross Domestic Investment to GDP at Current Market Prices 1950-86	75
6.7	External Finance as a Percentage of GDP at Current Market Prices 1950-86	76
6.8	Years of Education Per Person Aged 15 and Over	78
6.9	Rates of Population Growth 1900-87	79
6.10	Comparative Output, Inputs and Productivity Performance 1950-73	81
6.11	Per Capita Growth Indicators 1950-73	82
7.1	Economic Growth Experience of 126 Countries 1950-87	85
7.2	OECD Productivity Growth (GDP per Man Hour) 1900-86	88
7.3	Comparative Levels of OECD Productivity (GDP per Man Hour) 1900-86	89
7.4	Domestic Energy Requirement and Net Imports 1973-86	90
7.5	Comparative Output, Inputs and Productivity Performance 1973-84	91
7.6	Import Experience of OECD Countries 1950-86	92
7.7	External Debt 1973-86, Debt and Exports Per Capita in 1986	93
7.8	Productivity Growth (GDP per Person Employed) in Latin America 1950-86	94
7.9	Comparative Levels of Productivity in Latin America 1950-86	94
7.10	Ratio of Asian and Latin American Manufactured to Total Commodity Exports 1953-86	96
7.11	Productivity Growth (GDP per Person Employed) in Asian Countries 1950-86	98
7.12	Comparative Levels of Productivity in Asia 1950-86	99
8.1	Hypothetical Levels of GDP, Population and GDP Per Capita in the Year 2010 in Top 10 Countries if 1973-87 Trends Continue	107

Appendices

A-1	Real GDP Per Capita, Population and Total GDP Levels in 1980 in International Dollars	112
A-2	Total GDP in International Dollars (1980 Prices) 1900-87	113
B-1	GDP Indices for 16 OECD Countries, Selected Years, 1700-1912	119
B-2	GDP Indices for 16 OECD Countries 1913-49	120
B-3	GDP Indices for 16 OECD Countries 1950-87	122
B-4	GDP Indicators for 9 Asian Countries 1900-87	124
B-5	GDP Indicators for 6 Latin American Countries and USSR 1900-87	125
B-6	GDP Indices for 6 Other OECD Countries 1900-87	126
B-7	GDP Indices for Eastern Europe 1913-87	126
C-1	Population of OECD Countries 1820-1987	128
C-2	Population in Our 32 Country Sample	128
C-3	Population of Asian Countries 1820-1987	129
C-4	Population of Latin America and USSR 1820-1987	130

C-5	Population of Other OECD Countries 1820-1987	131
C-6	Population of Eastern Europe 1913-87	131
C-7	Employment in OECD Countries 1900-86	132
C-8	Hours Worked Per Person Per Year in OECD Countries and the USSR 1900-86 .	132
C-9	Employment in Non-OECD Countries 1950-86	133
C-10	Distribution of Employment by Sector 1950 and 1980 : OECD Countries	134
C-11	Distribution of Employment by Sector 1950 and 1980 : Developing Countries . .	135
C-12	Average Years of Formal Educational Experience of Population Aged 15-64 in 1950 and 1980	136
D-1	Value of Exports f.o.b.	138
D-2	Volume of Exports : OECD Countries 1900-86	139
D-3	Volume of Exports : Non-OECD Countries 1900-86	140
D-4	Exports at 1980 Prices 1900-38	141
D-5	Exports at 1980 Prices 1950-86	142
D-6	Ratio of Merchandise Exports to GDP at Current Market Prices	143
D-7	Average Ratio of Exports f.o.b. to Imports c.i.f. 1900-86	144
D-8	Carrying Capacity of World Merchant Shipping 1800-1950	145
D-9	Exchange Rates 1900-73	145
D-10	Total International Reserves of OECD Countries 1950-87	146
D-11	Capital Flows from DAC Countries to Developing Countries 1950-87	147

LIST OF GRAPHS

1.	GDP of the OECD Countries and the USSR 1900-87	16
2.	GDP of 9 Asian and 6 Latin American Countries 1900-87	16
3.	GDP Per Capita in 16 OECD Countries	17
4.	Exports at 1980 Prices 1900-86	28
5.	Share of Exports in GDP	28
6.	World Export Unit Value Index 1870-1986	87

PREFACE

The world we live in is changing rapidly. Long held stereotypes about West and East are disintegrating. The idea of a homogeneous Third World is no longer tenable, given rapid growth in Asia, negative growth in Africa, and stagnation in Latin America. The instruments and goals of economic policy have changed drastically in the past decade. If we are to understand the present and develop future policy options in a creative way, it is essential to have as clear a view as we can on how we got to where we are.

Most studies on economic and social development experiences are undertaken on a cross section basis, i.e., a comparison at one point in time of how different countries perform economically and socially. Much rarer are the studies that pool comparative and time series analyses. In the Alternative Development Strategies programme of the Development Centre, we have set out to do both types of studies. The present study is unique in the sense that it looks at the development experiences of different parts of the world throughout the twentieth century.

Angus Maddison has thus provided a succinct view of twentieth century experience in the major parts of the world economy–East and West, North and South. He has managed to develop and apply the same sort of quantitative tools to assess past performance which OECD uses to assess the present. He provides an illuminating perspective on the "phase" in which we now operate. Although it is full of political promise–for peace and democracy–it is an economic second-best compared with the golden quarter century we enjoyed until 1973. In most parts of the world economy, there is clearly scope for improvement in performance through better policy.

I can therefore commend this bold and imaginative study to readers interested in policies for growth and development and to all those interested in the application of quantitative analytic methods to comparative economic history.

Angus Maddison can draw on wide experience in surveying the world economy. He was head of the Economics Division in OEEC, responsible for analysing developments in Member countries in the 1950s. He was a director in the development department of OECD and one of the first fellows of our Development Centre. He has been a policy advisor to government in Brazil, Greece, Ghana, Pakistan. He returned to OECD in the 1970s to work on problems of unemployment, education and income distribution. Since 1978 he has been professor of economics at the University of Groningen in the Netherlands, working on problems of growth and development.

Louis Emmerij
President, OECD Development Centre

June 1989

9

INTRODUCTION

This is an essay in comparative economic history, using quantitative growth accounts to marshal much of the evidence. It involves a systematic confrontation of levels of performance and rates of growth across countries, as well as an attempt to give an aggregate picture and examine interrelations between different parts of the world economy.

Although there is heavy emphasis on measurable supply-side influences, strong emphasis is also given to the role of policy and institutions, both national and international. It analyses changes in macroeconomic momentum in the course of the century and defines the policy mix which characterised these phases.

Whilst there is systematic scrutiny of the evidence to hand, there is little reference to the experience of countries outside our sample for which quantitative evidence is generally poorer. This involves some loss of generality, but the procedures and analysis are more transparent than is the case with maximalist approaches or typological clustering, where performance of individual countries and weaknesses in their statistics sometimes disappear behind a veil of anonymity.

The systematic accumulation of standardised data has progressed a good deal in the past forty years but there are still substantial gaps and variations in the quality of the information. This made it impossible to cover countries in Africa and the Middle East for which long run historical estimates are as yet skimpy.

The sample of 32 countries represents about four fifths of world output and population. It probably embraces the full range of twentieth century growth experience. We are unlikely to discover countries which had faster per capita growth than Japan or which made less progress than Bangladesh. It also covers practically the whole span of per capita income levels, with a range of 32:1 from the United States to Bangladesh. However, the exclusion of very small countries, of Africa and the Middle East, mean that the full array of policy experience has not been explored.

Sources and measurement procedures are described rather fully in the appendices so that the reader may judge the quality of the evidence. For the GDP series, a good deal of annual data are given for the benefit of those who may wish to deploy a different periodicity, or look more closely at business cycle phenomena. Those who wish to make alternative regional aggregates can do so easily, as the country information and weights are given in full.

Our OECD group is limited to sixteen high income countries, but figures for GDP and population for six other member countries are included in the appendix (Tables B-6 and C-5) for those who wish to get a fuller picture for the OECD as a whole. Estimates of GDP and population in seven East European countries are also included (Tables B-7 and C-6) for those who wish to trace developments in the communist world, outside the USSR. Table 7.1 gives estimates of GDP and GDP per capita for 126 countries for 1950-87.

I am very grateful to Louis Emmerij for commissioning this study, for the freedom he gave me in writing it, and to his patience in waiting for the results. Michèle Fleury-Brousse and Dirk Pilat were very helpful in putting the statistical material into graphical form. William Baumol, Colm Foy, Charles Kindleberger and Jan Pen gave me useful comments on drafts of the study. Riitta Hjerppe, Olle Krantz and Malcolm Urquhart provided the latest revisions for GDP series for Finland, Sweden and Canada. Bevan Stein gave me useful advice on DAC statistics. Whilst writing it I also benefitted from comments received in seminars in the universities of Berlin, Bielefeld, Geneva, Groningen, Lund and Yale, the Colegio de Mexico, the International Development Centre of Japan, the ISS in the Hague and ECLAC in Santiago. I am also grateful for the hospitality of St. Antony's College Oxford and the Library of the Oxford Institute of Statistics from which I benefitted in the Summer of 1988.

Chapter 1

ECONOMIC GROWTH IN THE TWENTIETH CENTURY

This study analyses twentieth century growth–its magnitude, characteristics and causes. It concentrates on a sample of 32 countries in Latin America, Asia, the OECD area and the USSR. They are only a fifth of the 160 nations in the UN, but in 1980 they represented 85 per cent of world GDP, 76 per cent of world population and 79 per cent of world exports, i.e. around four fifths of the world total in each major dimension. Their aggregate growth experience is probably reasonably representative for the world as a whole[1].

Table 1.1 summarises performance in the major regions. "World" GDP (i.e. the aggregate for our 32 countries) rose thirteenfold between 1900 and 1987, i.e. a compound growth of 3 per cent a year. Latin America did best. It was least affected by the two world wars, and had the quickest population growth; there the aggregate product increased 32 fold–an average of 4.1 per cent a year. Aggregate growth in the OECD countries was 3 per cent a year. Asia showed the least progress with a rise of 2.7 per cent a year.

Absolute levels of per capita income have increased very substantially. They were more than three times bigger in Asia, on average, in 1987 than in 1900, and nearly five times as high in Latin America. In OECD countries they rose nearly sixfold, and in the USSR more than sevenfold.

Table 1.2 shows the record for individual countries. Taiwan and Brazil had the fastest GDP growth, with rates of 5.1 and 4.8 per cent respectively. The slowest, with 1.6 per cent a year, was Bangladesh. In per capita terms, Japan did best, at 3.1 per cent a year, followed by Taiwan, with 2.8 per cent. The slowest were Bangladesh with virtually no net progress and India which averaged only 0.6 per cent a year. Six developing countries had less per capita growth than Australia, the laggard within the OECD group, and only three (Brazil, Korea and Taiwan) did better than the OECD average.

In all areas, performance accelerated in the second half of the century. Total output of the 32 countries grew by 2.1 per cent a year to 1950, and has since averaged 4.2 per cent. The acceleration was most marked in Asia, where growth since 1950 has been eight times as fast as in 1900-50. It was least marked in Latin America and the Soviet Union, but was nevertheless appreciable in both cases.

A central and striking feature differentiating nations is the disparity in per capita income levels. The average OECD level was nearly five times that in Asia and three times the Latin American level in 1900. These regional gaps have widened since, even though OECD GDP growth was the same as the 32 country average[2]. The apparent

13

Table 1.1. **The "world" economy and its components, 1900-87**

	16 OECD countries	9 Asian countries	6 Latin American countries	USSR	32 country total
a) GDP in billion "international" dollars at 1980 prices					
1900	603.1	303.5	30.3	98.0	1 035.0
1987	7 759.3	3 203.1	982.2	1 683.8	13 628.5
b) Population (million persons at mid-year)					
1900	310.0	749.9	47.0	123.0	1 230.0
1987	700.7	2 405.3	316.1	283.1	3 705.2
c) Per capita GDP in "international" dollars at 1980 prices					
1900	1 946	405	645	797	841
1987	11 073	1 332	3 107	5 948	3 678
d) Rate of growth of GDP (annual average compound rate)					
1900-87	3.0	2.7	4.1	3.3	3.0
e) Rate of growth of population (annual average compound rate)					
1900-50	1.3	0.8	1.9	0.8	1.0
1950-87	0.5	2.1	2.6	1.2	1.7
1900-87	0.9	1.3	2.2	1.0	1.3
f) Rate of growth of per capita GDP (annual average compound rate)					
1900-50	1.1	− 0.2	1.5	2.1	1.1
1950-87	3.3	3.5	2.2	2.6	2.5
1900-87	2.0	1.4	1.8	2.3	1.7

Sources: Appendix tables. In this table regional per capita incomes are weighted averages as distinct from the arithmetic averages of Table 1.3.

contradiction is resolved when we look at population growth. In OECD countries this was notably slower, particularly after 1950, when it was only 0.5 per cent a year compared with 2.6 per cent in Latin America and 2.1 per cent in Asia.

In 1987, the average gap between OECD per capita income and that of Asia was over 8:1; the gap was 3.6:1 for OECD compared with Latin America. In 1987 the gap between the poorest country, Bangladesh, and the richest was 36:1; in 1900, the spread was much smaller, at 8:1.

Within the OECD group there has been income convergence[3]. The rich countries of 1900, i.e. Australia, the United Kingdom, the United States, Netherlands and Belgium had slowest growth in per capita product, whereas the poorest, Japan, Finland and

Table 1.2. **Individual country growth performance, 1900-87**

Annual average compound growth rates

	GDP	Popu-lation	GDP per capita	GDP	Popu-lation	GDP per capita	GDP	Popu-lation	GDP per capita
		1900-87			1900-50			1950-87	
Australia	3.1	1.7	1.4	2.4	1.6	0.8	4.0	1.9	2.1
Austria	2.2	0.3	1.9	0.8	0.3	0.5	4.2	0.2	3.9
Belgium	2.1	0.4	1.6	1.3	0.5	0.8	3.2	0.4	2.8
Canada	4.1	1.8	2.3	3.9	1.9	2.0	4.4	1.7	2.0
Denmark	2.8	0.8	2.0	2.7	1.0	1.6	3.1	0.5	2.6
Finland	3.3	0.7	2.6	2.7	0.8	1.9	4.1	0.6	3.6
France	2.4	0.4	2.1	1.3	0.1	1.2	4.0	0.8	3.2
Germany	2.8	0.7	2.2	1.7	0.8	1.0	4.4	0.5	3.8
Italy	2.8	0.6	2.2	1.8	0.7	1.1	4.3	0.5	3.7
Japan	4.3	1.2	3.1	2.3	1.3	1.0	7.1	1.0	6.0
Netherlands	2.9	1.2	1.7	2.4	1.4	1.0	3.6	1.0	2.6
Norway	3.4	0.7	2.6	2.9	0.8	2.1	4.0	0.7	3.4
Sweden	2.8	0.6	2.3	2.6	0.6	2.0	3.1	0.5	2.7
Switzerland	2.8	0.8	2.0	2.6	0.7	1.9	3.2	0.9	2.2
United Kingdom	1.8	0.4	1.4	1.3	0.5	0.8	2.5	0.3	2.2
United States	3.2	1.3	1.8	3.1	1.4	1.7	3.2	1.3	1.9
OECD average	2.9	0.9	2.1	2.2	0.9	1.3	3.9	0.8	3.0
USSR	3.3	1.0	2.3	2.9	0.8	2.1	3.9	1.2	2.6
Bangladesh	1.6	1.5	0.1	0.7	0.8	−0.1	2.7	2.4	0.3
China	2.9	1.1	1.7	0.3	0.6	−0.3	6.5	1.8	4.5
India	2.1	1.4	0.6	0.8	0.9	−0.1	3.8	2.1	1.7
Indonesia	2.7	1.7	1.0	1.1	1.2	−0.1	4.9	2.3	2.5
Pakistan	2.8	1.9	0.9	1.2	1.3	−0.1	4.8	2.7	2.2
Philippines	3.3	2.4	0.9	2.5	2.0	0.4	4.3	2.9	1.4
South Korea	4.2[a]	1.8	2.4[a]	1.8[a]	1.7	0.1[a]	7.6	2.0	5.5
Taiwan	5.1	2.2	2.8	2.4	2.0	0.4	8.8	2.5	6.1
Thailand	3.8	2.3	1.5	2.1	2.0	0.1	6.3	2.8	3.5
Asian average	3.2	1.8	1.3	1.4	1.4	0.0	5.5	2.4	3.1
Argentina	3.3	2.2	1.1	3.9	2.6	1.2	2.6	1.7	1.0
Brazil	4.8	2.4	2.4	4.0	2.1	1.8	6.0	2.7	3.2
Chile	3.2[a]	1.7	1.5[a]	3.3[a]	1.4	1.8[a]	3.0	2.0	1.0
Colombia	4.2[a]	2.3	1.9[a]	3.9[a]	2.2	1.7[a]	4.7	2.6	2.1
Mexico	3.7	2.1	1.6	2.6	1.4	1.2	5.3	3.0	2.3
Peru	3.6[a]	2.0	1.6[a]	3.0[a]	1.4	1.6[a]	4.3	2.7	1.5
Latin American average	3.8	2.2	1.7	3.5	1.9	1.6	4.3	2.5	1.9

a) For the years 1900-13, growth estimates are proxies derived from average per capita growth in the rest of the region.
Sources: See Appendix tables.

Graph 1. GDP OF THE OECD COUNTRIES AND THE USSR

(billion international $ at 1980 prices)

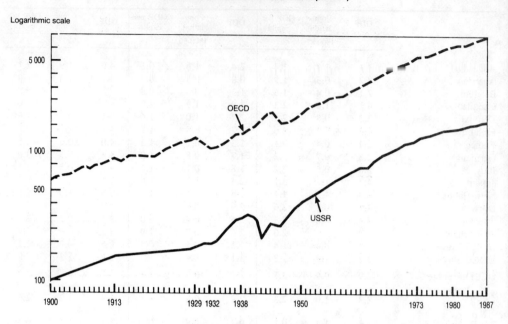

Graph 2. GDP OF 9 ASIAN AND 6 LATIN AMERICAN COUNTRIES

(billion international $ at 1980 prices)

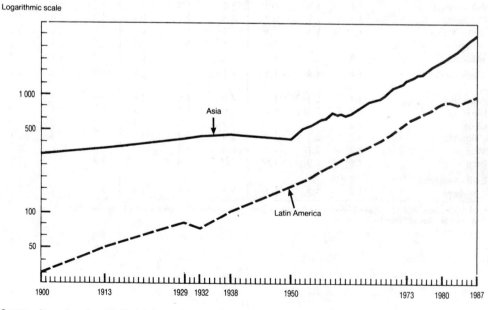

Source: Appendices A and B. Straight line segments are interpolations between benchmark years.

16

Graph 3

GDP PER CAPITA IN 16 OECD COUNTRIES
(in thousand international 1980 $)

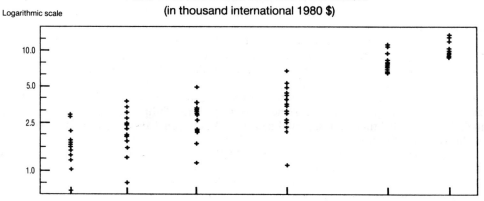

GDP/CAPITA IN 6 LATIN AMERICAN COUNTRIES
(in thousand international $)

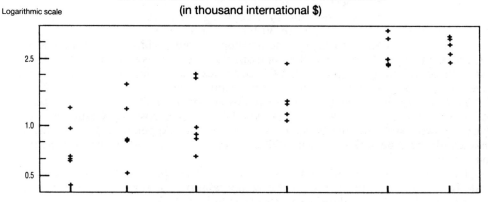

GDP/CAPITA IN 9 ASIAN COUNTRIES
(in thousand international $)

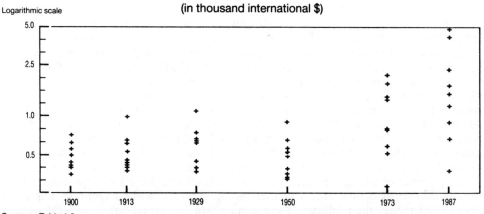

Source: Table 1.3.

Norway had the fastest. As a result the income spread within these 16 OECD countries narrowed from 4:1 in 1900 to 1.5:1 in 1987. However, this convergence has not been monotonic. It has been a postwar phenomenon. The spread of income levels is shown in Graph 5 for benchmark years. The USSR's per capita income growth over the century was somewhat faster than the OECD average. In this sense its experience fits into the convergence pattern.

Within Latin America the income spread in 1900 was about 3:1 between the richest, Argentina, and the poorest, Brazil. As in the OECD countries, the income spread between Latin American countries narrowed a good deal in the course of the century. Argentina had the slowest per capita growth and Brazil the fastest. The spread was therefore reduced to 1.4:1 by 1987. In Asia, there was growing divergence. In 1900 there had been a small 2:1 spread between the richest country, the Philippines, and the poorest, Bangladesh. By 1987 there was a gap of nearly 13:1 between Taiwan, the most prosperous and Bangladesh, the poorest.

A very significant difference between the OECD countries and the developing world lies in their demographic experience. OECD population growth from 1900 to 1987 was only 0.9 per cent a year compared with 1.9 per cent for the developing countries. There has been growing disparity over time. OECD population growth rates have declined, and those in developing countries have risen. Both areas have seen a major fall in death rates and a rise in life expectation; in OECD countries from an average of 49 years at birth in 1900 to 76 in the mid-1980s, in developing countries from 35 years in 1900 to 63. In the OECD group, there were 30 births per 1 000 inhabitants in 1900. By the mid-1980s, this had fallen to 13, but the developing country birth rate in the mid-1980s still averaged 29 per 1 000. Thus the population growth rate is now about four times as fast in the developing world as in OECD countries, and higher than OECD countries have ever experienced–a fact which makes per capita income growth harder to achieve[4].

The comparative estimates of absolute income levels in Tables 1.1, 1.3 and 1.4 are not converted at exchange rates, but use special OECD/Eurostat/UN estimates of purchasing power parity for the benchmark year 1980 (see Appendix A), which are then linked with the time series for real GDP and population to give estimates over time at constant prices.

The sources for the GDP estimates are described in Appendix B. Adjustments were made in several cases to ensure greater comparability, but some of the estimates are weak, particularly for the developing countries before 1913.

Throughout this study (except for foreign trade) the figures for the 32 individual countries are adjusted to exclude the impact of boundary changes, which were particularly important in Austria, Germany and India, and affected 18 countries to some degree. The figures refer throughout to GDP and population within the 1987 boundaries.

The growth process has been accompanied by major structural change. Statistical monitoring of this can be carried back furthest in the OECD countries. In 1900 38 per cent of their employment was in agriculture, and 31 per cent each in industry and services. Since then there has been a steady decline in agricultural employment, which represented only 6 per cent of the total in 1987, and a very substantial rise in services, which by 1987 represented 64 per cent of total employment. The share of industry has moved much less: first rising slowly, and, since 1950, declining. By 1987 it was back to where it was in 1900, i.e. 30 per cent of the total. These countries are often characterised as industrial, but in fact industry has never dominated the employment picture.

The patterns of change in output shares are similar to those for employment, with a secular decline in agriculture, a secular rise in services, and an umbrella curve for industry (first rising, then falling). The output share for agriculture is generally lower

Table 1.3. **GDP per capita in international dollars (1980 prices)**

	1900	1913	1929	1950	1973	1987
Australia	2 923	3 390	3 146	4 389	7 696	9 533
Austria	1 651	1 985	2 118	2 123	6 434	8 792
Belgium	2 126	2 406	2 882	3 114	6 937	8 769
Canada	1 808	2 773	3 286	4 822	9 350	12 702
Denmark	1 732	2 246	2 913	3 895	7 845	9 949
Finland	1 024	1 295	1 667	2 610	6 804	9 500
France	1 600	1 934	2 629	2 941	7 462	9 475
Germany	1 558	1 907	2 153	2 508	7 595	9 964
Italy	1 343	1 773	2 089	2 323	6 824	9 023
Japan	677	795	1 162	1 116	6 622	9 756
Netherlands	2 146	2 400	3 373	3 554	7 754	9 197
Norway	1 218	1 573	2 184	3 436	7 071	11 653
Sweden	1 482	1 792	2 242	3 898	8 288	10 328
Switzerland	2 077	2 474	3 672	5 256	10 556	11 907
United Kingdom	2 798	3 065	3 200	4 171	7 413	9 178
United States	2 911	3 772	4 909	6 697	10 977	13 550
OECD average	1 817	2 224	2 727	3 553	7 852	10 205
Bangladesh	349	371	372	331	281	375
China	401	415	444	338	774	1 748
India	378	399	403	359	513	662
Indonesia	499	529	660	484	786	1 200
Pakistan	413	438	441	390	579	885
Philippines	718	985	1 091	898	1 400	1 519
South Korea	549[a]	610	749	564	1 790	4 143
Taiwan	434	453	631	526	2 087	4 744
Thailand	626	652	616	653	1 343	2 294
Asian average	485	539	601	505	1 061	1 952
Argentina	1 284	1 770	2 036	2 324	3 713	3 302
Brazil	436	521	654	1 073	2 504	3 417
Chile	956[b]	1 255	1 928	2 350	3 309	3 393
Colombia	610[b]	801	975	1 395	2 318	3 027
Mexico	649	822	835	1 169	2 349	2 667
Peru	624[b]	819	890	1 349	2 357	2 380
Latin American average	760	998	1 220	1 610	2 758	3 031
USSR	797	973	1 044	2 265	5 066	5 948

a) Korean per capita GDP assumed to have moved like the average for the other 8 Asian countries from 1900 to 1913.
b) Chilean, Colombian and Peruvian per capita GDP assumed to have moved like the average for the 3 other Latin American countries from 1900 to 1913.
Sources: Derived from Appendices A, B and C.

Table 1.4. Long term changes in structure of employment and output

	Employment			Value added		
	Agriculture	Industry	Services	Agriculture	Industry	Services
	OECD average					
1870	49	27	24	39[a]	26[a]	35[a]
1900	38	31	31	28[a]	31[a]	41[a]
1950	25	36	39	13[b]	11[b]	11[b]
1980	7	34	59	4	37	59
1987	6	30	64	4[c]	36[c]	60[c]
	Latin American average					
1950	50	22	28	23	30	47
1980	29	26	45	12	37	51
1986	24[d]	28[d]	48[d]	11	38	51
	Asian average					
1950	73	8	19	49	15	36
1980	57	17	26	28	34	38
1986				25	34	41

a) Excludes Australia, Belgium, Finland, Netherlands, Norway, Sweden and Switzerland.
b) Excludes Australia and Switzerland.
c) 1986.
d) Excludes Peru, figures refer to 1985.
Sources: See Appendix C for employment. 1980 and 1986 value added shares of GDP from World Bank, *World Development Reports* (except Taiwan and Chile which are from national sources). 1950 GDP shares for OECD countries from A. Maddison, "Economic Growth and Structural Change in the Advanced Countries" in I. Leveson and J.W. Wheeler, *Western Economies in Transition,* Croom Helm, London 1980, p. 51, supplemented for Canada and Belgium from OECD national accounts. 1870 and 1900 OECD GDP shares from national sources for GDP cited in Appendix A. Whenever possible, the GDP shares were calculated at current prices. 1950 GDP shares for developing countries from national sources.

than the employment share, for this is the sector with lowest productivity levels. Industry has had higher than average productivity, markedly so in developing countries which have favoured the flow of capital to this sector. Services generally have higher than average productivity.

The reasons for structural change are complex. The rate and direction of technical progress (slowest hitherto in services) has obviously played a substantial role, but so has the hierarchy of consumer tastes. As incomes rise, the relative demand for food drops, and the increase in consumer demand is directed more strongly to the products of other sectors. The level of government consumption, the rate of investment, the share and pattern of foreign trade, and the rate of depletion of natural resources have all played a role.

The proportion employed in agriculture is inversely related to levels of per capita income, and hence is lowest in the OECD countries and highest in Asia. In 1980 the income level of Asian countries was below that of OECD countries in 1900, and Asian employment in agriculture, at 57 per cent of the total was higher than that of OECD countries in 1900. The Latin American proportion in agriculture in 1986 was like that of OECD countries in 1950, but Latin American income levels were somewhat lower than those in OECD countries in 1950.

In industry and services there is less evidence of a straightforward relation between per capita income level and employment proportions. The developing world is not replicating the employment patterns of OECD countries. The Latin American industrial employment share is lower and the proportion employed in services higher than was the case in OECD countries when they were at comparable income levels.

The productivity gap between modern best practice and that in traditional activities is much wider than it used to be, so modern industrialisation is less labour intensive than it used to be. Furthermore, as developing countries have experienced much faster population growth than OECD countries ever did, there is probably more disguised unemployment in the service sector than was historically the case in OECD countries.

The twentieth century has been one of high inflation by historical standards, particularly by comparison with the nineteenth century when the long run price trend was stable (after 1815). The world export price index (expressed in dollars) rose by 2.7 per cent a year from 1900 to 1986. In the OECD countries, excluding Austria and Germany which had hyperinflations in the early 1920s, the average rise in consumer prices from 1900 to 1986 was 5.7 per cent–with a range from 2.6 per cent a year in Switzerland to 12.6 per cent in Japan. In Asia, India had the slowest inflation (4.1 per cent a year), whilst China, Indonesia and Taiwan had hyperinflations. Inflation was most persistent in Latin America, with average annual rates over 9 decades of 20 per cent in Brazil and Peru, and over 30 per cent in Chile and Argentina.

Table 1.5 provides an illustration of the forces which influenced economic performance in the five biggest OECD economies from 1913 to 1984.

The reasons for intercountry or intertemporal variation in growth are extremely complex and still open to considerable dispute, particularly as the quantitative historical record is incomplete in some major dimensions for most of the countries in this survey. For the moment, the purpose is simply to illuminate the main measurable elements of growth causality.

The first column of Table 1.5 shows the most fundamental indicator of growth performance, GDP, for 1913-50 (when growth was slow), 1950-73 (when it accelerated in all the countries), and 1973-84 (when growth slowed down again).

One of the earliest analysts of growth dynamics, Thomas Malthus, concentrated on the man/land ratio (the second column in the table). The inevitably negative long-run character of this indicator with rising population was the source of Malthusian pessimism. However land scarcity was not the drag Malthus predicted. In these advanced economies, where agriculture, the major land intensive activity, now represents about 4 per cent of output, land is no longer a significant factor in growth. Its importance is bigger in developing countries, where agriculture provides a larger share of income, and where land warrants a higher weight in the production function (see Chapter 6).

Land availability has not been a serious growth constraint because its productivity has been augmented by improvements such as irrigation and other investment, as well as growth of knowledge about cropping and breeding, and use of intermediate inputs such as fertilisers. In fact, the general tendency in these countries with relatively low population growth and fast growing technology has been to reduce the proportion of land which is cultivated.

The second column shows the other major traditional factor of production, labour input. The relation of labour input to population depends on the proportion of people of working age (generally higher in OECD countries than in developing countries because of differences in demography), the proportion of women who work, the proportion of people in education or retirement, the proportion of the labour force which is unemployed, and even more significantly, the length of the working week and annual

21

Table 1.5. Growth accounts for 5 OECD countries, 1913-84

Annual average compound growth rates

	GDP	Cropped land	Hours worked	Labour quality improvement due to education	Gross capital stock	Total factor productivity
			1913-1950			
France	1.15	−0.59	−1.05	0.43	1.94	1.30
Germany	1.30	−1.08	0.25	0.30	0.74	0.74
Japan	2.24	0.07	0.55	0.72	1.55	0.92
United Kingdom	1.29	0.00	−0.28	0.39	1.16	0.87
United States	2.79	0.37	0.35	0.49	1.82	1.57
Average	1.75	−0.25	−0.04	0.46	1.24	1.08
			1950-1973			
France	5.13	−0.49	0.12	0.43	3.62	3.69
Germany	5.92	−0.52	−0.05	0.23	5.35	4.14
Japan	9.29	−0.92	1.55	0.62	7.98	5.47
United Kingdom	3.02	−0.16	−0.15	0.24	3.28	1.98
United States	3.65	0.11	1.22	0.48	3.38	1.49
Average	5.40	−0.40	0.54	0.40	4.72	3.35
			1973-1984			
France	2.32	−0.01	−1.23	0.71	4.00	1.47
Germany	1.72	−0.16	−1.27	0.12	3.39	1.48
Japan	3.72	−0.67	0.57	0.52	3.41	1.99
United Kingdom	1.10	−0.18	−1.33	0.38	2.51	1.19
United States	2.42	0.09	1.33	0.65	2.79	0.25
Average	2.26	−0.11	−0.39	0.48	3.22	1.28

Source: The basic approach is the same as in A. Maddison, "Growth and Slowdown in Advanced Capitalist Economies", *Journal of Economic Literature,* June 1987, with slightly modified weights as land was not incorporated in the 1987 analysis. National sources and FAO Yearbooks were used for cropped land information. There are also some minor modifications as noted in the Appendices, e.g. revised GDP figures for France.

holidays. Between 1913 and 1984 the average working year fell from around 2 600 to 1 700 hours. As real incomes rise, people have a strong desire for more leisure. The net result of all these influences has been a slower rise in labour input than population or even falls in labour input. The United States and Japan have had faster population growth than the other three countries, which partly explains their faster growth of labour input, but the United States also had a strong rise in female activity and Japan has stuck to very long working hours.

The role of education as investment in human capital and as an important factor in growth performance was emphasised strongly by T.W. Schultz in the 1960s[5]. Although this is not the only purpose of education and its economic role is difficult to identify with precision, there is in fact a strong correlation between level of per capita income and levels of education (as can be seen in Chapter 6), and countries with particularly fast economic growth such as Japan, Korea and Taiwan have also had very fast growth in education. However, the demand for and supply of formal education is not geared closely to the general pace of economic growth. The pace of educational progress was no faster in the period of fast growth, 1950-73, than in the other two periods of slower growth.

The postwar development literature gave heavy stress to the importance of investment in growth. Accelerated growth would require a "big push", a "critical minimum effort", or a "take-off". Indeed, none of the countries which had accelerated postwar growth has done so without an increase in investment rates, and the highest rates are generally found in the countries which have had the fastest growth. It is in fact preferable to analyse the role of capital by looking at the growth of the capital stock rather than at ICORs (incremental investment output ratios) which were a fashionable and sometimes misleading proxy in the days before capital stock measures were available[6].

Investment is the major instrument for harnassing the the fruits of technical progress. Without technical progress, these countries would not have found it profitable to maintain high rates of capital formation, because they would have run into diminishing returns. Generally speaking it is much easier for follower countries to maintain high rates of increment in capital per person engaged, than the leader, the United States, which is at the technical frontier, and has to bear most of the costs of research and experimentation with new technology. In 1950-73 the follower countries were able to benefit from more rapid growth of capital stock per worker than the lead country, the United States, because they were in a catch-up phase of growth where they were largely mimicking the leader's technology and did not have to bear the same burden of innovation. In this catch-up period the follower countries did a number of things to improve resource allocation which made their total factor productivity increase at historically unprecedented rates of a once-for-all character. It is noteworthy that total factor productivity in the United States did not accelerate as it did in the follower countries. Hence there is no strong evidence that the acceleration of postwar growth involved any quickening of progress at the frontiers of technology.

In the period since 1973, growth rates of GDP have dropped substantially, for a variety of reasons analysed in Chapter 7 below. There is evidence that, since 1973, OECD countries have been growing below their potential, as their labour input has been lowered by unemployment, and the growth of their capital stock has been high relative to the growth attained, which suggests that capacity is not being fully used.

The indicators so far discussed are simply the proximate supply-side elements in growth. A sophisticated analysis also requires consideration of deeper causal influences deriving from national institutions and policy, the nature of the international economic order, and the degree of socio-economic and political conflict of interest within and between nations. All of these have been subject to major change in the course of the twentieth century, and have had a substantial impact on the pace of investment and international trade. These causes will be analysed in subsequent chapters[7] in order to provide a richer explanation of why the pace of growth has changed.

NOTES AND REFERENCES

1. In 1900, world population is generally estimated to have been 1 650 million, which means that our 32 countries were around 75 per cent of the total compared with 76 per cent in 1980. For years prior to 1950 figures on GDP growth are not available for most countries outside our sample. For 1950-87, the weighted average GDP growth for 94 countries outside our sample was 4.3 per cent per annum, which is virtually identical with the 4.2 per cent of our sample. For the same 94 countries, the weighted average per capita growth for 1950-87 was 2.1 per cent a year which was lower than the 2.5 per cent for our sample. See Table 7.1 below. The 126 countries in Table 7.1 cover 98 per cent of world population.

2. These statements are based on Table 1.1 which shows weighted averages for areas as if they were national units. Tables 1.2 and 1.3 give arithmetic averages. The gap widened whichever way one looks at it. The weighted average for OECD is strongly influenced by the large weight of the richest country, the United States. The weighted average for the developing countries is strongly affected by the heavy weight of China and India.

3. The sixteen OECD countries in the sample represented 93 per cent of OECD product in 1980. Greece, Iceland, Ireland, Luxembourg, New Zealand, Portugal, Spain and Turkey were excluded because GDP indicators were either lacking or weak. Hence the foregoing statements on income levels and convergence apply only to the sixteen countries we cover. In fact 5 of the excluded countries have income levels below the OECD average.

4. The statistics quoted above for OECD countries can be found in A. Maddison *Phases of Capitalist Development*, Oxford, 1982 for 1900 and OECD *Labour Force Statistics* for the mid-1980s. For developing countries, the figures are taken from World Bank, *World Development Reports*, and from the UN, *Demographic Yearbooks*.

. See T.W. Schultz, "Investment in Human Capital", *American Economic Review*, March, 1961.

. See E.F. Denison, *Why Growth Rates Differ*, Brookings 1967, pp. 121-2 on this point.

. See A. Maddison, "Ultimate and Proximate Growth Causality: A Critique of Mancur Olson on the Rise and Decline of Nations", *Scandinavian Economic History Review*, No. 2, 1988.

Chapter 2

THE INTERNATIONAL ECONOMY IN
THE TWENTIETH CENTURY

National economies do not grow in a vacuum. Their performance is strongly influenced by the opportunities or constraints which arise from relations with other countries.

These are of several kinds: trade, capital flows, migration, foreign exchange mechanisms, transmission of fashions in economic policy and ideology, pressures from friendly or unfriendly neighbours, foreign rule, and various kinds of shock which interrupt these relations.

From 1900 to 1986 the export volume of our 32 countries expanded more than twentyfold, at 3.6 per cent a year. This was faster than the 3 per cent growth of output[1]. For trade as for total product, the picture in the second half of the twentieth century was one of much faster growth (see Table 2.1). In 1950-86 the export volume of the 32 countries rose by 6.5 per cent a year, i.e. more than four times as fast as in the first half of the century.

Table 2.2 shows individual country growth performance, the comparative level of their exports and the importance of trade in their economies. Within the OECD group, Japan had the fastest growth rate (7.5 per cent a year) and the United Kingdom the slowest (2.2 per cent). Excluding these two extremes, long term growth rates were rather closely clustered within a range from 3.3 to 4.8 per annum.

Within the non-OECD group, the fastest growth rates were in Taiwan (8.2 per cent per annum) and Korea (7.9 per cent) and the slowest in India at only 1 per cent a year. Thus the range of performance within Asia was more dispersed than in the OECD countries. Long run export growth was slowest in Latin America, and the range of variation in performance was narrower than in other regions.

The gap between levels of trade per capita is bigger than in real product per head. In OECD countries, average trade per head in 1986 (Table 2.2) was $3 411 (measured in US dollars converted at official exchange rates), compared with $369 for the 9 Asian countries, and $206 in Latin America. Within the OECD, the highest exports per head were in Belgium, at $6 740 in 1986, and the lowest in the United States with 899, i.e. a range of somewhat under 8:1. Within the developing group, per capita exports varied from $9 in Bangladesh to $2 056 in Taiwan, a range of 228:1!

The ratio of exports to GDP (both in national prices) tends to be inversely related to the size of the country, but the relation is not close. Policy differences have clearly had an enormous influence, whose direction has changed substantially over time (we come back to this point in subsequent chapters).

The relative size of individual countries in terms of population and output does not correspond with their importance as traders. Thus the United States was by far the

Table 2.1.   **World trade and its components, 1900-86**

		16 OECD countries	9 Asian countries	6 Latin American countries	USSR	32 country total
a)	*Exports in $ million at current prices*					
	1900	6 920	653	500	369	8 442
	1950	35 234	3 538	3 937	801	44 510
	1986	1 415 352	147 656	57 315	97 336	1 717 659
b)	*Exports in $ million at 1980 prices*					
	1900	69 431	7 900	6 131	3 193	86 655
	1950	149 340	17 050	13 212	5 657	185 259
	1986	1 446 549	168 451	75 085	92 503	1 771 889
c)	*Exports per capita, $ at 1980 prices*					
	1900	186	10	130	25	70
	1950	258	15	108	31	92
	1986	2 078	72	243	330	487
d)	*Growth (annual average compound rate) of total export volume*					
	1900-50	1.5	1.6	1.5	1.2	1.5
	1950-86	6.5	6.6	4.9	7.8	6.5
	1900-86	3.6	3.6	3.0	3.9	3.5
e)	*Growth (annual average compound rate) of export volume per capita*					
	1900-50	0.7	0.8	− 0.4	0.4	0.5
	1950-86	6.0	4.5	2.3	6.6	4.7
	1900-86	2.8	2.3	0.7	2.9	2.3

Sources: Appendices B and D. These figures are aggregates for each region. They differ from the arithmetic averages shown in Table 2.2.

biggest economy in terms of output throughout the century, but in 1900 British exports were bigger than those of the United States; in 1986 Germany had bigger exports than the United States, and Japan was very close behind. So influence on the world economy is not a straightforward question of economic size. This is even more true of the three big non-OECD economies. The USSR exports about the same value of goods as Italy, China less than Korea, and India about half as much as Norway.

In so far as growth influences are transmitted through world trade, it is clear that the OECD countries have had the major influence throughout the twentieth century (and, indeed, much earlier), with 73 per cent of world exports in 1900, and 67 per cent in 1986. Their exports and commercial policy have had a major influence on world economic performance.

Another major dimension in which the external world affects development of national economies is through flows of foreign capital. Flows from the advanced to the developing countries are useful in helping to increase the growth of the capital stock and to transfer

Table 2.2. **Export performance of individual countries, 1900-86**

	Export volume annual average compound growth, 1900-86	1986 per capita exports ($)	1986 ratio of exports to GDP
Australia	3.4	1416	13.5
Austria	2.7	2975	24.0
Belgium	3.8	6740	61.4
Canada	4.7	3524	24.8
Denmark	4.2	4142	25.8
Finland	4.0	3326	23.2
France	3.7	2256	17.3
Germany	3.5	3984	27.3
Italy	4.6	1716	16.3
Japan	7.5	1735	10.8
Netherlands	4.5	5451	45.3
Norway	4.8	4373	26.5
Sweden	4.3	4452	28.6
Switzerland	3.3	5701	27.7
United Kingdom	2.2	1885	19.5
United States	3.3	899	5.2
OECD average	4.0	3411	24.8
Bangladesh	1.1[a]	9	5.6
China	3.4	30	12.1
India	1.0	12	4.3
Indonesia	3.8	89	19.7
Pakistan	1.9[a]	34	10.3
Philippines	4.5	87	15.5
South Korea	7.9	835	35.4
Taiwan	8.2	2056	55.7
Thailand	4.3	169	21.0
Asian average	4.0	369	20.0
Argentina	2.2	221	8.7
Brazil	3.1[b]	163	8.3
Chile	3.2	345	25.1
Colombia	4.8	176	15.6
Mexico	3.2	204	12.5
Peru	3.3	124	9.9
Latin American average	3.3	206	13.4
USSR	3.9	347	5.5[c]

a) Assumes 1900-50 growth to be the same as in India.
b) 1901-86.
c) Ratio of dollar value of exports to GDP in "international" dollars.
Source: Appendix D.

Graph 4. EXPORTS AT 1980 PRICES
(billion $)
(OECD, Asia and Latin America)

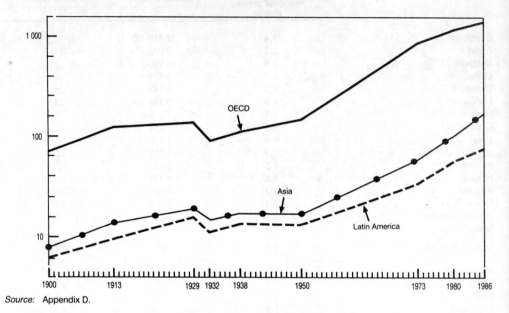

Source: Appendix D.

Graph 5. SHARE OF EXPORTS IN GDP
(OECD, Asia and Latin America, in %)

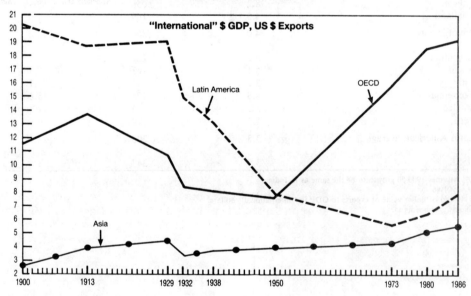

Source: Numerator from Table D-5, denominator from Table A-2. Figures are in effect weighted averages at constant 1980 dollars. For unweighted figures at current prices see Table D-6.

Table 2.3. **Ranking of top 10 countries in 1900 and 1987**

	GDP	Rank	Population	Rank	Exports	Rank
	($ 1980 prices)		(000s)		($ 1980 prices)	
			1900			
United States	221 714	1	76 094	4	12 368	3
China	160 434	2	400 000	1	1 967	12
United Kingdom	111 586	3	41 155	7	20 545	1
India	107 072	4	284 400	2	4 418	5
Russia	98 029	5	128 687	3	3 193	7
Germany	89 678	6	56 046	5	12 404	2
France	62 288	7	38 940	9	5 657	4
Italy	43 981	8	32 416	10	2 101	9
Japan	29 840	9	44 103	6	346	23
Indonesia	20 060	10	40 209	8	1 005	18
			1987			
United States	3 308 401	1	244 171	4	193 678[a]	2
China	1 869 945	2	1 069 608	1	35 994[a]	15
USSR	1 683 764	3	283 100	3	92 503[a]	7
Japan	1 198 943	4	122 897	7	182 617[a]	3
Germany	606 404	5	60 858	14	248 805[a]	1
France	527 602	6	55 685	17	129 953[a]	5
India	521 772	7	787 930	2	10 651[a]	32
United Kingdom	520 270	8	56 687	16	136 589[a]	4
Italy	515 158	9	57 094	15	97 858[a]	6
Brazil	480 752	10	140 692	6	27 178[a]	20

a) 1986.
Source: Generally from Appendix Tables, except that 1900 GDP and population refer here to the boundaries of that year, whereas the appendix figures are adjusted to refer throughout to 1987 frontiers. Ranking of GDP from Appendix A, population from Appendix C and INED, *Population et Sociétés,* September 1987, and export ranking from Appendix D and IMF, *International Financial Statistics.*

modern technology (particularly through direct investment) as well as smoothing over temporary payments problems.

By 1900, the stock of foreign capital[2] was already very substantial in relation to total third world product. As can be seen from Table 2.4, the total was $108 billion (revalued at 1980 prices), probably equal to about a quarter of their GDP at that period. In per capita terms, this investment was most heavily concentrated on Latin America, and was relatively smallest in the big Asian countries. Not all of it originated from transfer of funds. Quite a lot represented claims built up by reinvestment of profits made locally by foreign firms or settlers, who had often acquired access to natural resources on favourable terms. At that time, virtually all such capital was on a commercial basis and involved substantial service charges in the form of interest and dividends. In several important cases repayment difficulties led to major default. Nevertheless this capital did play a role in the development of Latin America, and was even more important in countries of recent settlement such as Australia and Canada in the decades before the first world war.

Table 2.4. Gross value of foreign capital in developing countries, 1870-85

$ billion at year end

	1870	1900	1914	1938	1950	1973	1985
Total in current prices	5.3	11.4	22.7	24.7	13.6	172.0	1 118.0
Total in 1980 prices	33.2	108.3	179.2	143.4	46.6	319.1	944.0

Sources: UK, French and German investment 1870-1914 and area breakdowns from H. Feis, *Europe: The World's Banker 1870-1914*, Kelley, New York, 1961, United States from C. Lewis, *America's Stake in International Investments*, Brookings, Washington D.C., 1938 and other countries from *International Capital Movements in the Interwar Period*, UN, Lake Success, 1949. 1938 from C. Lewis, *The United States and Foreign Investment Problems*, Brookings, Washington D.C., 1948 and Bank of England, *United Kingdom Overseas Investments 1938-1948*, London, 1950. 1950 estimated mainly from United Kingdom and US official sources. 1973 estimated from OECD *Development Cooperation*, various issues (includes $119 billion debt plus an estimated $53 billion of direct investment). 1985 figure includes $948 billion of debt, see OECD, *External Debt Statistics*, Paris 1987, and an estimated $170 billion of direct investment. Deflator is US consumer price index.

In the years 1914 to 1950, the stock of foreign capital fell drastically because of world depression and two world wars, so that by 1950 it was less than half of what it had been in 1900. Since 1950, it has grown very fast, rising by about 9 per cent a year in real terms from $47 billion in 1950 to $944 billion in 1985. A significant part of this modern flow was in the form of aid, and it played a helpful role in the postwar acceleration of investment in the third world, as we shall see in more detail in subsequent chapters. Nevertheless, its size in relation to third world GDP is probably smaller now than in 1900 (compare Tables 2.4 and A.2).

NOTES AND REFERENCES

1. In the nineteenth century, world exports grew about 3.1 per cent per annum, and world output probably around 2 per cent–see Table D.8 for nineteenth century world trade.
2. There has been some recent controversy about the stock of British foreign capital before 1914 (which was the largest individual component of the total). However Charles Feinstein has made a good case for sticking with the traditional estimates I used in Table 2.4, see his "Britain's Overseas Investments in 1913", *Economic History Review*, forthcoming.

Chapter 3

PHASES OF DEVELOPMENT

We saw in Chapter 1 that economic growth has not been steady in the twentieth century. It has been very much faster in the second than in the first half. In fact, there have been four distinct and important phases of development since 1900. These were the liberal, market oriented order which ended with the first world war; the period of conflict and autarky from 1914 to 1950; the golden age of fast growth to 1973; and the phase of slower growth and accelerated inflation since then. The chronology of these four phases serves as an organising framework for subsequent Chapters 4, 5, 6 and 7, and indeed for most of the quantitative evidence in our tables.

Phases are identified, in the first instance, by inductive analysis and iterative inspection of empirically measurable characteristics. Each phase must have a different and distinctive momentum, in dimensions which are analytically significant; these changes must extend to a substantial majority of countries under examination, and be sustained longer than a business cycle. They are not conceived as an analytical sequence of progressively interrelated "stages" such as one finds with Rostow, or members of the German historical school like List or Bücher, nor are they derived from a theoretical model of business cycle rhythm or Kondratieff style long waves–which is one reason why their length is uneven.

Successive phases have not been initiated by collective planning decisions, innovative ideas, or changes in the ideology of domestic and international economic policy. The transition from one phase to another has, in practice, been determined by some kind of exogenous system shock. However, the need to devise policy appropriate for new circumstances where old rules of thumb no longer work, or work less efficiently because of previous institutional collapse (e.g. in the international monetary system, international capital markets, or in trade barriers), or the emergence of new political elites representing the interests of a different clientele (as in postcolonial Asia), has created a tendency for each phase to be characterised by distinctive (and often fairly oecumenic) "establishment" views about the efficacy of different kinds of policy instruments. These policy views (and the institutions in which they were incorporated) have had at least as much influence on performance as the autonomous play of market forces, or the atomised decision processes of individual economic agents. Thus performance in different phases does not have an ineluctable quality of the kind assumed in Schumpeterian long wave analysis, but is the outcome of processes which may underexploit growth potential or push it to its limits.

The interrelatedness of different parts of the world economy limits the policy options which each nation state is able or willing to take. Hence each phase has demonstrated a distinctive orbit, which puts some constraints on feasible national trajectories of growth and change. These constraints must be part of the explanation for the surprising generality of the phase phenomenon.

These qualitative differences in policy orientation and weaponry are analysed in detail in subsequent chapters in order to identify the nature of the polity and its payoff more fully. At this stage it is necessary to reinforce our periodisation mainly by quantitative evidence.

If phases are to be acceptable units of analysis, they must a) be identified by quantifiable characteristics; b) the characteristics must change in some recognisable pattern from one phase to the next, so that successive phases can be shown to be different in nature; c) there should be a clear indication of when phases begin and terminate and why[1].

Later chapters are heavily peppered with quantitative indicators. Table 3.1 therefore provides only a summary characterisation of the different phases. It provides 4 major indicators for each phase–showing the average experience of the 16 OECD

Table 3.1. **Quantitative evidence of the existence of separate phases**

Annual average compound growth rates

Arithmetic averages	1900-13	1913-50	1950-73	1973-87
	GDP			
16 OECD countries	2.9	2.0	4.9	2.4
15 developing countries	2.6	2.1	5.3	4.7
32 countries	2.8	2.1	5.1	3.4
	GDP per capita			
16 OECD countries	1.6	1.2	3.8	1.9
15 developing countries	1.2	0.7	2.7	2.5
32 countries	1.4	1.0	3.2	2.2
	Volume of exports			
16 OECD countries	4.8	1.0	8.6	4.2[a]
15 developing countries	4.8	1.1	5.9	6.9[a]
32 countries	4.8	1.1	7.4	5.5[a]
	Change in price level			
16 OECD countries	1.4	− 0.7[b]	4.1	8.2[a]
15 developing countries	3.0[c]	− 0.5[b, e]	17.5	38.8[a]
31 countries	2.0[d]	− 0.6[b, f]	10.6	23.0[a]

a) 1973-86.
b) 1920-38.
c) 9 countries.
d) 25 countries.
e) 13 countries.
f) 29 countries.
Source: Annexes B, C, D and sources cited for Table 6.2.

countries, the 15 developing countries, and the 32 country total (including the USSR). The best aggregative measure of total economic output is GDP, which is the first of these measures. In terms of aggregate welfare the most significant is GDP per capita. Growth of trade provides an indicator of the degree of stimulus countries get from their interaction. The price climate gives some idea of the degree of strain on resources involved in the growth process, and may also be a significant trigger for modifications in policy.

In terms of GDP per head, the picture provided by Table 3.1 is clear. The postwar golden age 1950-73 was the best with GDP per capita growing 3.2 per cent a year, 1973-87 was second best at 2.2 per cent, the old liberal order 1900-13 was third best at 1.4 per cent. The period of conflict and disharmony, 1913-50, was the worst, at 1.0 per cent. The GDP figures show the same alternating growth momentum, with a slowdown in the second and fourth phases, but for OECD countries, phase IV was third best, rather than second best.

Export volume, the third key indicator, confirms the same alternating pattern of growth and deceleration for the 32 countries combined, though for developing countries, the latest phase was best.

Inflation, our fourth indicator, also shows very distinct changes in pace from one phase to another, with the same direction of change being operative for each group of countries, i.e. very mild inflation in 1900-13, deflation in the peacetime part of our second phase (1920-38), significant price rises in the golden age, and a price explosion in the fourth phase. Although the same alternating pattern of average rates of change is visible for prices as for output, and this phenomenon is general for the 32 countries, the status order of the different phases is different, with Phase IV clearly the worst.

Phase I.   The Liberal World Order to 1913

It is obvious that the first of these phases, the old liberal world order, was brutally terminated by the first world war, but its initial point, 1900, is arbitrary because this study is concerned only with the twentieth century. In fact its characteristic feature of respectable and sustained growth in the advanced OECD countries goes back to the 1820s[2] and the more modest diffusion of growth, through trade and capital flows, to third countries goes back to 1870[3]. What we are looking at is the heyday of a much longer phase.

Phase II.   Conflict and Autarky 1913-50

The second phase, 1913-50, was a "time of troubles" which encompassed two world wars and the world's greatest depression in 1929-32. Each of these "system shocks" was much bigger than anything that occurred in the first phase. There were successive breakdowns of the liberal world order in 1914-18, and of its reconstructed facsimile after 1929. There was a collapse of the international monetary system, liberal trade regimes were replaced by autarky and discriminatory blocs, the world capital market shrivelled up as a result of default and the era of free migration came to an end. The Russian revolution abolished capitalist property relations and market allocation mechanisms in the USSR in conditions of international isolation, and there were also changes in the balance of social forces and significant modification of domestic policy in the capitalist countries, with much greater government intervention and dirigisme.

33

The unifying characteristics of this period were international disharmony, slow growth in GDP and trade and an absolute fall in foreign investment. There was a sharp decline in the status and influence of European countries and the emergence of the United States as an economic superpower. By 1918 the Austrian and Turkish empires had collapsed. The German overseas empire was reallocated and there was some expansion of new colonial empires (by Italy and Japan). However, by the end of this phase it was clear that colonialism was doomed.

There can be little quarrel about the initial point of phase II, but the choice of 1950 as a terminal point is more arguable. 1945 was the year the second world war ended, and one might make a case for stopping there. But at that date the economies of many European and Asian countries were in ruins, and the shape of the postwar international order was not clear. By 1950, the recovery from the second world war was over in most European countries, it was clear that colonialism was finished in Asia, and the major new international institutions had been established and defined their role. Hence there are pragmatic reasons for regarding 1950 as the end of the era. Choice of an earlier terminal year for Phase II would make its performance worse, a later date would make it look better, but neither of these alternatives would have much impact on the character of the subsequent Phase III.

Phase III.   The "Golden Age" 1950-73

The years 1950 to 1973 were a "golden age". A new liberal world order was re-created on a much sounder institutional and political basis than the flawed efforts of reconstruction after the first world war. Colonialism was dismantled. The international order was buttressed by the creation of new and influential agencies–OECD, IMF, the World Bank, and the GATT–and involved a high degree of articulate economic co-operation, at least amongst OECD countries. There was a successful dismantling of trade barriers, an unprecedentedly fast growth of international trade, a restoration of private international capital flows, and the inauguration of large scale official aid programmes.

Domestic policy objectives and weapons also changed, with more explicit emphasis on growth and employment objectives in the developed countries, more activist fiscal and monetary policy, and a greatly increased role of the state in economic life. The newly independent countries of Asia adopted policy options consciously designed to accelerate growth and very different from those of earlier years. In Latin America, the change in policy attitudes and instruments was smaller. Latin America had done better than the rest of the world with inward looking dirigiste policies in the 1930s and 1940s, and stuck with them after the war, with much less integration in the world economy or commitment to the new liberalism.

The golden age saw a growth of GDP and GDP per capita on an unprecedented scale in all parts of the world economy, a rapid growth of world trade, a reopening of world capital markets and possibilities for international migration.

The character of phase III performance can be seen for each country in Tables 3.2 and 3.3. In all the OECD countries, per capita growth was much faster than in the 1913-50 period, and in 15 of them 1950-73 experience was also very much better than in 1900-13 (the exception being Canada). Average per capita growth in the OECD countries was 3.8 per cent compared with 1.2 per cent in 1913-50 and 1.6 per cent in 1900-13. This acceleration did contain some elements of recovery but it lasted so long, and involved such a massive and sustained improvement in performance that new forces were clearly at work in the growth process.

34

Table 3.2. Per capita real GDP growth: 1900-87

Annual average compound growth rates

	1900-13	1913-50	1950-73	1973-87
Australia	1.1	0.7	2.5	1.5
Austria	1.4	0.2	4.9	2.3
Belgium	1.0	0.7	3.5	1.7
Canada	3.3	1.5	2.9	2.2
Denmark	2.0	1.5	3.1	1.7
Finland	1.8	1.9	4.3	2.4
France	1.5	1.1	3.8	1.7
Germany	1.6	0.7	4.9	2.0
Italy	2.0	0.7	4.8	2.0
Japan	1.2	0.9	8.0	2.8
Netherlands	0.9	1.1	3.5	1.2
Norway	2.0	2.1	3.2	3.6
Sweden	1.5	2.1	3.3	1.6
Switzerland	1.4	2.1	3.1	0.9
United Kindom	0.7	0.8	2.5	1.5
United States	2.0	1.6	2.2	1.5
OECD average	1.6	1.2	3.8	1.9
Bangladesh	0.5	− 0.3	− 0.7	2.1
China	0.3	− 0.5	3.7	6.0
India	0.5	− 0.3	1.6	1.8
Indonesia	0.5	− 0.2	2.1	3.1
Pakistan	0.5	− 0.3	1.7	3.1
Philippines	2.5	− 0.2	1.9	0.6
South Korea	(0.8)	− 0.2	5.2	6.2
Taiwan	0.3	0.4	6.2	6.0
Thailand	0.3	0.0	3.2	3.9
Asian average	0.7	− 0.2	2.8	3.6
Argentina	2.5	0.7	2.1	− 0.8
Brazil	1.4	2.0	3.8	2.2
Chile	(2.1)	1.7	1.5	0.2
Colombia	(2.1)	1.5	2.2	1.9
Mexico	1.8	1.0	3.1	0.9
Peru	(2.1)	1.4	2.5	0.1
Latin American average	2.1	1.4	2.5	0.8
Developing country average	1.2	0.7	2.7	2.5
USSR	1.6	2.3	3.6	1.2
32 country average	1.4	1.0	3.3	2.2

Source: Derived from Table 1.3. The regional averages are arithmetic.

Table 3.3. Real GDP growth, 1900-87

Annual average rate of GDP growth at constant prices

	1900-13	1913-50	1950-73	1973-87
Australia	3.1	2.1	4.7	2.9
Austria	2.4	0.2	5.3	2.2
Belgium	2.4	1.0	4.1	1.8
Canada	6.3	3.1	5.1	3.4
Denmark	3.2	2.5	3.8	1.8
Finland	2.9	2.7	4.9	2.8
France	1.7	1.1	5.1	2.2
Germany	3.0	1.3	5.9	1.8
Italy	2.8	1.4	5.5	2.4
Japan	2.5	2.2	9.3	3.7
Netherlands	2.3	2.4	4.7	1.8
Norway	2.7	2.9	4.1	4.0
Sweden	2.2	2.7	4.0	1.8
Switzerland	2.6	2.6	4.5	1.0
United Kingdom	1.5	1.3	3.0	1.6
United States	4.0	2.8	3.7	2.5
OECD average	2.9	2.0	4.9	2.4
Bangladesh	1.0	0.5	1.7	4.5
China	0.8	0.1	5.8	7.5
India	1.0	0.7	3.7	4.1
Indonesia	1.8	0.9	4.5	5.4
Pakistan	1.0	1.4	4.4	6.1
Philippines	4.4	1.8	5.0	3.2
South Korea	(2.0)	1.7	7.5	7.9
Taiwan	1.8	2.7	9.3	7.8
Thailand	1.7	2.2	6.4	6.2
Asian average	1.7	1.3	5.4	5.9
Argentina	6.4	3.0	3.8	0.8
Brazil	3.5	4.2	6.7	4.8
Chile	(3.4)	3.3	3.7	1.9
Colombia	(4.2)	3.8	5.2	3.9
Mexico	2.6	2.6	6.4	3.6
Peru	(3.5)	2.8	5.4	2.6
Latin American average	3.9	3.3	5.2	2.9
Developing country average	2.6	2.1	5.3	4.7
USSR	3.5	2.7	5.0	2.1
32 country average	2.8	2.1	5.1	3.4

Source: Derived from Appendix B. The regional averages are arithmetic.

In Asian countries, the acceleration of economic progress in the golden age was even more marked. Eight of them achieved better (generally very much better) per capita growth rates than in the two earlier phases. Bangladesh was the only exception. Average growth of GDP per capita for the nine countries was 2.8 per cent per annum in 1950-73 compared with 1.0 per cent in the heyday of the colonial era (1900-13) and the average decline of 0.3 per cent a year between 1913 and 1950.

In Latin America, the improvement in performance in 1950-73 was also unequivocal. Average per capita growth was 2.5 per cent a year, compared with 2.1 per cent in 1900-1913, and 1.4 per cent in 1913-50. However, the degree of improvement was not as marked as in the other regions and per capita growth in Argentina and Chile was slower than in 1900-13.

Phase IV. Growth Deceleration, and Accelerated Inflation

As the latest phase is not yet over, its terminal point cannot be identified. It is also more difficult to characterise than earlier phases, because the Asian countries have successfully bucked the general trend.

The fast growth of the golden age clearly came to an end in 1973 in the OECD countries. The oil shock at the end of that year came when the OECD economies were generally stretched to capacity and already feeling strong inflationary pressures. Well-established policy guidelines had been undermined by the collapse of the Bretton Woods fixed exchange rate system in 1971. The added surge of inflation and payments uncertainty which came from the oil price explosion pushed domestic and world inflation to unprecedented peacetime dimensions, and made it clear that the possibility for finely tuned trade-offs envisaged by the popular Phillips curve analysis had evaporated. These shocks induced a new caution in economic policy and indeed a new set of objectives. The new policy was geared to breaking inflationary momentum rather than low unemployment and high growth. This caution in macroeconomic policy was reinforced by the second oil shock which struck in 1979.

The contrast between the two periods can be seen clearly in Table 3.4. GDP growth has been less than half as fast since 1973, the incidence of cyclical disturbance has been four times as great, and inflation accelerated sharply. Since 1983, there has been some mitigation in the last two characteristics, but the growth momentum is clearly lower than in Phase III.

Table 3.5 shows the change between the two phases in Latin America. Aggregate GDP growth fell from 5.2 to 2.9 per cent a year, the incidence of cyclical disturbance and the already high pace of inflation quadrupled.

In Latin America, the onset of Phase IV was marked by a rise of inflation to levels which would have been considered catastrophic in OECD countries. Unlike OECD governments, most of those in Latin America thought they could be successfully accommodated. Their typical policy posture was much less cautious. Expansion continued up to 1980 at similar rates as in Phase III, with substantial help from increased capital inflows at low or negative rates of interest. The cessation of these flows after the Mexican debt crisis forced a belated adjustment on governments with excessive budget deficits and low credibility as borrowers. As a result Latin America, since 1980, has been stuck in an orbit of low growth. The policy leeway for solving these problems and moving to faster growth is much smaller than in OECD countries. The welfare significance of growth deceleration is more significant, because of much higher Latin American population growth. In per capita terms, performance in Phase IV is the worst of all the phases for Latin America (see Table 3.2).

37

Table 3.4. Annual indicators of characteristics of phases III and IV for 16 OECD countries

	Average year-to-year percentage change in GDP	Number of countries experiencing recession	Average of individual country unemployment rates	Year-to-year percentage change in average GDP deflator[a]
1951	6.2	1	2.9	13.7
1952	3.2	2	3.4	5.9
1953	4.8	0	3.3	0.5
1954	4.9	2	3.3	2.2
1955	6.0	1	2.8	2.7
1956	4.6	0	2.8	4.6
1957	4.0	0	2.8	4.0
1958	1.7	5	3.3	2.8
1959	5.3	0	3.0	2.0
1960	6.6	0	2.5	2.6
1961	5.6	0	2.3	3.3
1962	4.9	0	2.1	3.7
1963	4.6	0	2.1	4.0
1964	6.3	0	1.9	4.5
1965	5.2	0	1.8	4.5
1966	4.3	0	1.9	4.5
1967	3.5	0	2.3	3.9
1968	5.6	0	2.5	5.1
1969	6.1	0	2.2	4.3
1970	5.0	1	2.2	6.1
1971	3.9	1	2.5	6.8
1972	4.7	0	2.7	7.1
1973	5.5	0	2.6	9.7
Annual average	4.9	0.6	2.6	4.7
1974	2.3	5	2.8	13.1
1975	−0.1	10	4.0	11.7
1976	4.2	1	4.4	8.9
1977	2.3	1	4.7	8.0
1978	2.9	0	5.0	7.2
1979	3.8	0	4.8	7.2
1980	2.3	3	4.9	9.1
1981	1.0	6	5.9	8.7
1982	0.6	6	7.1	7.7
1983	2.2	0	7.8	5.6
1984	3.6	0	7.3	4.8
1985	3.3	0	6.9	4.2
1986	2.7	0	6.6	3.4
1987	2.3	1	6.6	3.7
Annual average	2.4	2.4	5.6	7.4

a) 1951-66 excludes Australia, 1951 excludes Italy and Norway, 1950-52 excludes Japan, 1950-53 excludes Belgium.
Sources: Appendix B, Maddison (1982), OECD National Accounts and OECD Economic Outlook.

Table 3.5. **Annual indicators of characteristics of phases III and IV for 6 Latin American countries**

	Average year-to-year percentage change in GDP	Number of countries experiencing recession	Year-to-year percentage change in average GDP deflator
1951	5.5	1	20.1
1952	3.5	0	14.3
1953	4.8	0	10.7
1954	5.8	0	20.3
1955	5.7	0	19.6
1956	3.6	0	20.7
1957	5.4	0	15.5
1958	4.6	1	19.5
1959	3.8	1	36.2
1960	7.6	0	10.3
1961	6.2	0	13.6
1962	4.6	1	18.2
1963	3.0	1	26.8
1964	6.9	0	27.5
1965	5.2	0	25.0
1966	5.6	0	20.0
1967	3.8	0	16.8
1968	5.2	0	16.6
1969	6.2	0	14.2
1970	5.9	0	14.3
1971	6.6	0	16.2
1972	5.5	0	32.3
1973	5.3	1	89.6
Annual average	5.2	0.3	21.3
1974	5.1	1	145.1
1975	0.7	2	103.7
1976	4.0	1	133.7
1977	4.6	0	67.9
1978	4.4	1	58.4
1979	7.4	0	66.2
1980	5.9	0	55.9
1981	1.3	2	57.3
1982	− 3.0	3	74.0
1983	− 2.7	4	124.8
1984	3.9	0	178.6
1985	2.5	1	200.2
1986	4.4	1	69.1
1987	4.0	0	104.7
Annual average	2.9	1.1	102.8

Source: Appendix B and sources mentioned in Table 6.2.

Table 3.6. Annual indicators of characteristics of phases III and IV for 9 Asian countries

	Average year-to-year percentage change in GDP	Number of countries experiencing recession	Year-to-year percentage change in average GDP deflator
1951	3.4	2	
1952	6.5	0	
1953	9.4	0	
1954	4.1	1	
1955	5.1	1	
1956	5.1	0	
1957	2.9	3	
1958	5.2	1	
1959	1.9	2	
1960	3.8	1	
1961	3.1	1	
1962	5.1	1	
1963	7.2	1	
1964	6.7	0	
1965	5.2	1	
1966	6.8	1	
1967	3.9	2	24.3
1968	7.2	0	15.8
1969	7.3	0	6.9
1970	8.6	0	5.7
1971	4.7	1	5.3
1972	3.4	2	8.0
1973	9.4	0	21.1
Annual average	5.4	0.9	12.4
1974	5.2	0	27.1
1975	6.4	0	15.7
1976	6.2	1	5.6
1977	7.2	0	6.9
1978	9.0	0	10.9
1979	5.1	0	14.7
1980	4.9	1	15.8
1981	6.1	0	9.9
1982	3.9	1	6.6
1983	6.2	0	6.2
1984	5.7	1	11.6
1985	4.7	1	7.4
1986	5.9	0	3.5
1987	6.2	0	7.6
Annual average	5.9	0.4	10.7

Source: Appendix B and sources mentioned in Table 6.2.

Table 3.6 shows the change in pattern in Asia. Here the situation is different from that in other parts of the world. Phase IV was better than Phase III. Growth was faster, and the incidence of depression was halved.

The Asian countries suffered some disturbance from the oil price explosions, but generally had more flexible commodity and labour markets than either the OECD or Latin American countries and fewer institutional ratchets for magnifying external price shocks. Macropolicy was less adventurous than that in Latin America with firmer budgetary and monetary controls, and less reliance on foreign borrowing to fill gaps in domestic finance. Exchange rate and export policies were more realistically geared to export promotion and the investment effort in terms of physical and human capital was greater. The reasons for this marked contrast between Asia and the other regions is a major theme of Chapter 7 below.

Finally, it is worth noting that the USSR (together with Eastern Europe) experienced slowdown in Phase IV to a greater extent than the capitalist economies, though for somewhat different reasons. The contrast between Soviet performance and that of China, whose growth acceleration was due largely to its move towards market allocation and incentives, has obviously made some contribution to the recent Soviet review of economic policy options.

NOTES AND REFERENCES

1. See S. Kuznets' discussion of the problem of identifying significant breaks in growth trends in his comments on Rostow's analytical schema in W.W. Rostow, ed., *The Economics of Take-Off into Sustained Growth*, Macmillan, London 1963.

2. See A. Maddison, *Phases of Capitalist Development*, Oxford University Press, 1982.

3. See W.A. Lewis, *Growth and Fluctuations 1870-1913*, Allen and Unwin, London, 1978 for a masterly analysis of the 1870-1913 period.

Chapter 4

PERFORMANCE AND POLICY
IN A LIBERAL WORLD ORDER 1900-13

The first years of the twentieth century were ones of high prosperity in a world order that conformed to the tenets of classical liberalism. The pace of growth and general buoyancy of demand led to a general rise in domestic prices–about 1.4 per cent a year in the advanced countries, and 3 per cent a year in the developing world. It was the end of a long phase in which the advanced countries had had substantial growth and diffused it (to a milder degree) to the rest of the world through their demand for imports of food and raw materials and the outflow of their capital. Average export volume of the 32 countries rose by 4.3 per cent a year from 1900 to 1913. As prices were rising, the dollar value of their trade grew by 5.2 per cent a year. The stock of foreign capital invested in developing countries rose by 3.7 per cent a year in real terms. These were peak years for international migration with an outflow of 10 million people from Europe to the Americas and Antipodes. A similar number of Chinese and Indians moved to Burma, Ceylon, Malaya, Sumatra and Thailand where there were jobs as labourers on plantations, or menial work in cities which the native inhabitants of these land abundant countries were not willing to perform.

Growth in the advanced countries of Europe and its white settler offshoots in America and Australasia was faster–averaging 2.9 per cent a year–than in the nineteenth century (when it had been about 2 per cent). Growth was fastest in North America, (4 per cent in the United States and 6.3 per cent in Canada), and slowest in the United Kingdom (1.5 per cent a year). The United States had recently become the productivity leader, a leadership based partly on its huge natural resources, but also due to high rates of investment, an educated and rapidly expanding labour force, the beginnings of industrial R and D. European countries had notably lower rates of investment than the United States or Canada in this period, and a more slowly growing labour force (partly due to emigration to the Americas). Within the advanced group, the fast growth of exports was a further (ancillary) source of productivity increase, as it facilitated economies of specialisation and scale.

Within the third world, Latin America maintained a faster pace of GDP growth than the the advanced countries. Argentina's huge natural resources induced the fastest growth, with high investment and large immigration from Europe. Per capita exports from Latin America averaged $25 in 1913 compared with less than $4 a head for Asia (see Table 4.1). In the three biggest Latin American countries, foreign investment per head averaged $202, compared with less than $8 in the biggest Asian countries (see Table 4.2).

Table 4.1. **Exports per capita, 1900-86**

$ at current prices and exchange rates

	1900	1913	1929	1950	1973	1986
China	0.33	0.70	1.36	1.01	7	30
India	1.25	2.49	3.39	3.18	5	12
Indonesia	2.59	5.61	9.73	11.00	26	89
Korea	0.38	0.97	7.88	1.12	95	835
Philippines	3.14	5.12	12.70	16.50	47	87
Taiwan	2.37	7.49	27.82	9.26	290	2 056
Thailand	2.05	4.95	7.80	15.63	40	169
Asian average	1.73	3.90	10.10	8.24	73	468
Argentina	31.75	67.29	78.33	68.69	130	221
Brazil	10.12	13.40	14.05	26.16	62	163
Chile	20.51	42.68	65.72	46.13	124	345
Colombia	2.75	6.54	15.85	33.97	52	176
Mexico	5.51	10.02	16.89	19.43	40	204
Peru	5.80	9.54	20.98	25.29	77	124
Latin American average	12.74	24.91	35.30	36.61	81	206
France	20.36	33.39	47.66	73.67	703	2 256
Germany	19.98	36.64	49.61	39.87	1 090	3 984
Japan	2.31	6.10	15.32	9.95	341	1 603
United Kingdom	34.41	55.97	77.73	125.59	527	1 885
United States	18.63	24.48	42.35	67.52	337	899
Average for 5 countries	19.14	31.32	46.53	63.32	600	2 125

Source: Table D-1 for exports, Appendix C for population. As the trade figures are not corrected for changes in boundaries, population within the customs boundaries of the pertinent year were used as a denominator, Burma was included in the Indian customs area to 1937. We therefore have to add Burmese population to the Indian denominator.

Asian developing countries lagged well behind (with a GDP growth averaging 1.7 per cent a year). Except in Japan, Asian investment, technological capacity and educational levels were low. The only engine of growth for them in that period was the expansion of world demand for food and raw materials which gave new opportunities to peasant and plantation agriculture and to mining. Asian export volume rose by 4.9 per cent a year compared with 1.7 per cent for GDP, so the role of exports in incremental demand was obviously high[1].

On a per capita basis, growth was fastest in Latin America (2.1 per cent a year). OECD countries averaged 1.6 per cent per year and Asia only 0.7 per cent.

Domestic economic policy within the advanced countries was inspired by principles of fiscal responsibility and sound money. Taxes and government expenditure were low and generally in balance; spending was mainly confined to provision for domestic order and national defence. Social spending was small, covering elementary education and preventive health measures, with negligible provision for pensions or welfare payments. There was strong reliance on market forces for resource allocation. Government regulatory activity was minimal, and government participation in enterprise activity was small

Table 4.2. **Foreign capital (portfolio and direct) around 1913**

	Total $ million	Per capita $
China	1 600	3.72
India	2 100	6.91
Indonesia	600	12.47
Argentina	3 136	409.80
Brazil	1 932	81.66
Mexico	1 700	113.55
Australia	1 800	373.37
Canada	3 850	490.32
South Africa	1 650	346.06

Source: Total foreign claims, China from UN, *International Capital Movements During the Interwar Period,* UN, New York, 1948, p. 2. India derived from estimates of Keynes and Howard cited in A.K. Banerji, *India's Balance of Payments,* Asia Publishing House, Bombay, 1963, pp. 150-5. Indonesia (1915) from C. Robequain, *Malaya, Indonesia, Borneo and the Philippines,* Longmans, London, 1966, p. 323. Argentina from C.F. Diaz Alejandro, *Essays on the Economic History of the Argentine Republic,* Yale, 1970, p. 30. Brazil (1914) from M. de Paiva Abreu, *Brazil and the World Economy, 1930-1945,* Ph. D. dissertation, Cambridge University, February 1977. Mexico (1910) public debt from J. Bazant, *Historia de la Deuda Exterior de Mexico (1823-1946),* Colegio de Mexico, 1968; foreign direct investment derived from R.W. Goldsmith, *The Financial Development of Mexico,* OECD Development Centre, Paris, 1966, p. 73. Australia, Canada and South Africa from W. Woodruff, *Impact of Western Man,* MacMillan, 1966, p. 154.

even in countries where Gerschenkron stressed government activism (e.g. Germany with its government owned railways). The only real exception was Japan, where government had an important developmental role.

Stable institutions and market freedom also characterised international transactions. It was the heyday of the gold standard. In these years, stable exchange rates prevailed virtually everywhere, even in China which remained on silver. Chile was the only country with substantial inflation and floating rates. Otherwise, in Latin America, it was an interval of orthodoxy. Nineteenth century adventures with floating currencies, budget deficits and debt default in Argentina and Brazil were temporarily over. Brazil was having an uncharacteristic period of falling prices and exchange appreciation. With the Chinese exception, Asian countries were also on gold for most of the period.

It was a world which relied on simple rules and protection of property rights. There were no international organisations like the OECD, IMF, BIS and GATT to "manage" a world "system", and no equivalent of the World Bank, UN agencies, or indeed bilateral aid "donors" to direct capital flows in the light of developmentalist objectives.

There were no quantitative restrictions on international trade and negligible departures from most-favoured nation tariff treatment, international migration was virtually unrestricted and large.

One major asymmetry in this world system, was in tariff levels. On the one hand, there were the traditional free trade countries, the United Kingdom and the Netherlands with tariff levels of zero, and 2.5 per cent respectively. Free trade was imposed throughout the vast colonial empires they controlled as well as in nominally independent countries such as China, Egypt, Iran, Thailand and Turkey. The latter were subject to treaties which kept tariffs low and restricted their tariff autonomy.

45

France and Germany were moderately protectionist with tariff levels averaging 16 and 12 per cent respectively, geared particularly to protect their agriculture. France also applied a system of imperial preference within its colonial empire. Japan had been a compulsory member of the free trade club (maximum tariffs 5 per cent) until 1911 when she renegotiated the treaties restricting her sovereignty and raised them to a moderate range of 10-15 per cent.

The most heavily protectionist countries were the United States, Russia and the Latin American countries (which, unlike Asian countries, were politically free to impose high tariffs)[2].

Latin American countries had thrown off political dependency in the 1820s, and in the main their governments were free to pursue policies in what they perceived to be their national interest. This is already clear with respect to tariffs, but they were also freer in fiscal-monetary policy, banking, exchange rate, commodity stabilisation and debt default than countries which were colonies or quasi colonies[3].

Latin American policy was not very different in many respects from the European norm. Countries used tariffs as much for revenue as for protectionist reasons. Most adhered to the gold standard rules of cautious finance, had little government involvement even in infrastructure development, and gave unrestricted freedom for foreign investment and remittances. They did not have central banks, and much of their commercial banking, shipping and insurance activity was controlled by European interests. Their governments were generally landowner-exporter oligarchies with close ties to European or incipiently, to US trading interests. Brazil probably had the most activist and independent economic policy.

Table 4.3. **Gold/gold exchange standards, 1821-1936**

	On	Off	On	Off
India	1893-9	1914	1925	1931
Indonesia	1877	1914	1925	1931
Korea	1910	1917	1930	1931
Philippines	1903	1917	1919	1933
Taiwan	1895	1917	1930	1931
Thailand	1908[a]	1914	1928	1932
Argentina	1899	1914	1927	1929
Brazil	1906	1914	1926	1930
Chile	1895	1898	1925	1932
Colombia			1923	1933
Mexico[b]	1905	1913	1918	1932
Peru	1897	1914	1926-8	1932
France	1873-4	1914	1928	1936
Germany	1871-3	1914	1924	1933
Japan	1895	1917	1930	1931
United Kingdom	1821	1914	1925	1931
United States	1879	1917	1919	1933

a) Thailand went off silver in 1902 and experimented with a sterling exchange standard until 1908.
b) Mexico had a bimetallic system, using silver coins internally.
Source: W.A. Brown, *The International Gold Standard Reinterpreted 1914-1934*, NBER, New York, 1940; M. Friedman and A.J. Schwartz, *A Monetary History of the United States 1867-1960*, NBER, Princeton, 1963, p. 64, and various country monographs.

Within Asia, free trade imperialism generally provided some opportunities for growth in countries with enough good land to expand peasant crops or plantation agriculture, but this growth has generally been exaggerated by both Myint and Lewis. Both of these authors present a more rosy picture than is warranted by our evidence[4]. Apart from their poorer natural resources, economic growth performance in Asia was also adversely affected by some forms of colonialism.

Colonialism, by 1900, was near its peak dimension, having grown rather fast in Africa from 1870 to 1900 (during which the United Kingdom acquired 38 colonies). For that year, Hobson's "measure of imperialism" identified the United Kingdom as the major colonial power with 345 million subjects outside the metropole, France was second with 56 million, Netherlands third with 35 million, Germany 15 million, the United States 10.5 million, Turkey 15 million and Portugal 9 million[5]. Hobson mentioned the internal colonies of Russia (16 million) and China (17 million), but omitted to mention

Table 4.4. **Average tariff levels, 1913-25**

	1913	1925
Free traders		
United Kingdom	0.0	3.0
Netherlands	2.5	4.0
China	4.0	8.5
India	3.5	13.5
Indonesia	5.5	9.0
Thailand	3.0	3.0
Mild protectionists		
Germany	12.0	13.5
Japan	12.0	
France	16.0	10.5
Chile	10.0	16.0
Heavy protectionists		
United States	32.5	27.5
Philippines	32.5	27.5
Argentina	26.0	26.0
Brazil	34.2	21.4
Mexico	31.5	25.5
Peru	23.0	17.0

Source: Argentina, France, Germany, India, Netherlands and the United States are weighted averages of two League of Nations estimates in W.S. and E.S. Woytinsky, *World Commerce and Governments,* Twentieth Century Fund, New York, 1955, p. 276. China from Chi-ming Hou, *Foreign Investment and Economic Development in China 1840-1937,* Harvard, 1965, p. 108. Indonesia, ratio of import duties to imports from P. Creutzberg, *Changing Economy in Indonesia,* Nijhoff, The Hague, vol. 2, pp. 65-6 and vol. 5, p. 64. Thailand from J.C. Ingram, *Economic Change in Thailand 1850-1970,* Stanford, 1971, p. 13. The Philippines was incorporated within the US tariff from 1909, see D.K. Fieldhouse, *The Colonial Empires,* MacMillan, London, 1982. Brazil from *Anuario Estatistico do Brasil 1939/40,* IBGE, Rio, pp. 1359 and 1411 (ratio of import duties to imports). Chile and Peru from R. Thorp, "Latin America and the International Economy from the First World War to the World Depression", *Cambridge History of Latin America,* 1986, vol. IV, p. 77. Mexico from D. Cosio Villegas, *Politica Aduanal Mexicana,* p. 58 (ratio of import duties to imports).

Table 4.5. **Relative density of railway infrastructure in 1913 (end of year)**

	Kilometres of railway per 100 square kilometres	Kilometres of railway per 10 000 inhabitants	Kilometres of railway at end of 1913
Argentina	1.2	43.4	33 215
Brazil	0.3	10.6	24 985
Chile	0.8	18.4	6 370
Colombia	0.1	2.0	1 000
Mexico	1.3	17.1	25 492
Peru	0.2	6.1	2 766
Average/Total	0.7	16.3	93 828
China	0.09	0.3	9 854
India	1.1	1.8	55 761
Indonesia	0.5	1.0	2 854
Thailand	0.2	1.2	1 130
Average/Total	0.5	1.1	69 599
France	9.5	13.0	51 188
Germany	11.8	9.5	63 730
Japan (with Korea)	1.7	1.7	10 986
United Kingdom	12.0	8.3	37 717
United States	4.4	42.3	410 918
Average/Total	7.9	15.0	574 539
World			1 104 217

Source: *Statistisches Jahrbuch für das deutsche Reich*, 1915, p. 46-7.

Japan, which had already acquired Formosa and was to be the most expansionist imperial power in the twentieth century.

Colonialism meant that the colonies were deprived of economic and political sovereignty, but it was not a "system". Policies of the major colonial powers differed in their impact on growth in the colonies and the degree to which its benefits were siphoned off by the the metropole and the metropolitans. Colonial practice often varied within given colonial empires.

By 1900 colonialism had a long history. The monopolistic practices of eighteenth century mercantilism had already been abandoned by the United Kingdom before the formal abolition of the East India Company in 1857. However, the free trade, non-discriminatory British policies were accompanied by hangovers from mercantilism. British shipping, banking and insurance interests enjoyed a *de facto* monopoly. Administration was efficient and free from corruption, but it was by white men, living in white cantonments with British clubs, so there was an automatic *de facto* discrimination against local enterprise, which was reinforced by lack of education amongst the native population, and some direct discrimination in government purchasing policies. In the Netherlands, the East India Company had been abolished in 1800, but until 1870 in Indonesia it was followed by a system of royal monopoly in trade, forced deliveries and forced

48

labour. The mercantilist hangovers favouring metropolitan interests were very strong and the profitability of empire was much greater in the Dutch than in the British case. British income attributable to the colonial situation of India was around 1.5 per cent of British GDP, but Dutch income from Indonesia was 8 per cent of Dutch GDP[6].

Japan and the United States were colonial latecomers, and neither followed a free trade policy. Both created their own trade zones with commercial preferences. They pushed public investment and infrastructure in Taiwan, Korea and the Philippines.

In Asia, our sample includes one British colony (India), one Dutch colony (Indonesia), one US colony (the Philippines), and two Japanese colonies. Two of the three other Asian countries in our sample, China and Thailand were not colonies, but their sovereignty had been limited in tariff matters, and the Chinese customs revenues were controlled and impounded by foreign powers–a fact which made the Thais very cautious about incurring foreign debt. The only real counterfactual in Asia which provides some sort of test of what might have happened if power had been vested in a Westernising national bourgoisie is Japan, which achieved faster growth than the other Asian countries by colossal investment in education, by westernising its institutions[7], and by government activism in fostering industry. In fact, the economic growth performance of Japan was not very dramatic in the period under consideration, partly because a good deal of Japanese energy went into military modernisation and adventures to preserve its sovereignty. It could, of course, be argued that without Western expansionism and the challenge of Commander Perry's gunboats, Japan would not have set out on an activist development policy, so the overall impact of Western expansionism was probably positive for growth in Asia as it was in Latin America.

NOTES AND REFERENCES

1. See I.B. Kravis, "Trade as a Handmaiden of Growth: Similarities between the Nineteenth and Twentieth Centuries", *Economic Journal*, December 1970, who goes perhaps a bit too far in debunking trade's role as far as the Asian developing countries are concerned, though for the advanced countries it is a useful essay in iconoclasm.

2. Latin American tariffs were high partly because they were a major source of fiscal revenue, but rates were not uniform and already reflected the pressure of various groups pushing for import substitution. Before 1844, Brazil had had uniform *ad valorem* tariffs of 15 per cent, a limit imposed by treaty with the United Kingdom. When tariff autonomy was regained, Brazilian tariffs were raised immediately to 30 per cent on manufactured goods, but lowered to zero on raw materials and machinery. Hence they were both revenue and protective tariffs. The situation was similar elsewhere in Latin America.

3. Andre Gunder Frank, *Capitalism and Underdevelopment in Latin America*, Monthly Review Press, New York, 1969, has suggested that Latin American countries were significantly constrained by economic and political dependency on the advanced countries, but he has met strong dissent on this point from N. Leff, *Underdevelopment and Development in Brazil*, Allen and Unwin, London, 1982, vol. II, Chapter 4 and D.C.M. Platt in W.R. Louis, ed., *Imperialism*, New Viewpoints, New York, 1976. The situation in the Caribbean, Cuba or prerevolutionary Mexico where US influence was very strong was different from that of Argentina, Brazil or Chile.

4. See H. Myint, "The Classical Theory of International Trade and the Underdeveloped Countries", *Economic Journal*, June 1958. Arthur Lewis says "The period 1880-1913 has to be regarded as one in which many tropical countries grew as rapidly as many of the industrial countries", "Some of the tropical countries must undoubtedly have matched the *per capita* growth of Western Europe (1 to 1.5 per cent per annum)... The evidence for Burma, Thailand, Malaya, Ceylon or the Southern Gold Coast (to list only those which have been examined) yields the same results". W.A. Lewis, ed., *Tropical Development 1880-1913*, Allen and Unwin, London, 1970, p. 30. A. Hlaing, "Trends of Economic Growth and Income Distribution in Burma 1870-1940", *Journal of the Burma Research Society*, 1964, actually shows a fall in Burmese per capita GDP for 1900-13, we find a rise of only 0.3 per cent a year for Thailand. For Malaya we have no hard evidence, but Lewis may well be right. For Ghana, Lewis is also probably right, see Maddison (1970), p. 299. For Ceylon, I doubt whether he is right. He does not mention the Philippines where growth was faster.

5. See J.A. Hobson, *Imperialism: A Study*, Allen and Unwin, third edition, 1938, p. 23.

6. See A. Maddison, *Class Structure and Economic Growth: India and Pakistan since the Moghuls*, Allen & Unwin, London, 1971, A. Maddison and G. Prince, eds., *Economic Growth in Indonesia, 1820-1940*, Foris, Dordrecht, 1989, and A. Maddison, "The Colonial Burden: A Comparative Perspective", in M. Scott, ed., *Public Policy and Economic Development*, Oxford University Press, 1989.

7. In both India and Indonesia, there was a conscious decision not to push Westernisation of institutions and native princelings too far, after the experience of the Indian mutiny in 1857 and the Diponegoro revolt in Indonesia in 1825-30. Certainly much less was done to promote education than in Japan or in the Philippines.

Chapter 5

WARS, DEPRESSION AND AUTARKY 1913-50

The period 1913-50 contained three major disasters without precedent in modern history.

a) The first world war and its aftermath led to 25 million deaths in European countries–9 million in military casualties, about 10 million in the wake of the Russian revolution, the rest in abnormal disease such as typhus and influenza.

b) The world depression of 1929-32 brought an 18 per cent fall in the aggregate GDP of OECD countries, a collapse in world trade, capital markets, and the international monetary system. It accentuated nationalism, autarky, and international conflict.

c) The second world war produced a death toll of 42 million people in Europe, and 10 million in Asia.

These disasters dwarf the losses in the previous big European war–174 000 soldiers killed–in the Franco-Prussian conflict of 1870-71[1], and the 4 per cent fall in aggregate OECD GDP in the previous big depression of 1908.

All parts of the world economy suffered in some degree from these disasters and the pace of growth slowed down worldwide. Their impact was biggest for Europe and Asia, least for Latin America.

The Advanced Capitalist Countries

The first world war brought major disruption in the international order. During the war the international flow of capital was halted, the flow of goods and services drastically interrupted and the gold standard abandoned. Domestically, in the belligerent countries, the role of government in production was greatly expanded; monetary and fiscal discipline lapsed, there was widespread and often dramatic inflation. The war changed the relative position of the different imperial powers. The economic power of the United States and Japan were greatly strengthened. The European powers were weakened by war damage and loss of foreign assets. The Austrian, German and Turkish Empires disappeared. The Russian Empire was reduced in size and, as the USSR, became the first "socialist" economy.

Substantial new trade barriers were erected in Eastern Europe, where five new countries had been created (Poland, Czechoslovakia, Latvia, Lithuania and Estonia), the new Austria was cut off from the trading partners it had had in its old empire, and

51

the USSR had little contact with the outside world. But there was little change in trade barriers in the rest of the world. The wartime McKenna duties of the United Kingdom were continued and a mild imperial preference was instituted from 1919 but the United Kingdom remained a very open economy and the increase in US tariffs in 1922 was not dramatic.

After a period of floating rates, and some sharp postwar inflations, a gold exchange standard was reestablished in 1925-28. Great importance was attached to restoration of the old international order, but the new arrangements were a flawed replica of the pre-war system. The institutional lynchpin was less robust. There was no longer a single central banker as the United Kingdom had been before the war. France, the United Kingdom and the United States were the new "nucleus", but were not in harmony on key decisions. Neither France nor the United States played according to the old rules. These had required countries with a strong balance (gold inflows) to ease their monetary policy, which was expected to increase their domestic demand and reduce their competitiveness, thus creating eventual export (gold acquisition) possibilities for the deficit countries which were assumed to follow deflationary policies of tight money until their competitiveness was restored[2]. This mechanism had not worked perfectly before the war[3] but the United Kingdom had more or less adhered to it. Now both France and the United States decoupled their domestic from their international position by sterilising gold reserves.

There was major currency misalignment, with the franc significantly undervalued, and sterling overvalued, which produced a big gold drain to France. The new system required much bigger reserves than the old, because of the greater difficulty in finding a lender of last resort, and the expectational uncertainties deriving from the disturbing postwar experience of extreme inflation and exchange volatility.

International economic relations were made acrimonious by the effort to extract large reparations from Germany and the existence of large inter-allied debts (mainly France and the United Kingdom to the United States). These debts had less "legitimacy" in political and banking circles than those originating in market transactions. The spectre of large-scale default threatened the whole structure to a greater degree than before.

The pattern and nature of international capital flows were different from what they had been before 1914. Both France and Germany were borrowers rather than lenders in the 1920s, UK lending capacity had declined. The United States was the new giant.

In spite of disputes about debt and reparations, the actual course of international lending was stabilising in the 1920s. In the immediate postwar period, the United States and the United Kingdom provided relief supplies to continental Europe. From 1919 to 1929 the United States exported $12.9 billion of capital–mostly private–a good deal of which went to Europe.

The economic experience of the 1920s differed from country to country. In the United States there was boom and prosperity, with the beginning of widespread ownership of cars and consumer durables. In Belgium, France and Italy it was a period of rising prices, expansionary monetary and fiscal policy, reasonably rapid growth and low unemployment. In Germany, in the 1920s, there was high investment and rapid expansion, only temporarily interrupted by the 1923 hyperinflation. The Scandinavian countries followed rather deflationary policies, but they were not as extreme as that of the United Kingdom which was the only really stagnant Western economy in the 1920s.

The expansionary policies of Belgium, France and Germany were due more to political inability to re-establish 'sound' finance, than to substantial analytical differences from British officialdom. Everywhere there was a feeling that balanced budgets, price stability and restoration of the gold standard were prime aims. The major error peculiar to the United Kingdom was the insistence on returning to the exact prewar parity for sterling.

The 1929-32 depression upset this precariously restored order. It was in no way a normal cyclical phenomenon. It originated in the two biggest economies–the United States and Germany where the fall in production was deepest and earliest. In both countries the impact of depression was reinforced by bank collapses. The fragility of the international order magnified the transmission mechanisms. Between 1929 and 1932, the aggregate import volume of OECD countries fell by a quarter. The international capital market collapsed. The gold standard was abandoned. Expectations were dampened by a fall of almost a half in world export prices.

Governments compounded the trade recession by destroying the liberal trading order. The United States gave an unfortunate lead with the Smoot Hawley tariff legislation of 1929-30. This set off a retaliatory wave which not only raised tariffs generally, but abrogated the multilateral principle. The United Kingdom introduced imperial preference in 1932 and France, Japan and the Netherlands followed similar tactics in their empires. Even worse than this were the quantitative controls on trade which Germany pioneered, which were also practised in France, Italy, Japan, the Netherlands, Indonesia, Eastern Europe and Latin America.

Recession was accompanied by sharply declining prices. During the 1920s the advanced countries had made considerable sacrifices to achieve price stability. Average price levels had been falling in Japan, Netherlands and the United Kingdom from 1924 to 1929, and they were stable in the United States. German policy makers were petrified at the possibility of rekindling inflation which was the fundamental reason they met the recession with such deflationary weapons. Within the advanced countries expectations were geared to price declines and this was reinforced by publicly decreed wage cuts in France and Germany. Furthermore, there had already been signs of overproduction and excess stocks of agricultural commodities before the recession, so primary commodity prices were unusually sensitive to slackening demand. Consumer prices in the United States and Germany fell by a fifth from 1929 to 1932, and substantially in the other Western countries[4]. For developing countries the price falls were even bigger, because it was much more difficult to cut output of agricultural products than manufactured goods, and agricultural incomes were in any case much more downwardly flexible than those of industrial wage earners in the developed world.

The depression was exacerbated by perverse international capital flows. The steady flow of American private capital which Germany had received in the 1920s was reversed in 1928-29. France which had the strongest payments position was positively hostile to Austro-German liquidity problems which caused the collapse of the Austrian Kreditanstalt in May and Germany's Danat bank in June 1931. A US action intended to be helpful was President Hoover's 1931 moratorium on war debts and reparations payments. However, such tolerance of *de facto* default on official debt meant that willingness to lend capital internationally on private account dried up more or less completely.

The 1929-32 recession was very deep in OECD countries. GDP fell by 18 per cent from 1929 to 1932 and was only 6 per cent above 1929 by 1938. However, the depression was much more severe in the United States than in Europe and Japan. US GDP fell by 28 per cent and was still more than 6 per cent below the 1929 peak in 1938. In the 15 other countries taken as a group the 1929-32 fall in GDP was 8.5 per cent and 1938 GDP was almost 17 per cent above the 1929 level.

In the recovery from depression, expansion of government expenditure played a major stimulative role, particularly in Germany and Japan (see Tables 5.1 and 5.2).

Table 5.1.   **Fiscal outcomes - General government net lending as a proportion of GDP at current prices, 1929-38**

	France	Germany	Japan	United Kingdom	United States
1929	0.4	1.2	−2.1	−2.3	0.9
1930	0.4	1.2	−3.3	−3.0	−0.3
1931	0.2	−0.1	−6.1	−3.7	−3.8
1932	−1.1	−0.7	−8.6	−2.0	−3.1
1933	−3.0	−3.5	−8.1	−1.4	−2.5
1934	−2.9	−3.9	−5.5	−1.1	−3.7
1935	−4.1	−5.7	−6.0	−2.1	−2.7
1936	−5.1	−7.1	−4.8	−2.4	−3.7
1937	−6.7	−5.9	−7.1	−3.1	0.3
1938	−8.9	−10.3	−14.8	−4.9	−2.1

Sources:

France from L. Fontvieille, *Evolution et croissance de l'Etat français 1815-1969*, ISMEA, Paris, 1976, pp. 2086-2090. GDP from J.-C. Toutain, *Le produit intérieur brut de la France de 1789 à 1982*, ISMEA, Paris, pp. 155-7.

Germany 1929-33 from D. Keese, "Die volkswirtschaftlichen Gesamtgrössen für das deutsche Reich in den Jahren 1925-1936", in W. Conze and H. Raupach, eds., *Die Staats — und Wirtschaftskrise des deutschen Reiches*, Klett, Stuttgart, 1967, pp. 43, 47 and 53. 1934-38 from R. Erbe, *Die nationalsozialistische Wirtschaftspolitik 1933-1939 im Lichte der modernen Theorie*, Polygraphischer Verlag, Zurich, 1958, pp. 34 and 100.

Japan from K. Ohkawa and M. Shinohara, *Patterns of Japanese Economic Development*, Yale, 1979, total government expenditure (p. 371) minus total current revenue (p. 377) both for fiscal years divided by calendar year PNB (p. 268).

United Kingdom from C.H. Feinstein, *National Income Expenditure and Output of the United Kingdom 1856-1965*, Cambridge, 1972, consolidated current balance (T35) plus central (T79) and local (T81) capital expenditures as percent of GDP (T11).

United States Government balance (p. 135) and GNP (p. 1), from *National Income and Product Accounts of the United States, 1929-82*, Dept. of Commerce, Washington, 1986.

These were the countries with the biggest recovery in private investment. The only case where exports improved substantially was Japan which made a major drive to bolster trade within its colonial empire, and to penetrate other Asian markets by deep devaluation.

The 1930s brought a major departure from the old canons of sound finance which had reemerged fairly intact after the first world war. This was not altogether due to government volition. The old orthodoxy was abandoned with demurrance and misgiving, but the overall drift (see Table 5.1) was clearly in the expansionary direction which Keynes was urging in the United Kingdom against Hayek, Robbins and supporters of the old "Treasury view", who favoured sound finance rather than compensatory policies[5].

In the United Kingdom, the first reactions to the recession were mildly deflationary with tighter fiscal and monetary policy to protect the exchange rate. However, policy switched in 1931 when the United Kingdom managed an effective and large devaluation for a couple of years before the dollar was devalued. In 1932, tariff policy switched completely with effective protection for many industries for the first time, augmented by preferences in imperial markets. The UK banking structure was much sounder than that of the United States and Germany and consequently avoided the phenomenon of secondary deflation which they suffered.

Japan had followed rather deflationary policies in the 1920s preparatory to its belated adoption of the gold standard in January 1930, but in December 1931, it devalued the yen even lower than sterling had gone. It raised tariffs, increased its penetration of

Table 5.2. **Indicators of recession and recovery in western countries in the 1930s**

Volume movements, 1929 = 100

	France	Germany	Japan	Netherlands	United Kingdom	United States
			GDP			
1932	85.3	84.2	101.3	92.4	94.9	71.8
1938	96.5	139.6	137.4	103.0	118.4	93.8
			Exports of goods and services			
1932	58.7	55.2	124.8	70.8	67.8	55.1
1938	63.0	47.9	203.1	87.8	76.8	81.0
			Fixed investment			
1932	80.3	55.3	91.9	83.8	85.9	30.4
1938	74.4	156.3	215.1	91.4	128.4	53.9
			Private consumption			
1932	94.5	82.8	101.2	108.6	102.0	81.7
1938	104.5	109.8	119.2	101.6	116.7	97.0
			Public consumption			
1932	129.8	89.2	129.4	117.0	105.0	108.5
1938	144.7	290.2	197.7	121.7	225.4	146.4
			Unemployment as a percent of labour force			
1929	1.2	5.9	n.a.	1.7	7.2	3.1
1932	n.a.	17.2	n.a.	8.3	15.3	22.3
1938	3.7	1.3	n.a.	9.9	9.2	12.4

Source: GDP components J.-J. Carré, P. Dubois and E. Malinvaud, *La croissance française*, Seuil, Paris, 1972 and C.A. van Bochove and T.A. Huitker, *Main National Accounting Series 1900-1986, Occasional Paper NA-017*, CBS, The Hague, 1987. Otherwise from sources mentioned for Table 5.1. Unemployment from A. Maddison, *Phases of Capitalist Development*, Oxford, 1982.

Asian markets, extended its budget deficit, promoted an investment boom, and undertook major rearmament. It had already strengthened its banking system in the 1920s, and avoided problems in this direction[6].

In the initial stage of the depression in Germany, the Brüning government pushed deflation to masochistic lengths, cutting government spending in real terms, raising taxes and interest rates and decreeing compulsory wage cuts of 10 per cent. In 1932 there was a change in fiscal policy by the Von Papen–Schleicher governments, which was continued by the Nazis, who boosted demand by massive rearmament, and repudiated reparations. German "Keynesians" urged devaluation and a more expansionary policy from an early date[7]. However, Germany did not devalue, but created a tight network of exchange and import controls with complex bilateral discrimination. This innovation in the peacetime policy armoury had a wide influence in Latin America.

The United States was the centre of the crisis, had the deepest recession in 1929-32, the slowest recovery, and another sizeable recession in 1937-38 which most other countries avoided. The cyclical record had for decades shown intermittent deep (Kuznets) cycles due to changes in demographic momentum and the long swing in housing. There

55

was a housing boom in the 1920s at a time when demographic growth was decelerating and a deep reversal of this in the 1930s. The turnround in housing was exacerbated by institutional weakness in the mortgage market. Up to 1929, three year renewable mortgages were common. These were defaulted and foreclosed on a large scale in the crisis. One of the major institution-strengthening pieces of New Deal legislation was reform of the mortgage market with tight government controls, guarantees, and a government organised secondary market.

The recession was reinforced by the collapse of the banking system. The United States had a primitive unit banking structure, rather than a few big banks with many branches as in Europe. Even in the good years of the 1920s, 800 of these small banks closed every year. In 1930-1933, 9,000 closed. The New Deal legislation introduced deposit insurance, but like mortgage insurance this came too late.

The 1920s had also seen a boom in consumer durables (notably cars) which was reversed in the crisis. The end of the stock market boom and reduction in consumer wealth reinforced this. This is one of the reasons why US consumption levels declined so much.

Friedman and Schwartz have argued that the Federal Reserve System was mainly responsible for the crisis because it failed to supply massive liquidity when the economy was weakened. Temin disagrees and offers an entirely non-monetarist explanation. Any satisfactory explanation must embrace both real and monetary factors, though the latter involved long-standing institutional weakness as well as conjunctural policy error[8].

The Roosevelt approach to the crisis was inspired more by Irving Fisher than Keynes. The emphasis was on reflating prices as much as on production, in order to reduce the debt burden. Thus agricultural prices were strengthened by farm support legislation, trade union power was bolstered in an effort to raise wages, the dollar was revalued against gold and silver for the same reasons and early New Deal legislation tried to strengthen cartels (until the moves were declared unconstitutional). The public works measures, the proliferation of new government agencies, the 1935 social security system, and the moderate fiscal deficit were not enough to bring the economy anywhere near full employment. Fiscal and monetary tightness in 1937 sparked off the 1938 recession.

It was wartime demand which pushed the US back to full employment. The long term value of the New Deal was in strengthening institutions designed to prevent a recurrence of the 1930s.

Latin America

The first world war interfered with Latin American export markets, import availabilities, capital flows, migration and prices. But its adverse consequences were much smaller than in most of the world economy. As in the United States, the 1920s were a return to the prewar "normality".

The 1929-32 crisis was a much bigger shock. It brought a collapse in world trade and capital markets and sharply worsened terms of trade. It broke a pattern of integration in the world economy which had lasted for decades, and induced a whole new armoury of defensive inward-looking policy weapons.

The world depression produced several types of deflationary impact. The first was a decline in the volume of demand for primary export products, the second was the decline in terms of trade, i.e. the relative prices of primary exports compared with imports of manufactures, the third was the sudden cessation of the capital flow from Europe and the United States and the fourth was the general fall in the world price level which raised the real burden of debt service. As a result, Latin America had to cut its import volume by 60 per cent from 1929 to 1932.

The initial response to the depression was adherence to old policy weapons and gold standard rules, i.e. defence of the exchange rate by tighter monetary and fiscal policy and loss of reserves. But given the magnitude of external shock, new policy weapons were needed. Argentina dropped the gold standard in 1929, though it continued to use reserves to protect the peso, Brazil followed shortly thereafter, Chile, Colombia, Peru and Mexico waited for two years.

The new weapons were the exchange controls, quantitative restrictions, and discriminatory practices invented by Dr. Schacht at the Reichsbank in Germany. There was an increase in tariffs, and debt delinquency was a vital component of the new policy menu. By the end of 1935 there was 100 per cent delinquency on dollar debt by Chile, Colombia, Peru, and Mexico, 93 per cent by Brazil and 24 per cent by Argentina (by municipalities and provinces, not by central government)[9]. This action provided very substantial balance of payments relief, and aroused no effective sanctions.

The process of recovery was helped by abandonment of fiscal orthodoxy which would have involved deflationary action to achieve a balanced budget and service foreign debt. The new policy-mix was a muddled and stumbling reaction to new challenges[10]. It was not derived from any theoretical insight[11], but it had common components across Latin America involving rejection of the old liberal economic order, a switch to government intervention, national autarky and a dash of populism.

Monetary policy helped finance budget deficits which were swollen by the shortfall in revenue from import and export duties. The central banks set up in the 1920s with advice from Kemmerer and Niemeyer did not function as brakes on expansion after the abandonment of the gold standard[12]. They accommodated sectors of the economy which were in difficulty. The fiscal-monetary stimuli were backed by creation of development

Table 5.3. **Regional impact of world depression 1929-38**

Indices, 1929 = 100

	GDP	Export volume	Import volume	Terms of trade
		OECD countries		
1929	100.0	100.0	100.0	100.0
1932	82.3	64.7	76.5	113.7
1938	106.0	79.9	87.0	108.3
		Latin America		
1929	100.0	100.0	100.0	100.0
1932	90.3	70.6	41.0	71.4
1938	125.9	86.4	72.5	84.9
		Asia		
1929	100.0	100.0	100.0	100.0
1932	103.2	77.2	78.5	84.2
1938	108.3	90.1	81.0[a]	94.9[a]

a) 1936.
Sources: First column derived from Appendices A and B. Second column from Appendix D. Otherwise from A. Maddison, *Two Crises: Latin America and Asia 1929-38 and 1973-83*, OECD Development Centre, 1985, with Latin America adjusted to include Peru.

banks[13] whose subsidised credits provided increasingly specific incentives. Triffin[14] described development of monetary policy as follows:

"The domestic-credit expansion, at first, took the form of an outright increase in the loans and investments of the central bank, under piecemeal and haphazard legislation of a frankly opportunistic type. The loans went primarily to the government, to development *(fomento)* institutions, to official and semiofficial agricultural and mortgage banks, to various producers' associations, etc. This brought about a gradual expansion of the means of payment and of bank reserves and served as a basis for the succeeding revival of other banking credit, side by side with central-banking credit."

In the 1930s, state enterprise was minimal except in Mexico where the government nationalised electricity, oil, and insurance. However, in the second world war Brazil created state companies for the manufacture of steel, iron ore, airplane engines, tractors, trucks, automobiles, soda ash, caustic soda and electricity.

Before the 1929 shock, most Latin American countries were governed by oligarchic elites representing propertied interests content to leave a substantial part of banking and trade to foreign interests. In the disarray that followed the world crisis, their hold was shaken. In Brazil, Vargas, dictator from 1930 to 1945, strengthened the federal government and created new elements of bureaucratic power and patronage. The new elites were nationalistic and wanted to reduce foreign influence in banking, insurance and commerce, an objective whose implementation was accelerated by general delinquency on foreign debt. Vargas and other rulers of the epoch cultivated a new labour clientele with a minimum wage, 8 hour day, holidays with pay, job security, and social security.

The biggest change occurred in Mexico. By 1940 there was an entirely new state apparatus where legitimacy was vested in a dominant party with its roots in the new bureaucracy, peasantry and organised labour. In its political strength, commitment to land reform and indigenist symbolism, it had no real parallel elsewhere in Latin America, but the general economic philosophy which emerged from the Mexican revolution—a dirigiste commitment to industrialisation, a nationalist penchant for autarky, a large state sector without anything like the European socialist commitment to eliminate domestic capitalist production—was one which had gained fairly general acceptance in Latin America by the end of the 1940s.

Latin American countries had considerable reasons for satisfaction with their economic achievements in the 1930s and 1940s. All of them except Colombia had been deeply affected by the shock of 1929-32, but they made a strong recovery thereafter, which continued through the war years. In spite of supply shortages, they were able to grow successfully, and achieve rather easy import substitution without a large switch of resources to capital formation, or any massive effort at popular education (though some countries strengthened vocational training on German lines—particularly Brazil and Colombia). The average GDP growth for Latin America for 1913-50 was 3.3 per cent a year compared with 2.0 per cent for OECD countries and 1.3 per cent for Asia. In spite of faster demographic growth than elsewhere, this was also a period of greater progress in real per capita income than in the rest of the world.

The Asian Countries

The basic political and legal character of the Asian economies did not change until after the second world war. The British and French colonial empires grew after the first world war when they acquired Germany's old possessions and took the remnants of the

Ottoman Empire. Japan increased its empire in the 1930s. The Asian picture was much less dynamic in the 1920s than in Latin America.

The 1929-32 recession had a relatively mild impact in most of Asia. Aggregate Asian GDP actually rose a little in these years. Latin America had a worse terms of trade shock, and had been much more dependent on foreign capital inflow than Asia. The trade dependence of Asia on the United States was small, and Japanese dynamism had its biggest impact on Asia. However, Asian countries did not enjoy the recovery which Latin American countries had in the 1930s and they were badly hurt by the second world war.

The 1930s experience of Asian countries was heterogeneous and policy differences played a major role. British and Dutch policies in their colonies were deflationary, whereas Japanese policy in Korea, Manchuria and Taiwan, was a form of military develop-mentalism which produced fast growth. China's policy was *sui generis*, influenced by special factors such as the nature of its silver currency system and exigencies of war, which led to inflationary fiscal policies. Thailand, which was not a colony, generally pursued cautious policies, to avoid foreign indebtedness. None of our Asian countries, except China, defaulted on foreign debt in the 1930s.

There had been some increase in protection in Asia in the 1920s. India had regained its tariff autonomy and some degree of protection developed before the crisis. The 3 per cent treaty limitation on Thailand's tariff was removed in 1926. China regained its tariff economy in 1929. In the 1930s these tariffs were raised.

In Indonesia, official monetary and fiscal policy was particularly deflationary. The metropolitan government adhered to the gold standard until 1936. Tariffs were not raised, there were no exchange controls or debt default. The problem of payments adjustment was met by policies which attempted to squeeze down prices to competitive levels and by quantitative import restrictions. There were drastic cuts in expenditure and in government personnel.

Until after the second world war, the big contrast between the Asian countries and Latin America, was that they were colonies or virtual colonies. This meant that foreigners had a quasi monopoly of top level government jobs with generous expatriate pay scales. The monopoly of top jobs in private activity was not as complete as it was in government, but the big imperial powers (France, Netherlands and the United Kingdom) had created their banking, shipping, commercial and managerial agencies initially in the age of mer-chant capitalism and retained a substantially monopolistic position for this reason. The colonial powers had imposed their own legal systems which often prevented native capitalists e.g. moneylenders operating according to customary law, from breaking into the modern capitalist sector. Finally the colonial governments reinforced the inherently unequal partnership situation by spending very little on "native" education as compared with the facilities for their citizens resident in colonies.

These points can be documented rather easily for Indonesia around 1929 thanks to the availability of estimates for national income by ethnic origin and the rather good 1930 population census. Thus in 1930, literacy rates (for population as a whole) were only 6 per cent for Indonesians and 29 per cent for Chinese against 75 per cent for Europeans. On a per capita basis Indonesian incomes averaged 63 guilders a year, foreign Asiatics 373, and Europeans 3 720[15]. Thus the average European income was round 60 times the average Indonesian income. As European incomes were so large, this rein-forced the enclave character of the colonial economy, and biased consumption patterns towards imported manufactured goods to a greater degree than would have been the case with an indigenous elite. This tendency was reinforced by a strong governmental tendency to purchase capital goods in the home country.

59

Table 5.4. **Dimensions of foreign presence under colonialism**

	"Europeans", metropolitan nationals, and those of assimilated status[a]	Percentage of total population
Dutch Colony		
Indonesia	240 162	0.40
British Colonies		
Burma (1931)	34 000	0.23
Ceylon (1929)	7 500	0.15
India (1931)	168 134	0.05
Malaya (1931) (included Singapore)	33 811	0.77
French Colony		
Indochina (1937)	42 345	0.18
Japanese Colonies		
Korea (1930-35)	573 000	2.62
Taiwan (1930)	228 000	4.96
US Colony		
Philippines (1939)	36 000	0.15
China[b]	267 000	0.06

a) Includes Eurasians in Indonesia (134 000); in Malaya (16 043); and in Indochina (approx. 14 000). The Philippine figure includes 10 500 Japanese, but excludes US military personnel and 200 000 Hispano-Filipino mestizos.
b) China was not a colony in the sense in which the other countries were, but had surrendered national sovereignty in "Treaty" ports to Japan, the United States and European countries, as well as ceding territory to Japan and Russia and suzerainty over other areas to France, Japan, Russia and the United Kingdom.
Source: A. Maddison, "The Colonial Burden: A Comparative Perspective", in M. Scott, ed., *Public Policy and Economic Development,* OUP, 1989.

The Dutch presence in Indonesia was proportionately bigger than the British in India or Ceylon, the French in Indochina. It was smaller than the Japanese presence in Korea and Taiwan (see Table 5.4).

Japanese policy in Korea and Taiwan was much more developmentalist than that of other colonial powers as it involved serious efforts to improve technology in basic foodcrops, substantial investment in developing modern industry, migration of middle level skills from Japan and somewhat more technical education for the local population than in British, French or Dutch colonies.

One consequence of the concentration of entrepreneurship and economic opportunity in the hands of metropolitan nationals, was that most of the savings of the economy accumulated in the hands of the foreign population. There was a substantial and continuous drain of remittances to the metropole on this account as well as for pensions. In India this averaged about 1.5 per cent of national income over several decades. In Indonesia it was much bigger than this in the 1920s–about 13 per cent of national income.

In spite of this drain, and the very substantial export surpluses which most colonial countries maintained for decades, foreigners built up substantial asset claims in these

Table 5.5. **Per capita net foreign capital stock**

In 1938

PORTFOLIO AND DIRECT

	Net obligations per capita ($)	Total foreign obligations ($ million)	Total foreign assets ($ million)
Argentina	230	3 193	39
Brazil	51	2 030	5
Chile	258	1 288	21
Colombia	37	322	2
Cuba	176	807	26
Mexico	89	1 778	19
Peru	48	326	2
Uruguay	136	248	0
Venezuela	97	356	2
Average/Total	125	10 348	116
Ceylon	21	125	0
China	3	2 557	770
India	11	3 644	203
Indochina	17	391	0
Indonesia	35	2 378	7
Korea	73	1 718[a]	0
Malaya	164	696	1
Philippines	18	307	28
Taiwan	35	198[b]	0
Thailand	14	200	0
Average/Total	39	12 214	1 009
Australia	503	3 730	254
Canada	428	6 628	1 855

a) 1941.
b) 1939.
Source: Foreign obligations from C. Lewis, *The United States and Foreign Investment Problems,* Brookings, 1948, pp. 321-41, except for India which is from D.H.N. Gurtoo, *India's Balance of Payments 1920-1960,* Chand, Delhi, 1961, p. 69 and Korea from Sang-Chul Suh, *Growth and Structural Changes in the Korean Economy, 1910-40,* Harvard, 1978, p. 129.

countries. Most of these were the fruit of locally financed investment and reinvested profits. Actual inflows of capital to the colonies were generally rather small except in Korea and Taiwan.

USSR

The Russian economy was very badly damaged by the strain of the first world war. About a third of the labour force was mobilised in the massive ill-equipped army which suffered crushing defeats. Industrial output fell by a quarter from 1913 to 1917, agricultural output was down by a tenth, and inflation was rampant.

The economic crisis facilitated the acquisition of power by the Bolsheviks, but their widespread expropriation of private property, repudiation of foreign debt, repression of the church, and persecution of the old ruling class led to foreign blockade, intervention and civil war. The economic chaos and inflation of that period was so great that socialist transformation was temporarily dropped in favour of the "new economic policy" (NEP) which restored a market economy and some degree of private enterprise, particularly in distribution. This produced a period of substantial recovery.

In the period between Lenin's death in 1924 and Stalin's drastic moves to impose a new Soviet model in 1928, there was extensive debate on the policy options. The main protagonists were Bukharin and Preobrazhensky, and a major point was on tactics for squeezing a bigger investible surplus from the economy to accelerate the growth rate. Bukharin argued that an increase in the levy on the peasants was not necessary and would weaken support for the regime. Instead incentives for industrial production and savings should be raised. He was optimistic about capital saving possibilities through economies of scale and shift working. Preobrazhensky, by contrast, argued that the capital stock was in poor condition, already under great strain, and that large scale investment was necessary. He wanted to squeeze peasant incomes by the price mechanism rather than fiscal policy, arguing naively that "not a single kopek" would be used for "any special taxation apparatus"[16].

The path of development chosen by Stalin was more extreme than that envisaged by Preobrazhensky. Between 1928 and the second world war, the largely peasant agriculture was collectivised, consumption was squeezed, labour force participation increased, the rate of investment went up from 12.5 per cent of GDP in 1928 to 26 per cent in 1937, exports fell from 3 to 1 per cent of GDP, priority was given to heavy industry and the manufacture of investment goods. Education was expanded very fast. In industry the output mix, the allocation of inputs and prices were all decided centrally by government.

There is controversy about the rate of Soviet GDP growth in the 1929-38 period, but even if we take the lowest Western estimates, which we have done, the pace of expansion was remarkably fast, at 6 per cent a year, particularly in the circumstances of the 1930s. The Soviet statistical yearbook registered the change in social structure from 1929 to 1939, with a rise of collective farm workers from 3 per cent to 47 per cent of the labour force, a decline of peasant farmers from 75 to 3 per cent, the bourgeoisie (already reduced from 16 per cent in 1913 to 5 per cent in 1928) disappeared, and the working class rose from 18 to 46 per cent[17].

The costs of the Stalin strategy were very high. Per capita private consumption fell. The process of collectivisation was brutal and wasteful. The peasantry destroyed farm buildings, equipment, and livestock on a tremendous scale. It was not until 1953 that the 1928 levels of livestock production were regained. Many peasants died resisting collectivisation or from famine. Stalin killed off the old Bolshevik elite, a large part of the intelligentsia and the officer corps of the army. Large numbers of people were sent to forced labour camps. Urban housing space per capita dropped by a fifth, and the distributive network of the NEP was replaced by a system of rationing and queues.

In the second world war, the Soviet economy suffered greater losses than most. The most densely settled parts of the country were occupied and fought over, a scorched earth policy was carried out, dwellings and factories destroyed, and so many people were killed that the 1939 population was not restored for 15 years.

NOTES AND REFERENCES

1. The French revolutionary wars were the most costly earlier episode in terms of lives lost. See UN, *The Determinants and Consequences of Population Trends*, Vol. I, New York, 1973, p. 145 which estimates war deaths from 1789 to 1815 at 5 million.

2. Gold standard theory did not refer to levels of demand or employment but argued on more or less microeconomic lines as if country disequilibria were simply a question of relative prices which could be nudged into line along a flat trend by mild monetary medicine because wages and prices were assumed to be flexible upwards and downwards.

3. See A. I. Bloomfield, *Monetary Policy Under the International Gold Standard 1880-1914*, Federal Reserve Bank, New York, 1959.

4. See A. Maddison, *Phases of Capitalist Development*, Oxford 1982 for the figures.

5. It is interesting to note, now that the 1980s orthodoxy has swung back to Hayek's steadfast position, that Robbins and other "Austrians" retracted their judgements of the 1930s. See L. Robbins, *Autobiography of An Economist*, Macmillan, 1971, pp. 154-55 and 188 "I shall always regard my dispute with Keynes as the greatest mistake of my professional career, and the book, *The Great Depression*, which I subsequently wrote, as something I would willingly see forgotten... I let my judgement of possible remedies be distorted by inappropriate sense of proportion... Fluctuations of aggregate demand must not be left to look after themselves... it is an important function of government, national or international, to pay attention to such matters." In similar vein Fritz Machlup's survey of Hayek's contribution to economics for the Nobel prize committee (*Swedish Journal of Economics*, 1974, p. 506), had this to say "after several years of the Great Depression, it had become clear that Hayek's prescription of 'waiting it out' was inopportune. ...In those years of 'secular' stagnation and unemployment, a model for which full employment was the starting assumption could not compete with one that was based on unemployment equilibrium."

6. See H.T. Patrick, "The Economic Muddle of the 1920s", in J.W. Morley, *Dilemmas of Growth in Prewar Japan*, Princeton, 1971.

7. See W. Grotkopp, *Die Grosse Krise*, Econ-Verlag, Düsseldorf, 1954 and the material cited in G. Bombach *et al.*, *Der Keynesianismus*, Springer, Berlin, 1976.

8. See M. Friedman and A.J. Schwartz, *A Monetary History of the United States 1867-1960*, NBER, Princeton, 1963, and P. Temin, *Did Monetary Forces Cause the Great Depression?*, Norton, New York, 1976. See C.P. Kindleberger, *The World in Depression 1925-1939*, second edition, Berkeley, 1986 and R.J. Gordon and J.A. Wilcox, "Monetarist Interpretations of the Great Depression: An Evaluation and Critique", in K. Brunner, *The Great Depression Revisited*, Nijhoff, Boston, 1981, for a more eclectic view.

9. C. Lewis, *America's Stake in International Investments*, Brookings, Washington, D.C., 1938.

10. R. Prebisch, "Argentine Economic Policies Since the 1930s: Recollections", in G. di Tella and D.C.M. Platt, eds., *The Political Economy of Argentina, 1880-1946*, Macmillan, London, 1986.

11. Furtado has suggested that Brazil in the 1930s was promoting a Keynesian-type "anticyclical policy of much broader scope than any even suggested in any of the industrialized countries" (see C. Furtado, *The Economic Growth of Brazil*, University of California, Berkeley, 1963,

p. 211). This has been challenged by Pelaez, and Fishlow has stressed that policy was only adventitiously Keynesian. One should also remember that the cumulative impact of Brazil's 1931-38 destruction of coffee stocks was equal to 17.6 per cent of 1929 GDP. See A. Maddison, *Two Crises: Latin America and Asia 1929-38 and 1973-83*, OECD Development Centre, Paris, 1985, p. 26. The latter source contains a summary of policy responses to the 1929-32 depression in Argentina, Brazil, Chile, Colombia, Cuba and Mexico, as well as in China, India, Indonesia, Korea and Taiwan.

12. Central banks were set up in the following order in these countries: Colombia 1923, Chile and Mexico 1925, Peru 1931, Argentina 1935, and Brazil 1964. India acquired a central bank in 1934, Thailand in 1942. In Japan, by contrast, the central bank was created in 1882.

13. In order of their creation, the main ones were: Caja de Credito Agrario, Industrial y Minero, Colombia, 1932; Nacional Financiera, Mexico, 1934; Banco Industrial del Peru, 1936; Corporacion de Fomento de la Produccion, Chile, 1940; Banco Industrial de la Republica Argentina, 1944; Banco Nacional de Desenvolvimento Economico, Brazil, 1952. See Maddison, *Economic Progress and Policy in Developing Countries*, Norton, New York, 1970, p. 174.

14. R. Triffin, "Central Banking and Monetary Management in Latin America", in S.E. Harris, ed., *Economic Problems of Latin America*, McGraw Hill, New York, 1944, p. 98. On fiscal policy, see H.C. Wallich, "Fiscal Policy and the Budget", in Harris, *op. cit.*, 1944, and A.V. Villela and W. Suzigan, *Government Policy and the Economic Growth of Brazil 1889-1945*, IPEA, Rio, 1977.

15. See A. Maddison, "Dutch Income in and from Indonesia 1700-1938", in A. Maddison and G. Prince, eds., *Economic Growth in Indonesia 1820-1940*, Foris, Dordrecht and New York, 1989.

16. See A. Ehrlich, *The Soviet Industrialization Debate 1924-1928*, Harvard, 1960; S.F. Cohen, *Bukharin and the Bolshevik Revolution*, Knopf, New York, 1971 and E. Preobrazhensky, *The New Economics*, Oxford, 1965.

17. *Narodnoe Khoziastvo SSSR 1962*, p. 14.

Chapter 6

THE POSTWAR GOLDEN AGE: 1950-73

The years 1950 to 1973 were ones of unparalleled prosperity, with GDP of our 32 countries growing 5.1 per cent a year, and per capita income 3.3 per cent.

One can look for the explanation of this boom in three dimensions.

1) In the first place, there was a functioning international order with explicit and rational codes of behaviour, and a strong and flexible institutional underpinning which had not existed before. There was an East-West split, but it had elements of stability, and there was much greater harmony of interest between capitalist economies than in the interwar situation. North-South relations were transformed from the colonial tutelage of prewar years to a situation where more emphasis was placed (rhetorically and often substantively) on action to stimulate development. There was a modest but fairly steady flow of capital to developing countries, equal to about 2.5 per cent of their GDP.

This new order affected the options of most countries in a positive way, offering greatly enlarged opportunities for trade and specialisation, better access to foreign capital and technology, increased possibilities for international migration, as well as the reassurance and stimulus which came from operating in a world in steady expansion, free of deflationary shocks and providing fora for negotiation, consultation and mutual aid.

2) The second new element of strength was the changed character of domestic policies, which were self-consciously devoted to promoting high levels of demand and employment in the advanced countries, and usually oriented to development objectives elsewhere.

3) Finally, one can explain improved performance more directly by the general and large increase in investment ratios, the accelerated growth of capital stock, the rise in foreign aid and technology transfers, the accelerated educational effort of developing countries, improvements in international trade and specialisation and in domestic economic structure.

The Postwar International Order as it Affected OECD Countries

The first steps towards the postwar order were world-wide in character, i.e. the creation of the United Nations as a more effective peace keeping successor to the League of Nations, with several specialised agencies–FAO, UNESCO, ILO, the IMF and World Bank–to promote economic and social development.

Shortly after the war, the cold war between the two superpowers upped the costs of peaceful coexistence. Mutual deterrence involved large military spending and the creation of competitive military alliances (NATO and the Warsaw Pact). It also became clear that the scale of funding required to provide effectively for speedy economic recovery was well beyond that envisaged when the new UN organisations were created. Thus they were supplemented by new agencies with a narrower membership: OEEC in Western Europe and the CMEA in Eastern Europe.

The OEEC (Organisation for European Economic Co-operation) grew out of the Marshall Plan under which the United States provided aid equal to 3 per cent of its GDP for 4 years to the European countries which formed the new organisation. The aid was conditional on mutual removal of barriers to trade and payments and was intended to restore the strength and promote the unity of the most shattered part of the world economy. Initially, Marshall aid was also offered to the East European countries, and was refused by them. The communist countries also stayed out of the IMF and World Bank, which meant that these two organisations were also *de facto* part of the Western institutional setting.

Marshall Aid was spectacularly successful in removing trade barriers, promoting recovery of output, establishing international reserves and collective action to provide credit. Experience in OEEC also demonstrated the usefulness of regular and articulate discussion of policy options and intentions and established a pattern of co-operation in many dimensions that continued after the end of Marshall Aid.

When it was clear that the so-called dollar problem had disappeared, the removal of trade barriers was followed by the general establishment of European currency convertibility in 1958. The return to convertibility had been nurtured by the earlier EPU arrangements within OEEC. The United States was the lynchpin of the postwar international monetary order—the fixed rate dollar-based system established at Bretton Woods—but there was co-operation in managing this system in IMF and OECD committees as well as in the BIS (Bank for International Settlements). This complex network of co-operation was quite different from the simple unwritten rules which had governed behaviour before 1914, or the recurrent discord of the interwar years. In fact, intimate co-operative arrangements within the West, within the East, and (to a much lesser extent) between developing countries, coexisted with more exiguous worldwide interchange inside UN bodies with less conflict than might have been expected. These inner core arrangements tended to facilitate the modest progress there was on a worldwide basis by preliminary clarification of many issues.

In 1958 the European Community came into operation. It was a smaller grouping of six European countries, with higher ambitions for integration of their economies than the 17 members of OEEC. In 1960, EFTA (the European Free Trade Area) emerged. This group included seven European countries which successfully sought to eliminate barriers in industrial trade between themselves and the European Community; in 1973, three EFTA countries (Denmark, Ireland and the United Kingdom) joined the EC and other countries followed thereafter.

There is no doubt that European countries were the biggest beneficiaries of the reduction in these trade barriers. Nevertheless, there were several successive worldwide reductions of trade barriers within the GATT (General Agreement on Tariffs and Trade) which meant that many of the benefits of industrial trade liberalisation initiated in Europe were filtered worldwide. In the course of the 1960s an institutionalised dialogue on trade and aid issues began between Western and developing countries in UNCTAD, as a supplement to those which already took place between North and South, and East and West in the UN.

One of the tasks of Western co-operation which emerged in 1961 when OEEC became OECD[1] was the co-ordination of the bilateral development assistance programmes of the 17 advanced countries which were members of its Development Assistance Committee (DAC). These programmes had grown *ad hoc* in the wake of very divergent

Table 6.1. Variations in export performance 1900-86

Annual average compound growth rate in export volume

	1900-13	1913-50	1950-73	1973-86
Australia	4.3	1.3	5.8	4.2
Austria	2.5	− 3.0	10.8	6.1
Canada	5.8	3.1	7.0	4.2
Belgium	4.9	0.3	9.4	3.4
Denmark	4.5	2.4	6.9	4.4
Finland	5.2	1.9	7.2	3.6
France	3.8	1.1	8.2	3.3
Germany	6.4	− 2.8	12.4	4.4
Italy	3.4	0.6	11.7	4.9
Japan	9.9	2.0	15.4	7.6
Netherlands	4.6	1.5	10.3	3.1
Norway	5.6	2.7	7.3	5.5
Sweden	4.9	2.8	7.0	3.2
Switzerland	3.6	0.3	8.1	3.5
United Kingdom	4.2	0.0	3.9	3.7
United States	2.5	2.2	6.3	1.7
OECD average	4.8	1.0	8.6	4.2
Bangladesh	(4.2)	− 1.5	2.0	4.2
China	4.7	1.1	2.7	10.4
India	4.2	− 1.5	2.5	2.5
Indonesia	4.0	2.3	6.5	3.3
Pakistan	(4.2)	− 1.5	3.6	6.7
Philippines	2.8	3.7	5.9	5.9
South Korea	8.0	− 1.3	20.3	14.0
Taiwan	7.4	2.6	16.3	11.6
Thailand	5.0	2.3	4.4	9.4
Asian average	4.9	0.7	7.1	7.6
Argentina	4.2	1.6	3.1	4.4
Brazil	0.4[a]	1.7	4.7	6.8
Chile	3.8	1.4	2.4	9.1
Colombia	7.8	3.9	3.8	6.0
Mexico	4.6	− 0.5	4.3	11.1
Peru	6.7	2.7	5.8	− 2.2
Latin American average	4.6	1.8	4.0	5.9
Developing country arithmetic average	4.8	1.1	5.9	6.9
USSR	4.7	− 0.1	10.0	4.7
32 country total	4.3	0.6	7.7	4.5

a) 1901-13.
Source: Derived from Tables D-2 and D-3.

decolonisation experiences. By 1961 most of the decolonialisation was complete, and there was also competition for influence in the third world from the USSR. There was a desire to broaden the flow of aid by contributions from new donors such as Germany, Japan, and some of the smaller European countries which had not had colonies. The bilateral aid flows were substantially bigger than the multilateral flow via the UN and its specialised agencies. The total size of official bilateral assistance (ODA) and other flows from OECD countries can be seen in Table D.11. ODA averaged 0.42 per cent of the GDP of the countries providing it from 1950 to 1973, other flows 0.37 per cent.

The Postwar Order in Latin America

In spite of its linguistic and cultural homogeneity, there was less impetus towards regional co-operation in Latin America than in European countries. Latin American countries did participate in the United Nations and its specialised agencies, but there were no substantial moves to reduce their high mutual trade barriers, there was resistance to liberalism in commercial policy and frequent rejection of IMF advocacy of fiscal and monetary rectitude and fixed exchange rates. As these countries had suffered less than other regions from the war, there was no equivalent to Marshall Aid. There had been some loose hemispheric co-operation in the Pan American Union since 1890 (which became the Organisation of American States after the war) and after some hesitation ECLA, the regional commission of the UN, was established in 1948, largely as a think tank and analytical body.

At the end of the 1950s, and early 1960s, there were some important changes in Latin American and US willingness to co-operate which had something to do with both the success of European reconstruction and the advent of Fidel Castro in Cuba. In 1958, President Kubitschek of Brazil put forward ideas for an Operation Panamerica. In 1959, the InterAmerican Bank was created. In 1960, the Treaty of Montevideo set up the Latin American Free Trade Area (with 9 member countries initially), and Latin American countries began to pay more attention to export possibilities. In 1961, President Kennedy responded to the Kubitschek idea by creating the Alliance for Progress, which was intended to generate an additional $20 billion capital flow to Latin America over a 10 year period, initiate closer consultation on economic policy in a special committee (CIAP) of the OAS, and promote social progress in land reform and other areas.

In a few years the impact of these new initiatives faded, partly because policies remained strongly nationalist under increasingly authoritarian governments. Although trade grew faster from the 1960s onwards, the proportion of intraregional trade remained very low in Latin America and the habit of mutual consultation on economic policy did not catch on, though there was somewhat greater progress in these respects in Central America[2].

The Postwar Order in Asia

In the Asian countries, the postwar changes in the international order were, in some respects, bigger than in the European countries, with the general ending of colonial rule and the communist takeover in China. However, there was no counterpart to the regional co-operation and institutions created after the war in Europe, and the Asian Development Bank did not start operations until 1966. Though there were military alliances (SEATO and other national arrangements) which ensured a large flow of military and economic aid, particularly to Korea and Taiwan, there was also a great deal of military action in the area due to conflicts of interest between countries of the region, and between the superpowers.

Thus the major institutional strength of the postwar international order was concentrated on the OECD countries and what it offered worldwide was a steady and substantial growth of international trade, some degree of international price stability, a functioning international monetary system, and a significant flow of official development assistance and of private capital from OECD countries.

Government Promotion of Domestic Demand in the OECD Countries

The fundamental innovation in postwar policy in the OECD countries was the commitment to full use of resources through activist real output management. In the United States, the idea was enshrined in the Full Employment Act of 1946, though it was not fully implemented until the 1960s. In the United Kingdom, Scandinavia and Canada, the Keynesian gospel of fiscal activism and the primordial commitment to full employment enjoyed very wide support throughout the political, academic, and bureaucratic "establishments". In France, the objective of full resource utilisation involved a bigger emphasis on planning and supply-side dirigisme. Italy and Japan had not participated in the Keynesian tradition but they also aimed at rapid and ambitious rebuilding of their economies by government intervention whenever necessary. Germany gave greater emphasis to price stability and export competitiveness than to buoyant domestic demand, but proclaimed the full employment goal in its Stabilisation Law of 1967.

In all these countries these new postwar goals tended to be stated in terms of full employment rather than rapid growth. The basic motivation was to avoid the waste of resources caused by unemployment and deflationary policy in the interwar period. With full and sustained employment, investment and growth rose to new and unprecedented levels but this was a bonus which early postwar policy makers had not anticipated.

Before the war, great importance was attached to price stability in most countries. In the golden age, it was often cited as a rhetorical target, but the aim was generally to keep the pace of price increase within limits that did not put too great a constraint on international competitiveness. Price increases of 4 per cent a year were regarded as a tolerable trade off for full employment.

A major feature of the golden age was the substantial growth in the ratio of government spending to GDP. This rose from 27 per cent of GDP in OECD countries in 1950 to 37 per cent in 1973. The rise was due largely to increases in social security and spending on merit wants such as education and health. After the early postwar nationalisations, there was no rise in the share of employment in public enterprise, and all the Western countries remained basically capitalist, i.e. they had predominantly private ownership of the means of production.

Domestic Policy in Developing Countries

a)   Latin America

In developing countries, there was also a move towards self-conscious governmental responsibility for maintenance of high levels of activity. In Latin America, Raoul Prebisch's influential 1950 Manifesto *(The Economic Development of Latin America and Its Principal Problems)* proclaimed a powerful role for government in avoiding the deflationary policies of the interwar years, though his message was more dirigiste, more inward looking, less optimistic about the possibilities for restoring a liberal world economy than was the case in OECD countries. In Latin America there was a greater commitment to government microeconomic intervention, more controls, subsidies and protection, a greater emphasis on "planning" and a greater distrust of market forces than in OECD countries.

Within Latin America, there were two striking features of postwar development, where experience differed markedly from Asia or from OECD countries. One of these was the much larger and persistent inequality of income (with dispersions between the top decile and bottom two deciles more than twice as high as in Asia or OECD countries, and the other was the widespread incidence of inflation (see Tables 6.2 and 6.4).

Table 6.2. **Experience of inflation, 1900-86**

Annual average compound rate of increase in GDP deflator

	1900-13	1920-38	1950-73	1973-82	1982-86
Argentina	n.a.	−1.4	26.8	224.0	366.7
Brazil	−1.3	2.0	28.4	58.5	182.3
Chile	7.2	4.5	48.1^c	177.6	23.0
Colombia	n.a.	1.8	10.4	24.4	22.4
Mexico	5.6^a	0.2^b	5.6	26.3	70.8
Peru	4.7	−1.1	8.6	147.5	110.6
Latin American average	4.1	1.0	21.3	109.7	129.3
Bangladesh	(1.8)	(−3.4)	5.0	15.6	10.4
China	n.a.	5.4	1.0^e	1.5	4.9
India	1.8	−3.4	4.4	7.6	7.4
Indonesia	n.a.	−5.4^d	77.5^f	19.8	7.5
Pakistan	(1.8)	(−3.4)	3.4	12.5	6.5
Philippines	n.a.	n.a.	4.6	12.6	19.0
South Korea	n.a.	−1.1	30.1	19.9	3.5
Taiwan	4.0	−0.6	7.2^g	10.2	1.6
Thailand	1.6	−0.8^h	2.6	9.0	2.1
Asian average	2.2	−1.6	15.1	12.1	7.0
France	0.9	3.6	5.5	10.9	6.9
Germany	1.3	−0.1^i	3.8	4.7	2.5
Japan	2.8	−0.3	5.2^c	6.3	1.3
United Kingdom	0.9	−2.6	4.6	15.0	4.7
United States	1.3	−2.0	3.1	7.9	3.2
5 OECD countries	1.4	−0.3	4.4	9.0	3.7

a) 1900-10.
b) 1921-38.
c) Consumer price index.
d) 1920-37.
e) 1957-73.
f) 1955-73.
g) 1951-73.
h) 1913-38.
i) 1924-38.
Source: Consumer price indices for first two columns, GDP deflators thereafter. Maddison (1982) and national sources for first two columns. 1950 onwards for developing countries, World Bank, *World Tables*, 1980 edition for 1950-73, 1988 edition thereafter. China 1957-66 from IMF, *International Financial Statistics*. Bangladesh-Pakistan 1950-60 from A. Maddison, *Economic Progress and Policy in Developing Countries*, p. 93. 1950 onwards for OECD countries from OECD *National Accounts*.

Table 6.3.   **Total government expenditure as a percentage of GDP at current prices, 1913-86**

	1913	1929	1938	1950	1973	1986
France	8.9	12.4	23.2	27.6	38.8	53.2[a]
Germany	17.7	30.6	42.4	30.4	41.2	47.8[a]
Japan	14.2	18.8	30.3	19.8	22.9	35.5
Netherlands	8.2[b]	11.2	21.7	26.8	49.1	58.0
United Kingdom	13.3	23.8	28.8	34.2	41.5	45.9
United States	8.0	10.0	19.8	21.4	30.7	37.1
Average	11.7	17.8	27.7	26.7	37.4	46.3

a) 1985.
b) 1910.
Source: France, 1913-38, numerator from L. Fontvieille, *Evolution et croissance de l'Etat français 1815-1969*, ISMEA, Paris, 1976, pp. 2124-9 and denominator from J.C. Toutain, *Le produit intérieur brut de la France de 1789 à 1982*, ISMEA, Paris, 1987, pp. 155-7. United States, 1929-73, from *National Income and Product Accounts of the United States, 1929-82*, Dept. of Commerce, 1986, pp. 1-2, 43-4, 35-6. Otherwise from A. Maddison, "Origins and Impact of the Welfare State, 1883-1983", *Banca Nazionale del Lavoro Quarterly Review*, March 1984. Postwar years from OECD *National Accounts*, various issues.

Table 6.4.   **Inequality of pre-tax income of households around 1970**

	Year	Gini coefficient	Top decile per capita income as multiple of that in bottom 2 deciles
Argentina	1961	0.425	11.2
Brazil	1970	0.550	20.0
Chile	1968	0.503	21.3
Mexico	1969	0.567	25.5
Peru[a]	1960	0.591	39.4
Latin American average		0.527	23.5
China		[0.200]	[3.5]
India	1964-65	0.428	12.4
Philippines	1971	0.490	21.4
South Korea	1970	0.351	7.6
Taiwan	1959	0.396	7.0
Thailand	1969	0.504	19.9
Asian average		0.395	12.0
France	1970	0.416	14.4
Germany	1973	0.396	10.5
Japan	1969	0.335	7.5
United Kingdom	1973	0.344	9.1
United States	1972	0.404	13.5
Average for 5 countries		0.379	11.0

a) Inequality in the economically active population, not in households, as for the other countries.
Source: Developing countries from J. Lecaillon, F. Paukert, C. Morrisson and D. Germidis, *Income Distribution and Economic Development*, ILO, Geneva, 1984, pp. 26-7, except the Gini for Brazil which is from p. 361. Taiwan from J.C.H. Fei, G. Ranis and S.W.Y. Kuo, *Growth with Equity: The Taiwan Case*, Oxford University Press, 1979, pp. 64 and 66. China is a guess, assuming inequality to be half of that in Taiwan. OECD countries from M. Sawyer, "Income Distribution in OECD Countries", *OECD Occasional Studies*, Paris, July 1976, p. 14.

Inequality was a heritage from old colonial systems of labour exploitation, with slavery in Brazil and peonage elsewhere. The proportion of landowning peasants was never as widespread as in Asia or Europe, and the only significant land reform had been in Mexico where land was redistributed to collective ejidos rather than individual peasants. Restricted access to education was another root of inequality, which was more important than in many Asian countries. There are also bigger variations in regional inequality within Latin American countries than is the case in Asian and OECD countries[3].

The comparative inflation record is shown in Table 6.2. The Latin American average in 1950-73 was 21.3 per cent per annum. The slowest Latin American inflation, in Mexico, was faster than in all five OECD countries shown in the table, and faster than six of the Asian countries. In Asia, Indonesia had a hyperinflation which was successfully quelled, and Korea had a similar experience. In Latin America, inflation was rooted in widespread government policies pushing public expenditure well beyond taxable capacity, whereas Asian and OECD countries followed more cautious monetary and fiscal policies.

b) Asia

The changed postwar responsibilities of government were most marked in the Asian countries, most of which had newly emerged from colonialism. As these countries were very much poorer than the OECD countries and Latin America, the problem of raising per capita income was even more urgent, and they were all strongly committed to development. Three of these countries embarked on a socialist path.

India was the first to develop a distinctive approach towards the problem of development and has remained remarkably faithful to it over the past 40 years. This drew heavily on Soviet interwar experience in concentrating on heavy industry investment financed and managed by government with allocation of resources by government planning decisions rather than the price mechanism. There was also a Soviet type stress on autarky and self-sufficiency which led to very slow growth in India's international trade. However, the agricultural sector was not collectivised as in Russia, and there was a Gandhian stress on the virtues of handicraft and small scale industry. Private property relations did not undergo major change as in China, and there was no major land reform, though the property and incomes of native princes and some large zamindars were eroded by government action. In the early postwar years India was able to run down its wartime sterling balances to help development. Thereafter it got bilateral aid from both East and West and some help from international agencies. However, the size of the aid was modest. India did not encourage private foreign investment, nor did the government borrow much on international capital markets.

India's five year plans got a great deal of publicity in the 1950s, when planning was often regarded as an integral part of development strategy even by US aid agencies which were dedicated to private enterprise. It took time for the inefficiency of India in allocating massive capital resources, in managing large enterprises bureaucratically, and in allocating permits and licenses for thousands of detailed items to become clear. The early insouciance about planning is captured in Nehru's comment: "(Planning) for industrial development is generally accepted as a matter of mathematical formula. (Men) of science, planners, experts, who approach our problems from a purely scientific point of view (rather than an ideological one) agree, broadly, that given certain preconditions of development, industrialisation and all that, certain exact conclusions follow almost as a matter of course."[4]

Chinese policy after 1949 conformed very closely to the Soviet model, with confiscation of private property, collectivisation of agriculture, universality of government enterprise and allocation of resources by centralised governmental decision rather than the price mechanism. China gave more weight than India to raising physical investment, improving human capital, and controlling population growth. After the split with the USSR in 1960, China got no foreign aid, and was very inward looking, with very slow growth of foreign trade.

Indonesia until 1965, under Sukarno's leadership, had a "guided" economy, vague socialist ideals, and an antipathy to local Chinese entrepreneurs and foreign capital which led to outright confiscation of foreign investment in 1957 and neglect of plantation agriculture. There was little in the way of effective ideas or instruments for development, and the period ended with huge budget deficits and hyperinflation. In 1965, GDP per capita was lower than in 1938. Sukarno's only real achievement was to consolidate the political unity of a country which consisted of thousands of islands. Since 1965, Indonesia has followed a basically capitalist path, and its formerly large communist party was suppressed. Economic growth has been much faster and was helped substantially by the large multi-country debt cancellation agreement of 1965, which is still quite unprecedented in scope.

South Korea and Taiwan were both Japanese colonies before the war. One significant aspect of decolonialisation was their far-reaching reforms in landownership (designed in both cases–as in Japan–by the American adviser Wolf Ladejinsky). These reforms helped increase peasant incentives to produce, and rendered postwar growth much more egalitarian than in most developing countries of Asia (except China). Both countries have given strong emphasis to human capital investment and hard work, a high level of savings, aggressive pursuit of export opportunities, and technological development. Government has provided strong guidelines, subsidies and tax favours, but the basic structure of enterprise has been private (corporate in Korea, small scale in Taiwan). Both countries have been closely allied with the United States. They both received high levels of US aid and technical assistance in the 1950s and 1960s, which helps explain their very high growth performance. On the other hand, they both had very large military commitments to finance[5].

The Philippines and Thailand showed some of the same characteristics as Korea and Taiwan, but with a less intense commitment to development objectives.

Pakistan was the poorest country of the region. It got a great deal more foreign aid than India, and the West Wing of the country received an important transfer of resources from the East Wing (now Bangladesh) until the country split in two in 1970. Pakistan placed little emphasis on heavy industry and government ownership, and did not share India's socialist and Gandhian philosophy[6].

Domestic Policy in the USSR

Postwar policy in the USSR continued basically on the line which emerged under Stalin in the late 1920s. The main difference was that the country was no longer so isolated internationally. It had 6 communist countries in Europe with which it had very close ties in the CMEA (the seventh, Yugoslavia, having broken away in 1948) as well as a privileged relationship with the two European neutrals (Finland and Austria). Until 1960 it also had close ties with China. As a result, Soviet foreign trade grew enormously. However, the new trade opportunities did not offer as much real gain as those within the capitalist world, as they did not involve access to countries with sophisticated technology or competitive efficiency. In the case of its third world associates (like Cuba) such trade involved a large burden of subsidies. Whereas the USSR had had impressive economic

73

growth in comparative terms in the interwar period, the efficiency problems of an economy without a price mechanism for resource allocation became increasingly clear. Several Western countries surpassed Soviet postwar performance, with a smaller investment effort, and clearly superior efficiency in resource allocation (see Table 6.10).

Quantitative Indicators of Factors Underlying Growth Acceleration in the Golden Age

When one looks at the more detailed reasons for the postwar acceleration of growth, some features emerge quite strikingly. Table 6.5 shows clearly the major acceleration in the growth of capital stock in the post war period in all areas of the world.

Table 6.5. Rates of growth of fixed capital stock
Annual average compound growth rates

	1913-50	1950-73	1973-84
France	0.94	3.62	4.00
Germany	0.74	5.35	3.39
Japan	1.55	7.98	3.41
United Kingdom	1.66	3.28	2.51
United States	1.82	3.38	2.79
Average	1.24	4.72	3.22
China		9.22	7.92
India	1.34	5.79	4.86
Korea		5.93	10.80
Taiwan		7.65	10.00
Average		7.15	8.40
Argentina	1.81	3.49	3.20
Brazil	2.51	6.15	8.40
Chile		3.11	1.69
Mexico		6.08	6.81
Average		4.71	5.03
USSR	2.90	8.64	6.69

Source: See sources cited in Table 6.10 and 7.5 below. Otherwise India 1913-50 from Bina Roy, *Capital Formation in India,* Das Gupta, Calcutta, 1979, pp. 113-114. USSR from *Narodnoe Khoziastvo.* Central Statistical Office, Moscow. 1962 edition p. 52 and 1965 edition, p. 64 for 1928-50, 1913-29 per capita stock assumed stable.

One of the most generally emphasised features of the postwar development literature was the stress on the need to raise rates of investment and the growth of capital stock. In 1955, Arthur Lewis suggested a need to raise the rate of annual net investment "from around 5 per cent or less to 12 per cent or more", if a country was to move from stagnation at subsistence levels of income to a situation of sustained growth. Seven years later Rostow made the same point with his aeronautic metaphor of the "takeoff" in a book which received wider publicity[7]. The same point about the critical importance of raising investment was made by other observers in different idiom, e.g. Rosenstein Rodan's "big push" and Leibenstein's "critical minimum effort", and the priority to heavy industry and accumulation of capital which had been a major point in Soviet 5 year plans and in Mahalanobis' strategy for Indian planning.

In fact most of the available statistics refer to gross rather than net capital formation. Lewis's 5 per cent represents about 8 per cent gross, so it can be seen from Table 6.6 that most developing countries were already making a somewhat bigger investment effort in 1950 than Lewis and Rostow suggested. It is also abundantly clear that their investment

Table 6.6. **Ratio of gross domestic investment to GDP**

At current market prices, 1950-86
Percentages

	1950	1973	1986
Bangladesh	(5.5)	8.9	13.1
China	10.4[a]	29.7	36.7
India	9.9	19.2	25.3[b]
Indonesia	11.5	20.8	26.2
Pakistan	(5.5)	12.9	17.8
Philippines	15.0	20.2	13.1
South Korea	5.7	24.5	29.2
Taiwan	14.5[c]	29.3	16.2
Thailand	11.8	23.9	21.5
Arithmetic average	10.0	21.0	22.1
Argentina	13.3	18.3	9.1
Brazil	12.3	22.4	18.1
Chile	8.0	7.9	14.6
Colombia	16.9	18.3	18.3
Mexico	14.1	21.4	18.4
Peru	17.1	15.8	12.9
Arithmetic average	13.6	17.4	15.2
Developing country average	11.4	19.6	19.4
France	23.5	26.2	19.1
Germany	22.8	25.3	19.3
Japan	25.5	38.2	28.2
United Kingdom	11.5	21.6	17.3
United States	21.2	19.6	18.3
OECD average	20.9	26.2	20.4

a) 1952.
b) 1985.
c) 1951.

Source: Developing countries 1950 from World Bank, *World Tables,* 1980 edition, 1973 and 1986 from 1988 edition supplemented by national sources. China 1952 from T-C. Liu and K-C. Yeh, *The Economy of the Chinese Mainland: National Income and Economic Development 1933-1959,* Princeton, 1965, p. 68. Taiwan from *National Income in Taiwan Area, The Republic of China,* Executive Yuan, Taipei. OECD countries from *National Accounts of OECD Countries,* various editions, except for Japan 1950 which is from K. Ohkawa and M. Shinohara, *Patterns of Japanese Economic Development: A Quantitative Appraisal,* Yale, 1979, p. 254.

rates rose well beyond expectations. By 1973 their average investment rate had risen to nearly 20 per cent of GDP as compared with 11.4 per cent in 1950.

The advanced OECD countries had a higher average level than the developing countries, but China and Taiwan reached rates of investment near to 30 per cent of GDP, which were surpassed only by Japan.

Some of the success in raising investment levels in developing countries was due to receipts of foreign capital and aid. On average, as can be seen from Table 6.7, foreign resource transfers amounted to about two and a half per cent of GDP. This was a considerable improvement on the prewar situation. This cannot be demonstrated on the same basis as Table 6.7 which is based on balance of payments statistics, but Table D.7 demonstrates the point with trade statistics. In the 1950-73 period, developing countries generally received enough foreign capital of various kinds to run import surpluses, whereas in the first half of the twentieth century most of them had to run large export surpluses. Thus it is clear that their situation had changed for the better in the golden age.

Table 6.7. **External finance as a percentage of GDP**

At current market prices 1950-86

	1950-73	1974-81	1982-86
Bangladesh	2.54	9.40	11.58
China	0.19[a]	0.39	1.06
India	1.76	1.41	2.68
Indonesia	3.10[b]	−5.48	−0.60
Pakistan	4.41	10.08	11.40
Philippines	2.07	5.23	1.10
South Korea	8.39[a]	5.50	0.42
Taiwan	3.06[c]	−0.56	−10.08
Thailand	1.77	4.43	0.92
Arithmetic average	3.03	3.38	2.05
Argentina	0.63	−1.23	−4.21
Brazil	1.32	4.65	−3.45
Chile	1.29	2.41	−1.26
Colombia	2.03	−0.71	2.54
Mexico	1.90	4.30	−6.64
Peru	2.56	3.94	0.20
Arithmetic average	1.62	2.23	−2.20
Developing country average	2.46	2.92	0.35

a) Excludes 1950-52.
b) 1966-73.
c) Excludes 1950.
Source: *"External finance"* is the net balance on all goods and services divided by GDP, with sign reversed. Except as specified below, 1950-66 is from A. Maddison *Economic Progress and Policy in Developing Countries,* Norton, New York, pp. 310-11; 1967 onwards from *World Tables 1987,* fourth edition, 1988. China 1952-73 from *Statistical Yearbook of China 1984,* pp. 29 and 32 and is the difference between national income available and national income. Taiwan 1951-86 from *National Income in Taiwan Area, The Republic of China,* Executive Yuan, Taipei, 1987. Pre-1970 figures for Bangladesh and Pakistan are estimates based on total external finance of prepartition Pakistan, allocated in accordance with East and West Pakistan trade balance (including interwing trade) as reported in *Reports of the Advisory Panels for the Fourth Five Year Plan 1970-75,* Islamabad, July 1970, pp. 143-4.

It can be seen from Table 6.7 that the importance of these foreign capital inflows varied a good deal from country to country. South Korea was the most favoured with receipts equal to 8.4 per cent of GDP, whereas China received negligible help (getting some Soviet aid until 1960, and making net repayments thereafter).

If we juxtapose Tables 6.6 and 6.7, it is clear that in spite of foreign finance, developing countries made a very considerable and successful effort to raise their domestic savings ratios. In China, where most private property holdings were confiscated by the state n 1949, the massive savings effort was made largely by the government and involved a major squeeze on private consumption levels, siphoning off production surpluses or profits to the state, low paid or voluntary labour on public construction projects. Very little of the saving was done privately. In India, where government investment was relatively large, some contribution to savings was also made by the public sector. Elsewhere the bulk of the increased savings were due to wealth accumulation in the private sector. The secular boom, the predominantly unequal distribution of income, low wages, and the often protected domestic markets in most of these countries provided new opportunities which were widely exploited. The proportions of income saved also depended on the degree of frugality of the population, the effective rate of interest and the expectations of investors and savers about the prospects for growth and profitability.

The second major area, which postwar development theory stressed as important in influencing economic growth, was the accumulation of human capital[8].

One crude measure of this is the average number of years of education embodied in the population of working age, as a result of their previous schooling.

Table 6.8 shows how backward the developing countries were in human capital terms in 1950. The average level of Asian education was only a quarter of that in the advanced countries and only a third in Latin America. This was partly a heritage of previous poverty, but reflected the relative neglect of education in the colonial period or under the old oligarchic regimes in Latin America. Recognition of the importance of education for economic growth in prewar years was largely confined to Japan. As a result Japanese education levels were already, in 1950, near to those in Europe.

In the course of the golden age, the importance of education was recognised by most of the developing world, and their average level of attainment grew faster than that in the OECD countries. By the 1980s the gap between the developing countries and the advanced was much smaller than it was in 1950. The developing countries now have average levels of education about half of those in the OECD area. The highest levels in the developing world were attained by South Korea and Taiwan, which also had the fastest growth.

In most countries, the bulk of education is provided in public institutions, so to this extent the increase in formal education levels visible in Table 6.8 is a success of public policy. However, there is a significant amount of private education in many countries, and part of the cost of public education is borne privately, because families have to forego the potential earnings which their children might have had, if they had not been at school. The expansion in education cannot therefore all be laid at the door of government, and not all of the expansion was conceived as an investment in development.

There is systematic variation in the average earning level of people with different levels of education, and evidence of this kind[9] was used to produce the weighted estimates of education in Table 6.8. However, the economic impact of better education is not easy to measure. Education is correlated with intelligence and family background, and its quality varies a good deal from country to country, so that it would be hazardous to assume that the quality of labour inputs rises *pari passu* with levels of education[10]. Indeed all assumptions about the average contribution of education to growth must be

Table 6.8. **Years of education per person aged 15 and over**

Average for both sexes, in equivalent years of primary education

	1913	1950	1973	1984
France	6.99	9.58	11.69	13.65
Germany	8.37	10.40	11.55	11.86
Japan	5.36	9.11	12.09	13.56
United Kingdom	8.12	10.84	12.09	13.14
United States	7.86	11.27	14.05	16.18
OECD average	7.34	10.24	12.29	13.68
China		2.20	3.97	5.69
India		1.35	2.60	3.92
South Korea		3.36	6.82	11.39
Taiwan		3.62	7.35	12.61
Asian average		2.63	5.19	8.40
Argentina		4.80	7.04	9.28
Brazil		2.05	3.77	5.55
Chile		6.09	7.98	9.83
Mexico		2.60	5.22	7.09
Latin American average		3.89	6.00	7.94
USSR		4.10	8.30	11.50

Source: From Table C-12 except for rough estimates for the USSR derived by extrapolation of the 1959 figure in *Dimensions of Soviet Power,* Joint Economic Committee, US Congress, 1962, pp. 242-4, and from estimates of subsequent development in *Soviet Economic Perspectives for the Seventies,* Joint Economic Committee, US Congress, 1973, pp. 595 and 624, and Aganbegyan (1988), p. 46. See footnote 9 of this chapter for weights.

very rough. The main point is that education does play a positive role in economic growth and this role was important in developing countries in the golden age.

Another major feature of the human capital situation, which had much less direct connection with government policy, was the very substantial acceleration in population growth in developing countries from an average of 1.6 per cent a year in 1913-50 to an average of 2.6 per cent per annum, in 1950-73 (see Table 6.9). Except for immigrant countries, such rapid population growth had never been experienced before, and it was more than two and a half times as fast as in the developed world. This growth was due primarily to improvements in public health which cut death rates drastically. At the same time, fertility remained much higher than it had been in Europe where late marriage and some degree of celibacy had existed for several hundred years before death rates fell to the postwar levels experienced by developing countries.

Rapid growth of population did not have the adverse Malthusian consequences sometimes feared, because food production rose faster than population in spite of pressure on land resources in many countries. Several third world countries managed to increase their employment faster than population in spite of falls in the proportion of population of working age. Nevertheless, rapid population growth was regarded by many third world governments as an obstacle to faster growth because the rising proportion of dependents reduced the capacity to save and invest; a given rate of growth in output

78

Table 6.9. Rates of population growth, 1900-87

Annual average compound growth rates

	1900-13	1913-50	1950-73	1973-87
Bangladesh	0.7	0.8	2.4	2.4
China	0.6	0.7	2.1	1.3
India	0.5	1.0	2.1	2.2
Indonesia	1.4	1.1	2.4	2.3
Pakistan	0.1	1.7	2.6	2.9
Philippines	1.9	2.1	3.0	2.6
South Korea	1.2	1.9	2.2	1.6
Taiwan	1.5	2.2	3.0	1.7
Thailand	1.3	2.2	3.1	2.2
Asian average	1.0	1.5	2.5	2.1
Argentina	3.8	2.2	1.7	1.6
Brazil	2.1	2.1	2.9	2.5
Chile	1.2	1.5	2.1	1.7
Colombia	2.0	2.2	2.9	1.9
Mexico	0.7	1.6	3.2	2.6
Peru	1.3	1.4	2.8	2.7
Latin American average	1.9	1.8	2.6	2.2
Developing country average	1.3	1.6	2.6	2.1
USSR	2.0	0.3	1.4	0.9
Australia	2.0	1.4	2.2	1.3
Austria	1.0	0.1	0.4	0.0
Belgium	1.0	0.3	0.5	0.1
Canada	2.8	1.5	2.1	1.2
Denmark	1.2	1.0	0.7	0.1
Finland	1.0	0.8	0.7	0.4
France	0.2	0.0	1.0	0.5
Germany	1.4	0.5	0.9	−0.1
Italy	0.6	0.7	0.7	0.3
Japan	1.2	1.3	1.1	0.9
Netherlands	1.4	1.3	1.2	0.6
Norway	0.7	0.8	0.8	0.4
Sweden	0.7	0.6	0.6	0.2
Switzerland	1.2	0.5	1.4	0.2
United Kingdom	0.8	0.5	0.5	0.1
United States	1.9	1.2	1.4	1.0
OECD average	1.2	0.8	1.0	0.5

Source: Appendix B.

meant smaller per capita growth than if population growth were smaller; rapid population growth prolongs the period in which there is an "unlimited supply" of unskilled labour, which means that problems of unemployment, "dualism", and inequality tend to be chronic.

For these reasons, many developing countries tried policies of population control, but these had little success before the 1970s.

Table 6.10 attempts to pull together the comparative performance of 14 countries in the 1950-73 period. Unfortunately data limitations prevent such a presentation for all 32 countries, and indeed some of the information used is rather weak. Its purpose is to give a broad view of the success of different countries in resource mobilisation, and of the efficiency with which resources were utilised[11].

Several interesting conclusions can be drawn from the table, particularly from the broad comparison of developing and OECD countries. In the first place, the expansion of total product was somewhat faster in the developing than in the OECD countries (a point which was also true for the 32 country comparison in Table 3.3 above). Secondly, the developing countries had to expand their cropped area, by moving on to poor quality land, or at some cost in terms of irrigation and land development. The advanced countries, by contrast, were able to reduce the cropped area, abandoning marginal land. Thirdly, labour inputs were much higher in developing countries, because of faster population growth, but also in Korea, and Taiwan by increases in working hours. In the advanced countries generally, working hours have been cut, holidays increased, and older workers have been able to retire, so growth of labour input has been modest. Cuts in working hours mean that employment involves less strain than in the third world, which has probably helped the general efficiency of the advanced economies. Fourthly, the educational quality of the labour force has expanded much faster in developing than in OECD countries. A fifth point to note is that the capital stock grew faster in the developing than in OECD countries. This may seem strange as the average investment rate was higher in the advanced countries (see Table 6.6 above), but the rate of investment accelerated more in developing countries, and the initial level of their capital stock was low. Finally, the last column of Table 6.10 casts some light on the efficiency of these economies. Total factor productivity (obtained by dividing the growth of GDP by a weighted total of the three factor inputs–land, labour and capital–and the contribution of increased education to labour quality) grew twice as fast in OECD than in developing countries. This suggests that the strains of fast development and high resource mobilisation lessened efficiency of allocation, particularly of capital. Factor productivity was weakest in China and India amongst the developing countries, presumably because of the priority they gave to bureaucratic rather than market methods of resource allocation.

The picture which emerges for the USSR in Table 6.10 is closer to that for the developing than for the OECD countries, and like China, it had a weak record (negative productivity) in allocating capital resources.

Table 6.11 presents an alternative view of the growth process: looking at output and inputs on a per capita basis. On this basis, the advanced countries grew fastest: 4.4 per cent a year compared with 3.4 per cent for developing countries in this sample (see Table 3.2 for the full 32 country sample). In terms of land, there was little significant difference between the two sets of countries. They both achieved substantial growth per capita in spite of the declining use of agricultural land per head. Labour input per head grew in developing countries and fell in the advanced countries. The stock of education per head grew faster in the developing countries as already noted in Table 6.10, but the growth of capital per head was somewhat smaller in developing countries.

Table 6.10.   **Comparative output, inputs and productivity performance 1950-73**

Annual average compound growth rates

	GDP	Cropped land area	Quantity of labour input	Labour quality improvement due to education	Capital stock	Total factor productivity
China	5.84	0.23	2.97	1.30	9.22	0.49
India	3.69	0.99	1.78	1.45	5.79	−0.05
Korea	7.49	0.65	3.11[a]	1.56	5.93[b]	2.84
Taiwan	9.32	0.29	4.25[a]	1.56	7.65	3.51
Asian average	6.59	0.54	3.02	1.47	7.15	1.70
Argentina	3.78	0.03	1.41	0.84	3.49	1.38
Brazil	6.75	3.03	2.78	1.34	6.15	2.13
Chile	3.67	1.25	1.09	0.59	3.11	1.60
Mexico	6.38	2.39	2.48	1.54	6.08	1.91
Latin American average	5.15	1.68	1.94	1.08	4.71	1.76
USSR	5.05	1.69	1.42[a]	1.56	8.64	0.50
France	5.13	−0.49	0.12[a]	0.43	3.62	3.69
Germany	5.92	−0.52	−0.05[a]	0.23	5.35	4.14
Japan	9.29	−0.92	1.55[a]	0.62	7.98	5.47
United Kingdom	3.02	−0.16	−0.15[a]	0.24	3.28	1.98
United States	3.66	0.11	1.22[a]	0.48	3.38	1.49
OECD average	5.40	−0.40	0.54[a]	0.40	4.72	3.35
Developing countries	5.87	1.11	2.48	1.27	5.93	1.73

N.B.:   Weights for developing countries and USSR labour 0.60, capital 0.30, land 10; for OECD countries, 0.67, 0.30 and 0.03 respectively. Weights proportionate to average shares of factors in total income. Relative importance of land and other capital derived from relative asset values shown in R.W. Goldsmith, *Comparative National Balance Sheets,* Chicago, 1985.

a)   Labour input measured in hours. Other countries show movement in employment.

b)   1953-73.

Source: GDP and labour input from Appendix Tables. Education from Table 6.8 assuming an 0.5 per cent proportionate gain in labour quality from a 1 per cent increase in years of educational attainment of the population of working age. Capital stock as follows: China from World Bank, *China: Long Term Development Issues and Options,* Washington DC, 1985, Annex 5, p. 79 (1950 assumed to be same as 1952, 1973 interpolated from 1975 estimate). India from J. Kumar, R.P. Katyal and S.P. Sharma, "Estimates of Fixed Capital Stocks in India", November 1986, processed. Korea from H.K. Pyo, *Estimates of Capital Stock and Capital Output Coefficients by Industries for the Republic of Korea (1953-1986),* KDI Working Paper 8810, Seoul, September 1988; Taiwan from H.T. Oshima, *Economic Growth in Monsoon Asia: A Comparative Survey,* University of Tokyo Press, 1987, p. 140. Argentina from IEERAL, "Estadisticas de la evolucion economica de Argentina, 1913-1984", *Estudios,* July-September 1986. Brazil from R.W. Goldsmith, *Brasil 1850-1984: Desenvolvimento Financiero so um Secolo de Inflacao,* Harper and Row, Sao Paulo, 1986. Chile 1950-60 from V.J. Elias, "Sources of Economic Growth in Latin American countries", *Review of Economics and Statistics,* August 1978, 1960 onwards from E. Haindl and R. Fuentes, "Estimacion del Stock de Capital en Chile: 1960-1984", *Estudios de Economia,* April 1986. Mexico, 1950-67 from Bank of Mexico, *Cuentas Nacionales y Acervos de Capital 1950-1967,* 1969 and 1967 onwards from Bank of Mexico, *La Encuesta de Acervos, Depreciacion y Formacion de Capital del Banco de Mexico 1975-1985,* 1986. USSR from *Narodnoe Khoziastvo,* 1965 edition, p. 64 and 1984 edition, p. 60. OECD countries from A. Maddison, "Growth and Slowdown in Advanced Capitalist Economies", *Journal of Economic Literature,* June 1987. Land (cropped area) from national sources for China, Argentina, Brazil, Mexico, USSR. India, Korea and Taiwan from Asian productivity Organisation, *Productivity Measurement and Analysis: Asian Agriculture,* Tokyo, 1987. OECD: countries and Chile from FAO *Production Yearbooks.*

Table 6.11. Per capita growth indicators 1950-73

Annual average compound growth rates

	GDP per capita	Land per capita	Labour input per capita	Capital stock per capita	Export volume per capita
China	3.67	− 1.83	0.84	6.97	0.6
India	1.57	− 1.08	− 0.35	3.63	0.4
Korea	5.15	− 1.54	0.87[a]	3.62[b]	17.7
Taiwan	6.18	− 2.60	1.25[a]	4.55	12.9
Asian average	4.14	− 1.76	0.65	4.69	7.9
Argentina	2.06	− 1.63	− 0.28	1.77	1.4
Brazil	3.76	0.15	0.10	3.18	1.8
Chile	1.50	− 0.88	− 1.04	0.98	0.03
Mexico	3.08	− 0.79	− 0.70	2.79	1.0
Latin American average	2.60	− 0.79	− 0.48	2.18	1.1
USSR	3.56	0.25	− 0.01[a]	7.10	8.5
France	4.13	− 1.44	− 0.94[a]	3.63	7.2
Germany	4.94	− 1.45	− 0.98[a]	4.37	11.4
Japan	8.05	− 2.04	0.40[a]	6.76	14.1
United Kingdom	2.53	− 0.64	− 0.64[a]	2.79	3.4
United States	2.17	− 1.31	− 0.23[a]	1.90	4.8
OECD average	4.36	− 1.38	− 0.48[a]	3.89	8.2
Developing country average	3.37	− 1.28	0.09	3.44	4.5

a) Labour input measured in hours per capita. Other countries show movement in employment per capita.
b) 1953-73.
Source: Population from Appendix B, otherwise as for Table 6.10.

Experience with exports throws further light on the problem of efficient resource allocation. On average the OECD countries had a faster growth of exports, at 8.2 per cent per capita compared with 4.5 per cent in developing countries. Within the developing world, South Korea and Taiwan were quite exceptional in the degree to which they exploited the potential of world markets to develop their exports. This was probably a major reason why they had a relatively good record in resource allocation.

It is not possible to construct tables like 6.10 and 6.11 for earlier periods for developing countries, but the earlier record for OECD countries is shown in Table 1.5 above. From this it appeared that their postwar acceleration in output and productivity growth was primarily due to faster growth in their capital stock, and improved efficiency in resource allocation[12].

NOTES AND REFERENCES

1. The OECD (Organisation for Economic Co-operation and Development) was founded in 1961. It included the 17 original members of OEEC and Spain, with the United States and Canada as full members (rather than associate members as they had been in OEEC). Japan joined in 1964, Finland in 1969, Australia in 1971 and New Zealand in 1973.

2. For an analysis of the post-war international order in Latin America, see A.O. Hirschman, *Latin American Issues*, Twentieth Century Fund, New York, 1961; V.L. Urquidi, *The Challenge of Development in Latin America*, Praeger, New York, 1964; D.H. Pollock, "Some Changes in United States Attitudes Towards CEPAL over the Past 30 years", CEPAL Review, 1978; and A. Maddison, ed., *Latin America, The Caribbean and OECD*, OECD Development Centre, Paris, 1986.

3. In Brazil, the interstate range of per capita income was nearly 9:1, between the Federal district and Piaui (in 1980); in Mexico the range was 6.3:1 between Tabasco and Oaxaca in 1980. See A. Maddison *Poverty, Equity and Growth in Brazil and Mexico*, forthcoming. In the United States, the interstate range was 2:1 in 1985 between Mississippi and Alaska (*Survey of Current Business*, August 1986, p. 24). Within the EC in 1978, the range was 2:1 in France, 2.4:1 in Germany, 2.6:1 in Italy, 2.7:1 in the Netherlands, 2:1 in Belgium, 1.5:1 in the United Kingdom, see *Yearbook of Regional Statistics*, Eurostat, 1981, pp. 3-7. In China, the per capita income range was 2.4:1 in 1982, being 582 yuan in Shanghai, and 245 in Gansu, see World Bank, *China: Economic Structure in International Perspective*, Annex 5, 1985, p. 83. In India, the 1980 range was 3.8:1 from Pondicherry to Sikkim, see *Estimates of State Domestic Product 1970-71 to 1984-85*, CSO, Delhi, 1986, p. 7.

4. See G. Rosen, *Democracy and Economic Change in India*, Berkeley 1966, p. 105.

5. See T. Scitovsky, "Economic Development in Taiwan and South Korea: 1965-1981", *Food Research Institute Studies*, No. 3, 1985.

6. See A. Maddison, *Class Structure and Economic Growth: India and Pakistan since the Moghuls*, Allen and Unwin, London, 1971.

7. See W.A. Lewis, *The Theory of Economic Growth*, Allen and Unwin, 1955, p. 208, and W.W. Rostow, *The Stages of Economic Growth*, Cambridge, 1962, p. 39.

8. Professor T.W. Schultz (who got a joint Nobel prize with Arthur Lewis) was particularly influential here, see his "Investment in Human Capital", *American Economic Review*, March 1961.

9. One year of secondary education was taken to be equivalent to 1.4 year of primary, and one year of higher as equal to two years of primary in weighting the economic value of years of schooling. *Education, Inequality and Life Chances*, Vol. 1, p. 47, OECD, Paris, 1975, provided evidence of average earnings differentials of this size, by level of education for 10 OECD countries.

10. We assumed a 0.5 per cent proportionate gain in labour quality from a 1 per cent gain in the (weighted) educational attainment of the employed labour force.

11. Apart from the sources cited for Table 6.10, there have been several exercises in this type of growth accounting pioneered by Edward Denison in the United States, see A. Bergson, *Productivity and the Social System–the USSR and the West*, Harvard, 1978; B.H. Dholakia, *The*

Sources of Economic Growth in India, Good Companions, Baroda, 1974; K.S. Kim and J.K. Park, *Sources of Economic Growth in Korea: 1963-1982*; KDI, Seoul, 1985; C.G. Langoni, *As Causas do crecimento economico do Brasil*, Apec, Rio, 1974; D.W. Perkins, "Reforming China's Economic System", *Journal of Economic Literature*, June 1988. It should be noted that Perkins' estimates of the growth rate of the Chinese capital stock are a good deal lower than the World Bank figures we have used. For a detailed analysis of the problems of estimating the Chinese capital stock, see K. Chen *et al.* "New Estimates of Fixed Investment and Capital Stock for Chinese State Industry", *The China Quarterly*, June 1988, who show industrial gross capital stock growing at 12.3 per cent a year from 1952 to 1973 and at 7.3 per cent a year from 1973 to 1984.

12. For a more detailed analysis, see A. Maddison, "Growth and Slowdown in Advanced Capitalist Countries: Techniques of Quantitative Assessment", *Journal of Economic Literature*, June 1987.

Chapter 7

THE SLOWDOWN IN THE WORLD ECONOMY SINCE 1973

Since 1973, world growth has slowed dramatically. This is very clear in the OECD countries, where there was a sharp and widespread break in trend in 1974. It is true of the USSR and Eastern Europe. It was equally plain in Latin America, where the turning point came in the early 1980s. Except for Asia, the phenomenon has indeed been worldwide. In Africa and the Middle East there were even significant declines in per capita product after 1973 (see Table 7.1).

Table 7.1. **Economic growth experience of 126 countries 1950-87**

Annual average compound growth rates

	1950-73	1973-87	1950-87	1950-73	1973-87	1950-87
	GDP			GDP per capita		
	Our sample (weighted average)					
32 countries	4.8	3.3	4.2	3.0	1.7	2.5
	Rest of world (weighted average)					
41 Africa countries	5.1	2.2	4.0	2.5	−0.9	1.2
11 Middle East countries	8.2	2.4	6.0	5.1	−0.8	2.8
16 Other Latin America	4.8	2.2	3.8	2.1	−0.3	1.2
11 Other Asia	5.7	6.4	6.0	3.5	4.1	3.7
8 Other OECD countries	5.7	2.8	4.6	4.2	1.4	3.1
7 East European countries	5.0	1.8	3.8	4.2	1.2	3.1
94 Country - Total	5.5	2.3	4.3	3.4	−0.1	2.1

Source: Our 32 country sample from Tables A.2 and C.2. Other OECD and East European countries from Appendices B and C. Other countries supplied by OECD Development Centre. In 1987, our 32 country sample had a population of 3 705 million, the other 94 countries had 1 211 million, a total of 4 916 million, i.e. about 98 per cent of the world total. The figure for the 94 countries are aggregated at 1984 prices and exchange rates.

The suddenness of the slowdown points up the role of external shocks, i.e. the OPEC price explosion at the end of 1973 which had its biggest impact in OECD countries, and the debt crisis which hit Latin America in 1982, shortly after the second OPEC shock. However, the shocks are far from the whole story.

85

The OECD Countries

Policymakers in OECD countries already had reasons for a switch to cautious policy before the first oil shock. In the 1950s and 1960s there had been a cosy coexistence of high growth with modest, stable and accommodable rates of inflation (around 4 per cent a year – see Table 3.4), and a world export price index with zero growth from 1951 (after the Korean crisis) to 1969. In the early 1970s, inflation increased sharply. The average annual rate in OECD countries had risen to nearly 10 per cent by 1973. World export prices exploded to reach 23 per cent in 1973. Graph 8 shows clearly the unprecedented peacetime character of the price explosion of the 1970s. It was widely felt that inflation on this scale meant that hyperinflation was a real possibility if decisive action was not taken to break the spiral and change expectations.

A major cause of the worldwide inflation was the breakdown of the Bretton Woods arrangements which had provided a fixed exchange rate, dollar based, international monetary system. In 1971, because of domestic inflation, payments problems, erosion of its gold reserves, and huge speculative capital movements, the United States abandoned the link between the dollar and gold. This removed the monetary pillar of the postwar international order. Henceforth there was a non-system, with a clear dichotomy inside the group of five (the arbiters of any world system) between the United States, the United Kingdom, and Japan which favoured floating rates, and France and Germany which created an island of stability inside the European monetary system.

Liberalisation of capital movements started in the European OECD countries in 1958. Its assumed benefits were taken to be axiomatic, and over time, there was increasing proliferation of external asset holding by private business and banks. By December 1973, the foreign assets of banks in OECD countries in foreign currencies amounted to $248 billion, compared with official reserves of $182 billion. By end 1987 these had risen to $3 056 billion compared with official reserves of $789 billion[1]. The freedom of capital movements had costs as well as benefits. The scope for speculative movements was already massive in the early 1970s, and became increasingly so. The potential costs of being a key currency country were therefore greatly magnified, and the dichotomy about fixed rates reflected different exposure to such risks (the United Kingdom, the United States and Japan having the biggest private international banking involvements). This freedom for international investment and the dimensions it attained, were a major institutional change, with significant implications for macroeconomic policy. Policy now had to operate in a state of much greater uncertainty, which affected the expectations of employers, trade unions and traders. Bigger official reserves were needed (see Table D-10), real exchange rates became volatile, and it was clear that even mildly expansionary policies might provoke a payments crisis. This was a second reason why policy became much more cautious.

The acceleration of inflation and the breakdown of Bretton Woods undermined the previously general conviction (also under attack in the academic world from Milton Friedman) that governmental demand management could be finely tuned to achieve full employment with modest inflation.

The action of the OPEC oil cartel accentuated the inflationary momentum, caused substantial problems as relative prices changed drastically, and induced OECD countries to make a major energy saving effort (see Table 7.4). It created payments problems for oil importers, and seemed likely to cause major disturbances in capital movements as OPEC's large payments surpluses were recycled. Thus old guidelines and even objectives of policy changed. The consensus amongst the economic establishment (civil servants,

Graphique 6. WORLD EXPORT UNIT VALUE INDEX
(1913 = 100, in dollars)

Logarithmic scale

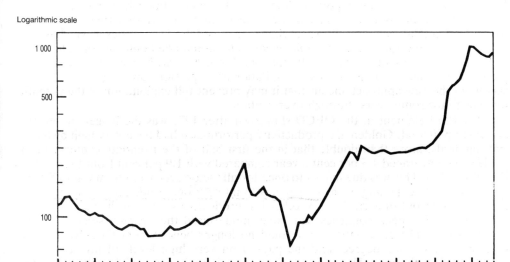

Source: 1870-1950: A. Maddison, "Growth and Fluctuation in the World Economy, 1870-1960", *Banca Nazionale del Lavoro Quarterly Review,* June 1962; 1950 onwards: *IMF International Financial Statistics.*

politicians, academic pundits) moved sharply away from the Keynesian mode. Full employment was no longer an objective of policy, economic growth had become a secondary goal. The top priorities were to stop inflation and avoid payments deficits.

There were three major elements in the OECD slowdown. On the one hand there were the inevitable costs of adjustment to the two system shocks, i.e. the twelvefold increase in oil prices at the end of 1973, and the earlier collapse of the monetary order. These were big enough to require changes in the discretionary weapons of macro-economic policy and in the rules of the game by which central bank and finance ministries had operated. Big enough too, to change expectations in the private sector. On any reasonable accounting, the most sophisticated governments could have been expected to lose output in dealing with these shocks, because they involved new risks and transition problems in devising and learning to use novel policy weapons, such as floating exchange rates. This is equally true of entrepreneurial and trade-union decision-makers whose reactions significantly affect macroeconomic outcomes.

The second reason for slower growth was the new consensus in economic policy. It emerged as a response to events, but it also helped to mould them. Thus, when oil prices collapsed and the momentum of world inflation was broken in the early 1980s, the new orthodoxy still continued to stress the dangers of expansionary policy in spite of widespread unemployment and strong payments positions. It looked for self-starting recovery rather than one stimulated by policy. I have attempted elsewhere[2] to characterise the

87

new "establishment view" of macropolicy objectives and weapons, and to identify its intellectual roots. The new "establishment view" is not identical in all countries. The United States has been an important deviant, with policy action which has been a quixotic version of the old Keynesian mode. The point is simply that there has been a widespread and far-ranging ideological change in most OECD countries in which stagnation of output and the rise in unemployment were an intended outcome of policy. This policy was successful in killing off inflation, and Latin American experience in the 1980s provides confirmation that the costs of inflationary explosions are very real. The very success of the new approach means that it may prevent full exploitation of the potential for growth for some years, through over-caution.

The third element in the OECD slowdown after 1973 was the longer run erosion of growth potential. Golden age productivity performance had been very high by historical standards, more than double that in the first half of the twentieth century. In the golden age it averaged 4.5 per cent a year compared with 1.9 per cent from 1913 to 1950 (see Table 7.2). This was due in part to once-for-all factors, recovery from war in Europe and Japan, the reopening of the economies to international trade and the large movement of labour out of agriculture or other less productive sectors of the economy. Furthermore as European countries and Japan modernised their capital stock and came closer to the technical frontier, they could no longer benefit from the advantages of catch-up to the same degree, and the pay-off on very high levels of investment was smaller than in the past. Hence some of the slowdown in productivity which occurred after 1973 would have happened anyway, and with some exceptions (notably the United States), productivity growth did remain higher than previous historical experience.

Table 7.2. **OECD productivity growth (GDP per man hour) 1900-86**

Annual average compound growth rates

	1900-13	1913-50	1950-73	1973-86
Australia	1.1	1.6	2.7	1.8
Austria	1.5	0.9	5.9	2.8
Belgium	0.9	1.4	4.4	1.7
Canada	3.5	2.4	2.9	1.5
Denmark	2.2	1.6	4.1	1.5
Finland	2.1	2.3	5.2	2.5
France	1.6	2.2	5.0	3.4
Germany	1.5	1.0	6.0	3.0
Italy	2.4	1.7	5.5	2.1
Japan	2.3	1.7	7.6	3.1
Netherlands	1.1	1.7	4.3	1.8
Norway	2.1	2.5	4.3	3.3
Sweden	1.6	2.8	4.4	1.6
Switzerland	1.6	2.7	3.3	1.6
United Kingdom	0.9	1.6	3.2	2.5
United States	1.7	2.4	2.4	1.2
OECD average	1.8	1.9	4.5	2.2
USSR			3.6	1.2

Sources: Appendix B for GDP, Appendix C for employment and hours.

Table 7.3. **Comparative levels of OECD productivity (GDP per man hour) 1900-86**

US GDP per man hour = 100

	1900	1913	1950	1973	1986
Australia	94	87	64	68	73
Austria	47	46	26	57	70
Belgium	63	58	40	62	90
Canada	61	76	76	85	89
Denmark	52	56	42	61	63
Finland	30	31	30	55	65
France	41	41	38	67	89
Germany	49	48	29	64	79
Italy	39	43	33	66	74
Japan	16	17	13	40	51
Netherlands	72	67	51	78	84
Norway	39	41	42	64	84
Sweden	41	41	46	72	76
Switerland	53	53	58	70	73
United Kingdom	82	74	54	64	75
United States	100	100	100	100	100
15 country average (excluding United States)	52	52	43	65	76
USSR			28	36	36

Sources: Appendices A, B and C.

There is evidence that the slowdown did involve reduction in growth below potential. This is suggested by the general rise in unemployment. In 1973, it had averaged 2.6 per cent of the labour force, a figure characteristic of the golden age as a whole (see Table 3.4). Thereafter it rose steadily to a peak of 7.8 per cent in 1983. The decline in capital productivity (compare Tables 6.10 and 7.5) also suggests the existence of excess capacity[3]. Cautious policy therefore had a significant cost in terms of potential output foregone, although it did eventually succeed in reducing the momentum of inflation. By 1986, partly due to the collapse of oil prices, OECD inflation was again down to 3 per cent.

The OECD slowdown transmitted a deflationary impulse to the world economy because import volume decelerated from the 8.7 per cent annual growth of the golden age to 3.4 per cent. However, imports generally continued to grow faster than GDP, and import elasticities were little different from the earlier period (see Table 7.6). Except in agriculture[4], there were no very significant relapses into protectionism. Liberalism in trade, the first pillar of the postwar international order, remained intact. So did the second pillar, the freedom of capital movements. Until 1981, a greatly increased flow of private funds was funnelled at negative real interest rates to third country borrowers. OPEC surpluses were recycled and this capital flow helped offset the deflationary impact of slackening OECD imports. ODA increased modestly in real terms. Developing countries were able to pursue rather buoyant expansionary policies, with the help of these capital flows. However, from 1982, the international voluntary flow of private capital

Table 7.4. **Domestic energy requirement in tons of oil equivalent per $10 000 of GDP, (in 1980 international dollars) and net imports 1973-86**

Million tons of oil equivalent

	Energy consumption: equivalent tons of oil per $10 000 of GDP		Net trade: million tons of oil equivalent	
	1973	1986	1973	1986
France	4.62	3.85	− 146.6	− 114.9
Germany	5.66	4.61	− 149.5	− 150.2
Japan	5.40	3.28	− 321.3	− 314.4
United Kingdom	5.30	4.18	− 115.5	+ 37.2
United States	7.56	5.49	− 292.3	− 253.5
Average/Total	5.71	4.28	− 1 025.2	− 795.8
Argentina	3.63	4.53	− 5.8	− 1.6
Brazil	2.32	2.65	− 35.6	− 33.2
Chile	2.39	2.28	− 3.7	− 3.6
Colombia	2.22	2.52	+ 2.9	+ 10.1
Mexico	3.61	4.72	− 7.2	+ 71.1
Peru	2.08	2.05	− 2.0	+ 2.8
Average/Total	2.71	3.13	− 51.4	+ 45.6
Bangladesh	0.79	1.21	− 1.0	− 1.8
China	3.93	3.35	+ 3.6	+ 36.4
India	2.44	2.92	− 17.0	− 16.0
Indonesia	1.18	1.74	+ 50.8	+ 65.5
Pakistan	2.08	2.38	− 3.3	− 6.7
Philippines	1.84	1.56	− 9.3	− 8.2
South Korea	3.60	3.87	− 13.7	− 45.8
Taiwan	4.27	4.41	− 9.1	− 25.0
Thailand	1.83	1.50	− 8.3	− 9.1
Average/Total	2.44	2.55	− 7.3	− 10.7
USSR	6.72	7.71	+ 109.5	+ 246.5

Source: International Energy Agency, *Energy Balances 1970-85,* and subsequent quarterly supplements for OECD countries, *World Energy Statistics and Balances 1971-1987* for other countries. Domestic requirement equals domestic final consumption and intermediate use of energy.

came to an abrupt halt in Latin America (for reasons examined below). As already mentioned, the third pillar of the postwar order, the Bretton Woods fixed exchange mechanism had collapsed in 1971, but the fourth pillar, the close and regular consultation between OECD countries remained robust, prevented the emergence of beggar-your-neighbour policies, and helped preserve a positive momentum for the world economy.

Latin America

In Latin America, the Bretton Woods collapse and the acceleration of inflation in early 1970s did not have the same effect on the policymaking establishment that it did

Table 7.5. Comparative output, inputs and productivity performance 1973-84

Annual average compound growth rates

	GDP	Cropped land area	Quantity of labour input	Labour quality improvement due to education	Capital stock	Total factor productivity
China	6.85	−0.27	2.35	1.66	7.92	2.10
India	4.29	0.93	1.97	1.90	4.86	0.50
Korea	7.38	−2.10	2.49[a]	2.39	10.80	1.42
Taiwan	7.63	−1.70	3.44[a]	2.51	10.00	1.23
Asian average	6.54	−0.79	2.56	2.12	8.40	1.31
Argentina	0.69	0.05	0.91	1.27	3.20	−1.58
Brazil	4.33	3.77	3.88	1.79	8.40	−1.97
Chile	1.24	0.72	1.68	0.96	1.69	−0.92
Mexico	4.55	2.35	3.45	1.41	6.81	−0.64
Latin American average	2.70	1.72	2.48	1.36	5.03	−1.28
USSR	2.16	−0.10	1.10[a]	1.50	6.69	−1.40
France	2.32	−0.01	−1.23[a]	0.71	4.00	1.47
Germany	1.72	−0.16	−1.27[a]	0.12	3.39	1.48
Japan	3.72	−0.67	0.57[a]	0.52	3.41	1.99
United Kingdom	1.10	0.18	−1.33[a]	0.38	2.51	1.19
United States	2.42	0.09	1.33[a]	0.65	2.79	0.25
OECD average	2.26	−0.11	−0.39[a]	0.48	3.22	1.28

N.B.: Weights as for Table 6.10.
a) Labour input measured in hours. Other countries show movement in employment.
Source: As for Table 6.10, except for Argentine capital stock which is from S. Goldberg and B. Ianchilovici, "El Stock de Capital en la Argentina", *Desarrollo Economico,* July-September 1988. For some countries (China, India, Taiwan and Brazil) rough estimates had to be made to update the capital stock to 1984 because the original source was available only to 1980 or 1981

in OECD countries. Five of the six countries in our sample had never seriously tried to observe the fixed rate discipline of Bretton Woods. Except for Mexico, they had currencies whose exchange rates were only a fraction of their 1950 level (see Table D-9 below). National currencies had been repeatedly devalued and high rates of inflation had become endemic. The new disturbance was simply a new variation on a familiar theme, and was not regarded as a razor's edge situation, calling for drastic policy change.

The direct non-price effects of the OPEC shock itself were unfavourable for a large oil importer like Brazil, but they brought windfall profits to Mexico and Colombia and were fairly neutral for self sufficient oil producers like Argentina, Chile and Peru. There was little effort to economise on the domestic use of energy. The general policy posture was one of accommodating inflation rather than trying to break its momentum, though there were unsuccessful and temporary monetarist experiments in Argentina and Chile. Growth continued to be strong up to 1980 and the only recessions (in Chile and Argentina) were due to internal causes–the switch from neo-Marxism, and from Peronism, to neo-conservatism. Imports expanded fast, and the payments problems were met by large scale foreign borrowing, mostly by government from foreign banks at floating rates of interest and denominated in dollars. Between 1973 and 1982, the outstanding debt of

Table 7.6. **Import experience of OECD countries 1950-86**

Annual average compound growth rates

	Volume of imports		Import elasticity	
	1950-73	1973-86	1950-73	1973-86
Australia	5.1[a]	3.9	1.04[a]	1.39
Austria	10.5	4.5	1.98	1.96
Belgium	9.0	2.9	2.20	1.61
Canada	7.5	3.8	1.47	1.12
Denmark	7.3	1.5	1.92	0.75
Finland	8.4	2.2	1.71	0.79
France	9.3	3.7[b]	1.82	1.61[b]
Germany	12.4	3.4	2.10	1.79
Italy	11.2	2.3	2.04	1.00
Japan	15.7	2.3	1.68	0.62
Netherlands	8.0	3.0	1.70	1.67
Norway	7.9	5.0	1.93	1.19
Sweden	6.9	3.7	1.73	2.18
Switzerland	8.2	3.8	1.82	4.22
United Kingdom	5.1	3.0	1.70	2.14
United States	6.7	5.2	1.81	2.08
Average	8.7	3.4	1.74	1.63

a) 1955-73.
b) 1973-85.
Source: IMF, *International Financial Statistics,* for import volume. Import elasticity is the ratio of change in import volume to change in real GDP.

the six countries rose from $35 billion to $248 billion, a much bigger growth than in any earlier period and faster than in other parts of the world. As interest rates remained lower than the pace of world inflation in the 1970s, this strategy for continued growth did not seem too risky in the circumstances of the time.

However, the basic parameters changed in the early 1980s. By then, the OECD countries were pushing anti-inflationary policy very vigorously. The change to restrictive monetary policy initiated by the Federal Reserve pushed up interest rates suddenly and sharply. The dollar appreciated and world export prices started to fall. The average real interest cost of floating rate debt rose to nearly 16 per cent in 1981-3 compared with minus 8.7 per cent in 1977-80. Real interest rates remained high thereafter, mainly because of the unusual fiscal-monetary policy mix in the United States, where the stringency of Federal Reserve policy was enhanced because of the large fiscal deficits. These events in themselves created major new adjustment problems, but in 1982 they were capped by the Mexican debt moratorium which stopped the flow of voluntary private lending, and created a need for massive retrenchment in economies which were already suffering from inflation levels unknown in peacetime in OECD countries.

Table 7.7 shows the scale of the Latin American debt problem in comparative perspective. Per capita debt is three times as high in Latin America as in Asia, and per capita exports are lower. The debt service problem is serious for all of the countries except Colombia. None have repudiated foreign debt, all have negotiated rollovers of

Table 7.7. **External debt 1973-86, debt and exports per capita in 1986**

	1973	1982	1986	1986	1986
		External debt		Debt per capita	Exports per capita
		$ million		$	$
Argentina	4 890	43 634	46 167	1 490	221
Brazil	12 866	91 027	106 174	773	163
Chile	3 179	17 342	19 410	1 584	345
Colombia	2 320	10 302	14 619	505	176
Mexico	8 990	85 890	97 662	1 227	204
Peru	3 213	11 636	14 575	721	124
6 Latin American countries	35 467	248 195	298 607	1 050	206
Bangladesh	4 165	4 656	7 407	74	9
China	0	8 358	21 993	21	30
India	10 625	22 816	36 814	48	12
Indonesia	6 534	26 500	42 038	252	89
Pakistan	4 251	10 069	12 584	127	34
Philippines	1 936	23 483	27 000	491	87
Korea	3 968	36 495	43 560	1 048	835
Taiwan	(2 000)	9 654	12 693	655	2 056
Thailand	903	11 496	16 971	326	169
9 Asian countries	34 382	153 527	221 060	338	69
USSR	1 166	15 707	24 000	86	348

Source: World Bank, *World Tables,* 1988, except for Taiwan, which is from *Financing and External Debt of Developing Countries,* OECD, Paris, 1987 and 1988 editions. USSR debt from D.M. Nuti, "Perestroika: Transition from Central Planning to Market Socialism", *Economic Policy,* October 1988, p. 368. Exports per capita derived from Appendices B and D below.

amortisation, but except for Peru they have usually paid interest in full. Given the high level of real interest rates, this has involved transfers of interest amounting to several per cent of GDP and has been financed only with the help of involuntary lending by commercial banks under pressure from the IMF. The IMF action certainly helped the creditor banks and gave them the leeway to accumulate more adequate reserves. It also helped preserve the viability of international capital markets. However, Latin America has been faced with a debt service burden without historical precedent[5] This has created adjustment problems much bigger than those of the 1930s, when Latin America eased its burdens by a much heavier dose of debt delinquency.

The domestic cost of adjustment for Latin American countries has been very heavy. Their real GDP per capita fell appreciably in the 1980s, and incomes were squeezed further by worsened terms of trade. Their investment and imports have been cut drastically. The drop in living standards, and the acceleration of inflation have weakened the credibility of government to a degree which closes off most of the feasible policy options for a return to sustained growth. The damage which these economies sustained is shown dramatically by the fall in total factor productivity (Table 7.5) and in labour productivity (Table 7.8). Normally, productivity does not fall much in periods of prolonged stagnation in capitalist economies as redundant workers are laid off, or plants shut down completely, but in Latin America there are large numbers of self employed or family workers[6] who do not become overtly unemployed. There was therefore a good deal of labour hoarding.

Table 7.8. **Productivity growth (GDP per person employed) in Latin America 1950-86**

Annual average compound growth rates

	1950-73	1973-80	1980-86	1973-86
Argentina	2.3	1.2	-1.8	-0.2
Brazil	3.9	2.9	-1.2	1.0
Chile	2.4	1.6	-1.3	0.2
Colombia	2.9	2.5	-0.1	1.3
Mexico	3.8	2.6	-2.2	0.4
Peru	3.2	0.6	-2.0	-0.6
Latin American average	3.1	1.9	-1.4	0.4

Source: Derived from Tables B-2 and C-8.

The productivity setback was due in part to the collapse of investment. Total factor productivity has also been hurt by underuse of the capital stock. As the level of productivity in Latin America is only a quarter of that in OECD countries, the longer term OECD reasons for a slowdown are not applicable and Latin America still has the potential for a return to fast productivity growth.

Latin American countries have to solve four major (and interrelated) problems before they can resume a reasonable growth path. One is the alleviation of the debt service burden. So far this has only involved rollovers of amortisation, with no concessions by creditors on interest rates. Another is the fiscal crisis[7]. Only Chile and Colombia have dealt with this problem. The third problem is inflation. Argentina, Brazil, Mexico and Peru are all hovering on the brink of hyperinflation, and a whole series of desperate remedies has failed. The fourth problem is excessive reliance on subsidies, controls and detailed intervention which has messed up resource allocation. One aspect of this is the relatively low level of external trade, which in spite of recent progress is still well below levels for other parts of the world. The average Latin American export ratio in 1986 was 13 per cent of GDP compared with 22 in 1929. In OECD countries the 1986 ratio was 25 per cent compared with 19 per cent in 1929, and in Asia 20 per cent compared with 16 per cent (see Table D-6).

Table 7.9. **Comparative levels of productivity in Latin America, 1950-86**

	GDP per person employed (US = 100)			GDP per man hour (US = 100)		
	1950	1973	1986	1950	1973	1986
Argentina	35	38	34	33	33	28
Brazil	19	29	30	17	25	25
Chile	39	42	39	36	37	33
Colombia	25	31	33	23	27	28
Mexico	22	34	32	21	29	27
Peru	22	29	25	20	25	20
Latin American average	27	34	32	25	29	27

Source: Derived from Tables A-2, B-2 and C-8. The man hour estimates are very rough; they assume average annual working hours per person in Latin America of 2 000 in 1950, 1 950 in 1973 and 1 900 in 1986.

In many parts of Latin America, the postwar policy orthodoxy was to give top priority to economic growth, with little of the concern for conjunctural equilibrium or social welfare which always characterised policy in OECD countries, and not much effort to promote microeconomic efficiency. This was not true of Mexico in the 1950s and 60s, but Mexican policy changed under the Echeverria and Lopez Portillo administrations (1970-82) with a spending spree that produced a 17 per cent budget deficit in spite of booming oil revenue. Until 1982, the old Latin American orthodoxy had produced four decades of growth with virtually no interruption, but there was a huge build up of inflation, payments difficulties, social tension, fiscal-monetary disequilibria and microeconomic inefficiency which underlie the chaos of the 1980s.

In Latin America as in OECD countries, these new problems have led to a search for a new policy mix, but the tasks are much bigger, and their unprecedented nature means that the intellectual preparation for change has been more shallow than in OECD countries (where Friedmanites and Hayekians had been hovering backstage for decades with an alternative policy agenda). Furthermore, the political strains are bigger. Austere policies are difficult to sustain in countries which in many cases have only recently enjoyed a release from authoritarianism and where social cleavage runs deep. There has therefore been a search for softer heterodox options.

The simplest option, debt delinquency, has been used mainly in respect of amortisation and only in moderate degree with regard to interest payments. Indeed some countries, notably Chile and Mexico, took over service of private debt which could have been legitimately left in default. Brazil experimented briefly with the delinquency option on interest payments, Argentina fell into deliquency in 1988 through insolvency, but Peru is the only one of our six countries which has practised it on a prolonged basis. In other respects, Peru retained the old orthodoxy. As a result, it got a short spurt of growth, but ended up with galloping inflation, an import and fiscal crisis, no exchange reserves and a new depression in output. The Peruvian experience makes it clear that the debt crisis is only part of the Latin American problem, and that elimination of the debt burden will not in itself be a panacea.

Argentina and Brazil both experimented, in 1985 and 1986 respectively, with another type of heterodox package, attempting to break inflationary expectations by abolishing price indexation; establishing a freeze on prices, wages and the foreign exchange rate; modifying debt relationships with the help of tablitas; and creating new currency units (the austral and cruzado respectively)[8]. These schemes had some initial success for several months in changing expectations, but both broke down. The inertia of past inflation continued to raise costs and squeeze profits. Private demand expanded fast due to wage increases preceding the stabilisation, and pre-emptive buying began as inflationary anticipations revived. The fixed exchange rate led to a boom in imports, an erosion of the trade balance and reserves. The essentials of these programmes had to be scrapped, inflation bounded back to triple digits, with the credibility of government policy in ruins.

Chile has taken a very different, ultra orthodox, path which has dealt with the budgetary and inflation problems, swapped a quarter of the foreign debt for equity, liberalised the economy from most controls and opened it up to international trade. However, the cost has been very high. There have been very big recessions in output (15 per cent in real terms in 1982-3) and per capita income was barely above the 1973 level in 1987. The high costs were due in part to the sweeping character of change–moving from the very large budget deficits, controls and nationalisation of the Allende years to budget balance, deregulation, privatisation and low tariffs. They were also due to major policy errors such as maintenance of a fixed exchange rate and complete freedom

Table 7.10. **Ratio of Asian and Latin American manufactured exports to total commodity exports 1953-86**

Percentages

	1953	1986		1953	1986
Bangladesh	1	73	Argentina	10	22
China	n.a.	64	Brazil	2	41
India	48	62	Chile	2	9
Indonesia	0	22	Colombia	1	18
Pakistan	1	68	Mexico	8	30
Philippines	8	61	Peru	3	23
South Korea	0	91	Latin American average	4	24
Taiwan	6	91			
Thailand	2	42			
Asian average	8	64			

Source: 1953 from A. Maddison, *Economic Progress and Policy in Developing Countries,* Norton, New York, 1970, p. 205. 1986 from *World Development Report 1988,* World Bank, Washington D.C., pp. 244-5, and for Taiwan, from *Statistical Yearbook of the Republic of China 1987,* Taipei, p. 381.

of capital movements when domestic inflation far outstripped that in the outside world, and to the governmental assumption of large private debts. As a result the government reacquired bankrupt private enterprises and banks on a large scale, as well as generating a big depression and massive unemployment. After a short episode of more traditional accommodatory policy and higher tariffs, there was a return, in chastened form, to Chicago style policies of budget balance, low tariffs, low inflation and reprivatisation[9]. Now, however, the exchange rate has been kept realistic, and international capital movement is subject to control.

The Mexican approach to the crisis was less drastic than that of Chile, but more broadly based than that of Argentina, Brazil and Peru.

The government has reduced microeconomic inefficiency by abolishing most import licensing, joining GATT, and rationalising its tariffs at a low level. Its exports are now very varied and back to the same per cent of GDP as in 1929. It has privatised or abolished 700 of the 1 200 state enterprises, introduced more realistic pricing policies in those that remain, and reduced subsidies.

It achieved massive fiscal retrenchment by large cuts in investment and real salaries in the public sector, reductions in subsidies, more realistic public sector pricing, increases in tax rates and tougher tax collection. However, the fiscal problem is complicated by the demonetisation of the economy and the impossibility of levying an effective inflation tax. The government has to meet interest costs, not only on the foreign debt, but also on internal debt whose holders demand both compensation for inflation and high real interest yields as well. As Mexico's geographic position makes it impossible to impose effective exchange controls, high interest rates are necessary to prevent capital flight. As a result, the overall "financial" deficit remains very high, though the "primary" balance (excluding the inflationary component of interest) is in substantial surplus.

In the last year of the de la Madrid administration an attempt was made to break inflationary expectations with the help of an incomes and price policy. This *pacto* involved concertation between the government, business, trade unions, and peasant organisations

96

to freeze prices voluntarily, and maintain wage stability. To provide an anchor for expectations, the exchange rate was also frozen, as it had been in the 1985-86 experiments in Argentina and Brazil.

The Mexican approach succeeded in cutting inflation sharply in the course of 1988, but the freeze in the exchange rate reduced competitivity, produced a big fall in the trade surplus and a major rundown in reserves. If is to continue debt service without large new loans, it will need to devalue to a degree which will rekindle inflation.

The Mexican approach to adjustment has had a high economic cost, with per capita income well below its 1981 peak. It also had political costs. In the 1988 election, the ruling party's prestige was lower than it had been for six decades and the new President obtained only a bare majority.

Latin America's seven year effort at "adjustment" suggests that it will be impossible to resume satisfactory growth without a very large cut in foreign debt service.

Asian Countries

Unlike the rest of the world, the Asian countries managed to maintain and even raise their average growth performance after 1973. GDP growth was 5.9 per cent for 1973-87 compared to 5.4 per cent in 1950-73, and as population growth decelerated, per capita growth rose from 2.8 to 3.6 per cent a year. In contrast to the OECD countries and Latin America, there was no general productivity slowdown in Asia. In fact average productivity growth increased modestly (see Table 7.11). The only significant exception was the Philippines, where growth deceleration and indebtedness resembled Latin American experience.

The improvement was very striking in China, which moved into the supergrowth league with Korea and Taiwan. Some of the poorest countries, Bangladesh, Pakistan and Indonesia also did appreciably better than before, and India also did better than in the past (see Table 3.3).

The reasons for better Asian performance are complex and differ somewhat between countries, but we can identify three major reasons when their experience is put in comparative perspective:

a) In the first place, most Asian countries still have low levels of productivity compared with OECD countries, or even compared with Latin America (see Tables 7.3, 7.9 and 7.12). They are in a low-level catch-up stage of development where the pay-off from high levels of investment and high levels of education can be substantial. In general, they have fast growing capital stocks (Table 6.5), high rates of investment (Table 6.6) and are making rapid progress in raising educational levels (Table 6.8).

b) Their macroeconomic management has generally been prudent. They have been much more cautious about indebtedness to commercial banks, about inflation and fiscal policy than Latin America. They did borrow to facilitate growth when they faced payments difficulties in the wake of the oil crisis, but the increases were more modest than in Latin America, and some of the countries with high debt/export ratios like Bangladesh, India and Pakistan borrowed largely from foreign governments and international institutions on concessional or fixed terms rather than from commercial banks at floating rates.

   Most are countries with conservative fiscal policies and an aversion to inflation. This attitude is traditional in India[10], and was acquired in China, Indonesia, Korea and Taiwan after experience with hyper-inflation in earlier decades.

Their rates of inflation prior to 1973 were generally well below those in Latin America. Since 1973 they have experienced two bouts of inflation which coincided with the oil shocks, but they were subsequently able to reduce it successfully. This was due in good part to responsible fiscal policy, and to some extent to the fact that they had more flexprice markets than OECD countries or Latin America, i.e. negligible elements of social security, farm income support, and trade union activity, and a bigger role for agriculture. Bangladesh, China and India have all had postwar experience of years where the GDP deflator fell appreciably. Thus their growth path has been relatively smooth, smoother in fact than in the 1950s and 1960s. In the major significant case, when an adjustment programme was necessary (Korea in 1980) it was short, sharp and effective[11].

Generally speaking, the Asian countries are oil importers and less favourably placed than Latin American countries to face the oil shock. The most significant exporter was Indonesia, which had more inflation than most of Asia, but behaved much more responsibly than Mexico in terms of fiscal restraint, with major devaluations to keep its non oil exports competitive and avoid the "Dutch disease", more or less complete removal of the subsidy to domestic oil consumption, a small public sector, low levels of government employment and salaries[12].

c) The third important advantage of the Asian economies is that they generally had done more to develop an export orientation, to keep their exchange rates competitive and to diversify their exports. They had a higher degree of interregional trade than Latin America, and as theirs was a very buoyant region in the world economy, this also helped. Thus even in slower growing world markets, they succeeded in raising exports substantially. The high export orientation was most marked in the supergrowth countries. It was not true of India, Bangladesh or Pakistan.

A special feature of Chinese performance, was the substantial liberalisation of the economy after the death of Mao Tse Tung and the arrival of a more pragmatic leadership between 1976 and 1978. The freedom for peasants to pursue profit and make market

Table 7.11. **Productivity growth**
(GDP per person employed) in Asian countries, 1950-86

Annual average compound growth rates

	1950-73	1973-86
Bangladesh	0.3	2.2
China	2.8	4.6
India	1.9	2.4
Indonesia	2.7	3.3
Pakistan	2.7	3.1
Philippines	2.7	0.6
South Korea	4.9	4.7
Taiwan	5.8	4.2
Thailand	3.6	3.5
Asian average	3.0	3.2

Source: Derived from Tables B.2 and C.8.

98

Table 7.12. **Comparative levels of productivity in Asia, 1950-86**

	GDP per person employed (USA = 100)			GDP per man hour (USA = 100)		
	1950	1973	1986	1950	1973	1986
Bangladesh	6	4	5	5	3	3
China	6	7	12	5	6	9
India	5	5	6	4	4	4
Indonesia	7	8	11	6	6	8
Pakistan	7	8	10	6	6	8
Philippines	13	15	15	11	12	11
South Korea	11	21	33	10	15	21
Taiwan	9	20	30	8	13	20
Thailand	8	11	16	7	9	10
Asian average	8	11	15	7	8	10

Source: Derived Tables A-1, B-2 and C-8. The man hour estimates are very rough: they assume 2 200 annual hours per person employed throughout 1950-86, except for Korea and Taiwan. For Korea hours were taken to be 2 200 per annum in 1950, 2 550 in 1973 and 2 570 in 1986 (see Kim and Park, 1985, pp. 113-4 for 1973 and *ILO Yearbook* for 1986). For Taiwan, hours were taken to be 2 200 in 1950, 2 700 in 1973 and 2 500 in 1986 (see *Statistical Yearbook*, 1987, Taipei, p. 5).

sales had spectacular results in agriculture, and there was also a substantial measure of freedom to develop small scale private enterprise in services and the artisan sector. From 1978 to 1987 GDP growth averaged 9 per cent a year, and agricultural value added rose 6.5 per cent a year. The economy was opened up to foreign trade and investment, and intellectual and technical contacts with the outside world helped productivity. Greater freedom in personal habits relieved the previous drabness of existence and increased work incentives. There was some decentralisation of the state sector and greater freedom for state enterprises to pursue profit.

The potential for substantial gains was bigger than in the Soviet Union, for several reasons. The degree to which private enterprise was permitted was much greater than has so far been the case in the USSR, and there was a bigger proportion of people alive who remembered capitalist habits. The liberalisation was accompanied by a major cut in military expenditures. The potential for easy catch-up improvements was much greater because the economy was more primitive. In 1973 Soviet income per capita was more than 6.5 times that in China. The degree of distortion in the economy, the incompetence in management and Orwellian thought control was bigger than in the USSR, due to reckless Maoist experiments and terror in the Great Leap Forward and the Cultural Revolution. Before the reform, the country had very little foreign trade, had received no foreign aid, foreign capital or know-how since 1960. The universities had been closed and intellectuals humiliated. For all these reasons, there were probably considerable once-for-all elements in Chinese progress from 1978 to 1987, and official awareness that further liberalisation may bring inflation, inequality and threaten some of the basic institutions of communist rule, may slow the pace of change. Although more than a quarter of Chinese economic activity is now in the private sector, there certainly has not been a switch to a capitalist path. The dominance of the communist party remains and bureaucratic controls are still the dominant method of allocation in the state sector.

The USSR

The deceleration in Soviet growth since 1973 has been even more marked than in OECD countries but the causes have been different. The country was fairly insulated from the world economy. Although its growth in export volume was halved, its foreign earnings (at least until the early 1980s) were cushioned by the rise in oil and gold prices, and it was able to borrow nearly $23 billion on international capital markets between 1973 and 1986. As prices and incomes are determined by the state, and as there was no scope for speculative capital movements, the two major Western reasons for caution in macropolicy were not operative, and there was no sacrifice of output due to unemployment. As the USSR's productivity level is only about half of that in European OECD countries (see Table 7.3 above), the third reason for OECD slowdown, the erosion of once-for-all catch-up factors should not have applied to the USSR[13].

There was a deceleration in the growth of labour and capital inputs, but this was not as marked as in OECD countries. What was most striking after 1973 was that total factor productivity became substantially negative, with labour productivity slowing down dramatically, and capital productivity very negative indeed.

There seem to have been three major specifically Soviet reasons for the slowdown. One was an increase in microeconomic inefficiency, the second was the increased burden of military expenditure, and the third was depletion of some of the most favourable natural resource advantages.

There are many sources of microeconomic inefficiency in the Soviet system, deriving from its character as a command rather than a market economy. It has a chronic tendency to use capital and materials wastefully as these are supplied below cost, and management has an incentive to hoard them in case of future shortages. Thus the average and incremental fixed capital output ratios are higher than in capitalist economies, inventories are higher, the steel consumption/GDP ratio is four times as high as in the United States. The energy/GDP ratio is 1.4 times that of the United States and 2.4 times that of Japan[14]. Transfer of foreign technology is impeded by Western trade restrictions, the absence of foreign direct investment, and limited foreign contacts of technicians and scholars. There is no very hard evidence that these long-standing problems worsened, but it is frequently argued that they did, and there has certainly been an enormous change in Soviet perception of such shortcomings and their importance. They got little mention in the days of Kruschev who expected the USSR to overtake the capitalist economies, but now they have been clearly articulated by Abel Aganbegyan, the head of the economic department of the Soviet Academy of Sciences, and the main economic advisor to the government since 1985[15].

The quality of consumer goods is poor. Retail outlets and service industries are few. Prices bear little relation to cost. Bread, butter and housing are heavily subsidised. Cars are very expensive and difficult to get serviced. Consumers waste time queueing, bartering or sometimes bribing their way to goods and services they want to buy[16]. There is an active black market in scarce goods and services, with special shops for the *nomenklatura*. Work incentives are poor, malingering on the job is commonplace. Frustration produced widespread and growing alcoholism, accompanied by a decline in life expectation. The long Brezhnev years were ones of growing cynicism and awareness of these problems. The leadership considered moving to a more market oriented system in the mid 1960s, but dropped the idea when it realised the extent of the shake up required. Growing disillusion with the rewards the system offered has had a dulling effect on work incentives.

100

The fact that the economy is now operating at a higher level, with a more sophisticated output mix, trying to cater for more exigent consumers had made it more difficult to run the increasingly complex command system efficiently.

A second probable reason for slowdown was the rising share of resources going to a military and space effort which was increasingly sophisticated, and involved growing overseas commitments to Cuba, Afghanistan and Vietnam. Soviet military spending is estimated by US sources to have risen from around 13 per cent of GDP in the early 1970s to 16 per cent in the mid 1980s (compared with a rise from 5.6 to 6.6 per cent of GDP in the United States and a stable 1 per cent in Japan).

The third reason for the slowdown was the increased real cost of exploiting natural resources. In the 1950s a good deal of agricultural expansion was in virgin soil areas, whose fertility was quickly exhausted. From 1950-73 the cropped area increased by half. Thereafter it fell. New mineral and energy resources were located in Siberia and Central Asia and their exploitation required bigger infrastructure costs than the older sources in European Russia.

Since 1985, when power passed into the hands of Gorbachev, there have been major changes in policy. The most spectacular successes have been in foreign policy, with a measure of agreed nuclear disarmament, disengagement from foreign commitments in the third world, an end to confrontational policies vis-à-vis the West and China, and a switch in military doctrine to a policy of reasonable sufficiency. These changes promise some long run reduction in the defence burden, and also strengthen the regime's legitimacy in tackling other problems, but their economic effect has so far been negligible.

There has been a major increase in freedom to criticise official policy, to emigrate, practice religion, and have foreign contacts. Political prisoners have been released, many tabu areas of past Soviet history have been reopened. Some dead literary figures and economists (like Chayanov, Bukharin and Kondratieff) have been rehabilitated. The political system is being revamped to strengthen legal rights, provide for more competitive elections within the one party system, and to permit socialist pluralism which gives some hearing to non party pressure groups. *Glasnost* is a major departure from past policy, but its economic effects are so far very limited. In the long run it should increase the creativity of Soviet research, technology, and artistic endeavour. It has also increased the sensitivity of the system to public discontents.

Direct action on the economy has had several dimensions. There have been some limited moves to permit non state economic activity (by individuals or co-operatives–but not by enterprises hiring wage labour) in agriculture and services. This has broken some earlier tabus and involved legal changes, but has not yet attained significant dimensions. Aganbegyan suggests (p. 28) that co-operative and self employment might be expanded to meet half the needs in services, one third of catering and a quarter of consumer goods. He does not say what scope the new leasehold arrangements provide for development of private agriculture.

In the state sector, the central allocative bureaucracy has been cut. Some greater autonomy has been given to government plants to satisfy demand rather than commands and to trade abroad. It is hoped to reform the consumer price structure, allocate capital and materials more efficiently, and create something like a wholesale market. It remains to be seen whether the government will be willing or politically able to make major changes in relative prices, or effectively break the stranglehold of bureaucracy, given the strong vested interests which frustrated the 1965 Liberman type proposals. Price freedom is likely to lead to significant inflation in view of the fact that the government is running a substantial budget deficit and consumers have large liquid savings accounts.

It is not intended to allow land, natural resources or significant means of production to be privately owned. Enterprises may go bankrupt, but the possibility of unemployment, a stock exchange or Western style banking is not envisaged. Aganbegyan suggests reducing the number of prices set centrally (at present 500 000) and reviewing them more often. But his idea of price flexibility is "a review at least once every five years" (p. 135), and his continued commitment to state allocation techniques is clear from the inclusion in his book of two appendices of mathematical control models developed by his own institute in Novosibirsk, and that of Fedorenko in Moscow[17].

Apart from these longer run possibilities for change, shorter term practical measures have had mixed success. Formerly prominent and corrupt officials have been successfully prosecuted but the attempt to tighten labour discipline without increasing rewards has produced some resentment, compounded by the unpopularity of the cut in official alcohol production by half (which has since been substantially rescinded). Tighter quality control has not always been compatible with increases in output. There is also growing awareness of the magnitude of the problems in reforming the system (inflation, greater inequality, possible unemployment), so that less emphasis is now placed on the goal of *uskorenie* (accelerated growth). *Perestroika* (restructuring) and *glasnost* (openness) are rather stressed as improvements in the quality of life.

NOTES AND REFERENCES

1. The figures for bank assets are those for countries reporting to the Bank for International Settlements. See its *46th Annual Report*, Basle 1976, p. 78 for 1973 and its December 1988 report on *International Banking and Financial Market Developments*, p. 4.

2. See A. Maddison, "Economic Stagnation since 1973, Its Nature and Causes: A Six Country Survey", *De Economist*, 131, Nr. 4, 1983.

3. Not everyone would accept this diagnosis. There are those who argue that the increase in unemployment was due to structural change in labour markets and that official estimates of capital stock which we have used are misleading because of accelerated scrapping. I disagree with both of these viewpoints.

4. On agricultural protection in OECD countries, see the estimates of producer subsidies in *National Policies and Agricultural Trade*, OECD, Paris, 1987, p. 117. These averaged 32 per cent of farm income in the OECD and ranged from 5 per cent in Australia of 59 per cent in Japan.

5. For historical precedents of previous transfers see H. Reisen, "The Latin American Transfer Problem in Historical Perspective", in A. Maddison, ed., *Latin America, the Caribbean and the OECD*, OECD Development Centre, Paris, 1986. In the 1930s, when a similar problem hit most of Latin America, there was very widespread delinquency in payments, with eventual write-off of most debt, see A. Maddison, *Two Crises: Latin America and Asia 1929-38 and 1973-83*, OECD Development Centre, 1985.

6. The proportion of self employed and family workers is about 37 per cent in Latin America compared with 13 per cent in OECD countries (See ECLAC, *Statistical Yearbook for Latin America*, 1987, (p. 655). In Peru, where H. de Soto, *The Other Path*, Tauris, London, 1989, has stressed the importance of the informal economy, the proportion of self employed and family workers is highest at 50 per cent.

7. On the fiscal crisis and its link with the debt problem, see H. Reisen and A. van Trotsenburg, *Developing Country Debt: The Budgetary and Transfer Problem*, OECD Development Centre, Paris, 1988.

8. The theory behind the Brazilian heterodox experiment is set out by those who implemented it in L. Bresser Pereira and Y. Nakano, *The Theory of Inertial Inflation*, Rienner, London, 1987. They stress inertia as the main problem, without significant mention of other issues such as debt, fiscal crisis and micro-inefficiency. They advocated an incomes policy, deindexation and a price freeze, and promised virtually instant results. A similar approach can be found in P. Arida, ed., *Inflacao Zero: Brasil, Argentina e Israel*, Paz e Terra, Rio, 1986. In the latter book, as in some others, Israeli experience is held up as a model for Latin American stabilisation, without mention of the totally different foreign capital situation. Whilst Latin America generally has a foreign drain of around 5 per cent of GDP, Israel receives foreign aid on a tremendous scale from the United States. If Brazil received aid on the same scale per capita as Israel, the annual inflow would exceed $100 billion.

9. On the Chilean experiments, see A. Foxley, *Latin American Experiments in Neoconservative Economics*, University of California, Los Angeles, 1983; J. Ramos, *Neoconservative Economies in the Southern Cone of Latin America, 1973-1983*, Johns Hopkins, Baltimore, 1986; S. and A.C. Edwards, *Monetarism and Liberalization: The Chilean Experiment*, Ballinger, Cambridge, Mass., 1987.

10. See Vijay Joshi and I.M.D. Little, "Indian Macroeconomic Policies", *Economic and Political Weekly*, Feb. 28th, 1987 who characterise the Indian fiscal-monetary-exchange rate policy approach as conservative and suggest that India's relative isolation from foreign trade and capital markets because of extensive controls has given it greater immunity to external shocks. They stress the role of a "high minded elitist bureaucracy with a Gladstonian fiscal outlook" and characterise macro policy as more Friedmanite than Keynesian.

11. See R. Dornbusch and Y.C. Park "Korean Growth Policy", *Brookings Papers on Economic Activity*, 2, 1987.

12. See D. Bevan, P. Collier and J. Gunning, *Poverty, Equity and Growth in Indonesia: 1950-86*, Oxford, 1987, processed.

13. Our estimate of relative Soviet productivity levels in Table 7.3 is in line with Soviet findings, see V.M. Kudrov, "Problemi Sopostavlenii Proizvoditelnosti Truda v Promischlennosti, S.S.S.R. i S.Sch.A.", *Vestnik Moscovskovo Universiteta*, No. 1, 1969.

14. For energy, see Table 7.4 above. Steel consumption is from Aganbegyan, *op. cit.*

15. See his *The Challenge: Economics of Perestroika*, Hutchinson, London, 1988.

16. Aganbegyan provides an anecdote comparing the treatment of consumers in the West and the USSR of the type previously heard only from Western Kremlinologists. During a trip to Austria he found the shops "literally groaning" with goods, "hundreds of types of cheese, sausage etc. on sale". But he stayed in the Soviet compound in Vienna and found "no restaurant or cafe", "empty shelves", "bread had sold out, the choice was meagre, and I felt quite at home" (p. 119).

17. It is interesting to contrast Aganbegyan's approach with that of President Bush's economic advisor: "Thousands of price decisions are made daily and an attempt to keep a large subset of them under control would have led to a governmental nightmare–so costly as to be beyond any possible gain", see M.T. Boskin, "Macroeconomics, Technology, and Economic Growth: An Introduction to Some Important Issues", in R. Landau and N. Rosenberg, eds., *The Positive Sum Strategy*, National Academy Press, Washington D.C., 1986.

Chapter 8

CONCLUSIONS

There are several ways of concluding a survey of world history. The most prudent and parsimonious is to dispense with conclusions. Once the chronology is complete, most traditional historians feel their job is done. Economists are under greater pressure to draw on the past for insights into future trends or advice on policy. As long as one recognises frankly that futurology is a different "discipline" from history, such speculation may be useful in highlighting the major issues.

Forces Making for Growth and Slowdown

Throughout this analysis it was assumed that the major engine of growth has been advancing knowledge and technical progress which needs to be embodied in human and physical capital in order to have its impact. There is no reason to suspect that this will change.

At the frontiers of knowledge and technology, economic progress is necessarily rather gradual, and there have been no big leaps forward in productivity. The United States, the lead country throughout the century in terms of living standards and level of performance, had a rather steady pace of advance in both labour and total factor productivity until the 1970s. At that time there was a distinct slowdown, which has persisted now for nearly two decades. If it continues in the long term, it would have major influence on the pace of growth in the 21st century as a whole though it would not affect world growth in the next couple of decades, because the follower countries in a catch-up position need not be significantly affected.

Productivity growth rates in the European countries and Japan were much more uneven than in the United States in the twentieth century, but given the big spurt they achieved in the postwar golden age, most of them managed to do better than the lead country over the long haul, making good the handicaps imposed by the differential impact of two world wars. They still lag behind US income levels but not by very much, and all the signs suggest that they will continue to narrow the gap between themselves and the leader. One or some may replace the United States as the productivity leader in the course of time, but this seems unlikely to occur in the next two decades.

Within the world economy, there are large spreads in per capita income and productivity. Some countries which were well below the frontier of technology at the beginning of the century were able to grow much faster than the lead country when they mounted the necessary effort in terms of human and physical capital. Japan, Korea and Taiwan, did a fair amount of catching up, but they are still significantly below US productivity levels. Japan's experience suggests that supergrowth cannot be sustained indefinitely, for its productivity growth has not surpassed that of the top European performers in the past decade. Countries like Korea and Taiwan also seem likely to converge to slower growth paths within the next two decades.

Progress in many of the poor countries, particularly in Asia, was faster in the second half of the century than it was in the first, partly because the abolition of colonialism gave countries greater freedom to control their destiny–a freedom which was generally used in a very positive manner. Progress was also helped by buoyancy in the world economy, better opportunities for trade and transfer of technology and to a modest extent because the advanced countries provided some aid for development. Nevertheless, in spite of significant gains in income and productivity, many are not catching up or keeping up the pace of growth in the advanced countries. Convergence in per capita income levels is by no means inevitable, particularly in countries with rapid population growth.

It is clear that the eighth and ninth decades were not the twentieth century's best. Only the Asian countries grew fast. Latin America and Eastern Europe are in the middle of complex "adjustment" crises, and OECD performance is well below that of the postwar golden age.

The slowdown in the OECD countries was due in part to the erosion of once-for-all elements in the postwar golden age. It is nearer to being satisfactory than that in some other parts of the world economy. But growth and employment are below potential because of caution about inflation and balance of payments risks, induced in part by problems of living in a world with unrestricted freedom for international capital movements and fluctuating exchange rates. Growth did not accelerate significantly in the 1980s in spite of the waning of inflation and the reduced power of OPEC. Mutual consultation has been successful in avoiding beggar your neighbour policies, but very slow in getting remedial action to reduce payments disequilibria, or to induce changes in the US fiscal-monetary policy mix.

In Latin America, the general economic situation is one of major crisis–worse than anything previously experienced in the twentieth century. Since 1982 these countries have had seven years in the wilderness trying unsuccessfully to tackle a multiplicity of problems with desperate remedies. There are four characteristic and interrelated problems, a fiscal crisis, galloping inflation, very heavy external indebtedness, and distortions in resource allocation which derived originally from excessive protectionism, subsidies, and dirigisme and have been complicated by inflation and depression. To solve all of them in an enduring way by orthodox policy measures has proved too painful to be politically feasible in most of these countries, and heterodox alternatives have proved disastrous. It is not clear how or when Latin America will emerge from this crisis, but attempts on previous lines to provide a "managed" solution of the debt problem seem likely to break down.

In the USSR and in Eastern Europe there is also a crisis situation of different origin. The Stalinist model of authoritarian centralised controls has lost its legitimacy even for those in charge. It produces low growth, shoddy products, queues and shortages. The transition to a more market oriented economy, with more consumer choice and scope for entrepreneurial initiative is held back both by vested interests remaining from the old system, and the inherent difficulty of the task. The remarkable Chinese results from liberalisation are not much of a guide to what can be expected from reforms in European communism, because they were applied to a much more primitive economy. As the USSR liberalises, its problems will probably take on a closer resemblance to those of Latin America. It too has a fiscal crisis. Its repressed inflation will become overt if price controls are relaxed. It has bigger problems of resource allocation and integration in the world economy.

106

It is true that our survey did not cover the whole of the world economy, but the areas we missed–Africa and the Middle East–seem to be in no better shape than Latin America.

The Nature of the International Order

Wars and international hostility were a major impediment to growth in the twentieth century because of the destruction and deaths they caused and because they impeded the free flow of trade, ideas and capital. The recent lowering of tension between the superpowers is therefore a positive augury for growth, but absence of major wars is not new. Fortunately they have been absent since 1945. However, a lowering of defence spending will release resources for civilian research and development and perhaps offset in some degree the apparent decline in the rate of technical progress.

The nature of the world economic order and its institutions has a powerful effect on national options. In a good part of the 1913-50 period, there was no order. In its present form it is more managed than it was before 1913 with less reliance on natural harmony, more explicit rules of behaviour and much better institutional cooperation. However, in some areas the institutions carry burdens beyond their capacity to solve, particularly the debt problem.

There is likely to be some change in the nature of the international economic order and how it is run. Communist countries have abandoned the idea that institutions developed essentially by the West are beneficial only to capitalist countries. China has joined the IMF and World Bank. The USSR gives much greater support to the United Nations. This wider support may increase the problem-solving power of international institutions.

The nature of the international order will also depend on change in the relative influence of the major powers. The leverage of individual powers depends on their military and commercial role as well as the size of their economies, but economic weight may play an increasing role, if military competition wanes. Table 8.1 gives an idea of

Table 8.1. **Hypothetical levels of GDP, population and GDP per capita in the year 2010 in top 10 countries if 1973-87 trends continue**

International $ at 1980 prices

	GDP ($ billion)	Population (million)	GDP per capita
China	6 204	1 440	4 308
United States	5 859	307	19 084
Japan	2 780	151	18 413
USSR	2 723	348	7 826
Brazil	1 398	248	5 637
India	1 268	1 271	998
Germany	927	59	15 712
Italy	868	61	14 228
France	782	56	13 962
United Kingdom	749	58	12 926

Assumptions: Population assumed to grow at 1973-87 rates (see Table 6.9), GDP per capita assumed to grow at 1973-87 rates (see Table 3.2), except for China where per capita growth is assumed to be slower (4 per cent a year). GDP is derived from the population and per capita assumptions.

the weight of different countries may have if present trends continue (assuming only some slowdown in China's supergrowth). If Table 8.1 is compared with Table 2.3 it can be seen that the top 10 countries are likely to be the same in 2010 as they were in 1987, and virtually the same as in 1900. However, the relative weight of different countries will change, with China, Japan, Brazil and India moving up, and presumably exerting greater influence on world affairs.

The Nature of Domestic Policy

In our analysis, policy plays a prominent role. In the course of the century, economic policy has undergone secular improvement because of advances in analysis and better statistical information. But improvement has not been monotonic. Policy changes in response to events, policymakers operate under great pressure, and it takes time for them to get things right. Policies are not always rational and may harden into moulds, doctrines, rules of thumb or guidelines which are inappropriate for realising full growth potential or for solving other significant problems such as inflation, indebtedness, budgetary or balance of payments disequilibria. In many cases, it may be clear that policy is deficient, but alternative courses of action are often risky or subject to uncertainty, which makes for legitimate disagreement about the options. Some disagreement arises from the fact that alternative options represent the interests of different groups, but it is rare for policy disputes to be based entirely on interest group conflict.

Before 1913, policy had a similar flavour almost everywhere. In the interwar period consensus disappeared. In the postwar period, approaches to policy tended to be compartmentalised. There was a neoliberal OECD mainstream. "Development economics" and its concomitant prescriptions for policy and "planning" were usually considered a separate field with greater scope for dirigisme. In communist countries there was a firm belief that the objectives, problems and prescriptions were different from those of the first and third worlds.

This situation is now changing. There is some convergence of view about tasks and instruments in a more liberal direction, more markedly perhaps in communist than developing countries. There is greater scepticism about the efficacy of detailed government intervention in planning, more general acceptance of the dangers of ignoring price mechanism, more awareness of problems of efficiency, the dangers of isolation from the world economy, and the need for macroeconomic balance.

Research Agenda

Our brand of economic history can be improved when comparable historical figures are available for more countries. For the countries we cover, the quality of the GDP estimates can also be enhanced. Generally, the postwar data are better than the historical estimates, though we modified some of the official figures (adjusting Chinese, Soviet and Brazilian growth downwards). There will no doubt be further revisions which may affect the rating of some countries, but they are unlikely to be big enough to move countries beyond the upper and lower bounds of the present sample.

In order to compare income levels we used Eurostat, OECD and UN benchmark estimates of real output and purchasing power of currencies, which were linked with the time series. These estimates still do not cover many of the world's economies. We also need comparable measures of real product and purchasing power parity by industry of origin, to permit better measures of productivity by sector and to facilitate comparative structural analysis.

This study includes capital stock estimates for only 14 countries (see Table 6.10 for sources). For most of the developing countries these estimates are rather poor. Progress in this field is essential for total factor productivity analysis. As estimates of investment rates are now available for several decades for many countries, it will be feasible to improve the quality of the estimates and extend the country coverage in the future.

The quality of the labour market accounts could be substantially bettered. Improvement in the basic data situation will take many years but statistical authorities could improve the usefulness of what is already available by better integration and merger of data using the type of articulate analytical framework developed by national accountants.

Appendix A

ESTIMATES OF GDP LEVELS

In order to compare levels of output, income per capita or productivity in different countries or to add their output to form an aggregate index, it is useful to have a unit which expresses the comparative value of their currencies better than exchange rates. The latter mainly reflect purchasing power over tradeable goods and services, and are subject to a good deal of fluctuation as a result of capital movements. The OECD and Eurostat regularly make estimates of the purchasing power parity of OECD currencies and the United Nations Statistical Office makes such estimates for many other countries. Both sets of estimates follow a common methodology in the joint ICP Project. Here the latest available ICP benchmark estimates (ICP V for OECD countries and ICP IV for other countries) were used for 1980 expressed in 1980 "international" dollars, except for China, Mexico, Taiwan, Thailand and the USSR which were not included in ICP IV, and which were derived from other sources as indicated below. For reasons of historical consistency, the estimates for Bangladesh and Pakistan were benchmarked to their relation to India just after partition of the subcontinent in 1950.

Figures for GDP per capita in international dollars (ICP V) in OECD countries are from OECD, *National Accounts 1960-1986*, p. 145, with adjustment for Italy from 7 982 to 8 019 because of our lower population figure. GDP figures are rounded in the OECD source to the nearest billion. Here they are calculated to the nearest million, multiplying the OECD per capita figures by population. Total GDP for the 24 OECD member countries was $6 913.6 billion, so our sample covers 93.4 per cent of total OECD product. Total OECD population was 757.7 million, so our sample represents 88.6 per cent of this. Countries omitted were Greece, Iceland, Ireland, Luxembourg, New Zealand, Portugal, Spain and Turkey. It should be noted that the ICP V results for OECD countries involved substantial revision from the ICP IV results for reasons explained in D. Blades and D. Roberts, "A Note on the New OECD Benchmark Purchasing Power Parities for 1985", *OECD Economic Studies*, Autumn 1987.

For non-OECD countries, per capita real GDP in 1980 international dollars (ICP IV) are from UN/Eurostat, *World Comparisons of Purchasing Power and Real Product for 1980*, New York, 1986, pp. 7-8 for 9 countries. For Taiwan and Thailand, estimates were derived from R. Summers and A. Heston, "A New Set of International Comparisons of Real Product and Prices: Estimates for 130 Countries, 1950-85", *Review of Income and Wealth*, March 1988 using Taiwan/South Korea, and Thailand/South Korea relatives. Bangladesh and Pakistan combined were assumed to have had same per capita GDP as India in 1950, with distribution between the two countries as shown in A. Maddison *Class Structure and Economic Growth: India and Pakistan Since the Moghuls*, Allen and Unwin, London, 1971. China was derived from estimates in A. Maddison, "A Comparison of Levels of GDP Per Capita in Developed and Developing Countries, 1700-1980", *Journal of Economic History*, March 1983, Mexico from a bilateral comparison with Brazil by industry of origin, see A. Maddison and B. van Ark, *Review of Income and Wealth*, March 1989 for a description of the approach used. USSR from P. Marer, *Dollar GNPs of the USSR and Eastern Europe*, World Bank, 1985, p. 86.

Levels of GDP for the years 1900-87 shown in Table A-2 were derived by linking the 1980 benchmarks in Table A-1 with the time series for GDP in Appendix B.*

Table A-1. **Real GDP per capita, population and total GDP levels in 1980**

In international dollars

	GDP per capita $	Population 000s	Total GDP $ million
Australia	8 486	14 695	124 702
Austria	7 925	7 549	59 826
Belgium	8 166	9 847	80 411
Canada	11 131	24 070	267 923
Denmark	8 563	5 125	43 885
Finland	8 032	4 780	38 393
France	8 773	53 880	472 689
Germany	8 891	61 566	547 383
Italy	8 019	56 157	450 323
Japan	7 954	116 800	929 027
Netherlands	8 704	14 150	123 162
Norway	9 510	4 087	38 867
Sweden	9 173	8 311	76 237
Switzerland	10 891	6 385	69 539
United Kingdom	7 905	56 314	445 162
United States	11 804	227 757	2 688 467
Bangladesh	339	88 678	30 062
China	995	981 235	976 329
India	570	679 000	387 030
Indonesia	1 097	146 360	160 557
Pakistan	687	83 840	57 598
Philippines	1 740	48 320	84 077
South Korea	2 583	38 124	98 474
Taiwan	3 185	17 642	56 190
Thailand	1 847	46 455	85 802
Argentina	3 843	28 237	108 515
Brazil	3 349	118 518	396 917
Chile	3 650	11 104	40 530
Colombia	2 838	25 892	73 481
Mexico	2 946	69 655	205 204
Peru	2 508	17 290	43 363
USSR	5 550	265 500	1 473 525

Table A-2. Total GDP in international dollars (1980 prices) 1900-87

Adjusted to exclude impact of boundary changes

$ million

	1900	1913	1950	1973	1987
Australia	10 934	16 344	35 891	103 929	154 398
Austria	9 859	13 432	14 721	48 812	66 488
Belgium	14 293	18 443	26 908	67 556	86 479
Canada	9 864	21 775	66 240	206 386	329 525
Denmark	4 435	6 699	16 627	39 397	50 818
Finland	2 709	3 920	10 464	31 752	47 049
France	65 154	80 636	123 051	388 908	527 602
Germany	53 259	77 864	125 361	470 687	606 404
Italy	44 718	64 066	108 657	371 649	515 158
Japan	29 840	41 102	93 342	719 530	1 198 943
Netherlands	11 036	14 794	35 950	104 211	134 420
Norway	2 717	3 848	11 218	28 011	48 711
Sweden	7 610	10 106	27 447	65 435	86 403
Switzerland	6 852	9 559	24 672	67 994	78 268
United Kingdom	107 502	130 623	210 041	416 686	520 270
United States	222 352	368 132	1 019 725	2 326 225	3 308 401
OECD total	603 134	881 343	1 950 315	5 459 168	7 759 337
Bangladesh	10 131	11 780	14 265	20 874	38 661
China	160 434	178 260	184 855	682 557	1 869 945
India	88 789	100 553	129 111	297 236	521 772
Indonesia	20 060	25 457	35 182	97 627	204 928
Pakistan	8 152	8 756	14 693	39 315	89 917
Philippines	5 259	9 242	18 022	55 583	86 582
South Korea	4 816[a]	6 264	11 584	61 054	176 116
Taiwan	1 240	1 571	4 144	32 202	92 757
Thailand	4 579	5 666	12 704	52 789	122 430
Asian total	303 460	347 549	424 560	1 339 237	3 203 108
Argentina	6 028	13 546	39 865	93 560	104 004
Brazil	7 839	12 325	55 709	250 014	480 752
Chile	2 844[a]	4 382	14 316	32 756	42 362
Colombia	2 438[a]	4 161	16 174	52 322	89 297
Mexico	8 829	12 313	32 003	132 678	216 434
Peru	2 364[a]	3 693	10 296	33 817	49 397
Latin American total	30 342	50 420	168 363	595 147	982 246
USSR	98 029	154 134	407 840	1 265 598	1 683 764
32 country total	1 034 965	1 433 235	2 951 078	8 659 150	13 628 455

a) Rough estimates for Chile, Colombia, Peru and Korea based on per capita assumptions mentioned in Table 1.3.

113

Gross domestic product (GDP) is an aggregate measure which covers the output of the whole economy. It can be crosschecked in three ways, for it is the sum of value added in different sectors (e.g. agriculture, industry and services); it is also the sum of final expenditure, e.g. by consumers, investors, and government; as well as the total of incomes from wages, rents, profits, etc. In postwar years, the statistical offices of most governments have estimated GDP according to a standardised system for which guidelines have been laid down jointly by the OECD and the United Nations. This has added greatly to the comparability of the accounts. The major exceptions are the communist countries which follow a different procedure. In the case of the USSR and China, we therefore have to rely on estimates made by Western Kremlinologists and China-watchers, in order to get figures adjusted to the standardised UN/OECD basis. However, China has recently started to compile accounts on the UN/OECD basis, and this will probably occur in the USSR as well.

For OECD countries, official figures cover virtually all the postwar years, and in some cases official bodies have published retrospective estimates for earlier years, e.g. back to 1830 for Austria, to 1865 for Norway, 1900 for Australia and the Netherlands, 1926 for Canada and 1929 for the United States. For other countries and for earlier years, we relied on estimates made outside government by scholars who generally followed rather closely the internationally recognised guidelines. Some of these studies have been massive exercises such as the 14 volume study on Japan carried out by Hitotsubashi University, the multivolume studies on Finland sponsored by the Bank of Finland, the UK accounts deriving mainly from the work of the Cambridge Department of Applied Economics, or the French estimates of ISMEA. For some countries, the estimates have involved a succession of studies, each crosschecking and building on earlier ones, e.g. for Sweden there have been five such exercises since 1937.

For most OECD countries, therefore, the estimates we use, back to 1900, are reasonably reliable. The weakest estimates are those for prewar years for Belgium and Switzerland. There is, of course, still scope for improving the comparability of historical estimates by examining the impact of variations between countries in techniques of deflation and weighting, e.g. the Dutch official indices are based on a chain weighting system, whereas the official US estimates back to 1929 are based entirely on 1980 weights. It is not yet clear how sensitive the results are to such differences.

For developing countries, estimates are weaker, even for postwar years, more so for prewar years and particularly so for years before 1913. This is partly because the statistical record is poorer for these countries, or because archives are in worse condition, but it is also due to shortage of talent. The economic sophistication which is needed for constructing national accounts is also in high demand elsewhere. Thus Juan Sourrouille started in national accounts and became Minister of Finance in Argentina, Richard Webb became governor of the Bank of Peru, Leopoldo Solis became the President's economic advisor in Mexico! In spite of their shortcomings, the estimates we have used are in general based on the standardised system, the methods and sources of estimation in most cases are clearly described. They are not the fruit of rough hypothesis or regression. In my view they provide a reasonable basis for the present analysis of quantitative economic history. But they are obviously more likely to be significantly revised than those for the developed countries.

Sources for the 16 OECD Countries in Our Sample

Except as stated below, GDP growth taken from A. Maddison, *Phases of Capitalist Development*, Oxford 1982, updated from 1950 from OECD *National Accounts*. All figures are adjusted to eliminate the impact of territorial change. The following revisions or additions were made:

Canada: 1870-1960 from M.C. Urquhart, "New Estimates of Gross National Product in Canada 1870 to 1926, along with Official Estimates 1926 to 1985: Some Implications for Canadian Development", IARIW, Rocca di Papa, 1987, processed. Professor Urquhart kindly supplied ratios for conversion from GNP to GDP, and I adjusted the figures for 1949 onwards by .987 to offset the incorporation of Newfoundland in that year. 1960 onwards from OECD *National Accounts*.

Finland: 1820-60 per capita GDP assumed to increase by 22.5 per cent, as indicated in S. Heikkinen, R. Hjerppe, Y. Kaukiainen, E. Markkanen and I. Nummela, "Förändringar i Levnadsstandarden i Finland, 1750-1913", in G. Karlsson, ed., *Levestandarden i Norden 1750-1914*, Reykjavik, 1987, p. 74. 1860-1973 from R. Hjerppe, *The Finnish Economy 1860-1985: Growth and Structural Change*, Bank of Finland, Helsinki, 1989.

France: 1870-1913, 1920-38, and 1949-60 from J.-C. Toutain, *Le Produit Intérieur Brut de la France de 1789 à 1982, Economies et Sociétés*, Presses Universitaires de Grenoble, 1987 pp. 147-57 and 188 adjusted to eliminate the impact of boundary changes by use of the coefficients indicated in Maddison (1982). Interpolation between 1913-20, and 1938-49 as indicated in Maddison (1982).

Japan: 1885-1950 from K. Ohkawa and M. Shinohara, eds., *Patterns of Japanese Development: A Quantitative Appraisal*, Yale 1979, pp. 278-80 for 1885-1940, pp. 259 for 1940-50, adjusted from GNP to GDP basis using coefficients from pp. 268-9. 1945 GDP was assumed to be two-thirds of the 1944 level (see Y. Kosai, *The Era of High Speed Growth*, University of Tokyo, 1986, p. 34 for partial indicators for 1945). A rough estimate for 1870 was derived by assuming that per capita product rose by 1 per cent a year from 1870 to 1885. This is smaller than in later years, but 1870-85 saw major upheavals in which economic growth was probably slow. 1950-2 from *National Income White Paper*, (in Japanese) 1963 ed., p. 178, adjusted to a calendar year basis. 1952 onwards from OECD *National Accounts*. Adjustment for loss of Okinawa in 1946 as indicated in Maddison (1982). It was assumed that the official figures published by OECD are adjusted to exclude the effect of the reacquisition of Okinawa in 1973.

Netherlands: 1870-1900 from J.L. van Zanden, "Economische Groei in Nederland in de Negentiende Eeuw" *Economisch en Sociaal-Historisch Jaarboek*, 1987. 1900-60 from C.A. van Bochove and T.A. Huitker, "Main National Accounting Series, 1900-1986", *CBS Occasional Paper*, No. 17, The Hague, 1987. 1960-87 from OECD *National Accounts*.

Sweden: 1820-1973 figures supplied by Olle Krantz, see Olle Krantz, "New Estimates of Swedish Historical GDP Since the Beginning of the Nineteenth Century", *Review of Income and Wealth*, June 1988.

Switzerland: The estimates for Switzerland are weaker than for other OECD countries. The years 1890, 1913 and 1924-50 real product in international units from C. Clark, *Conditions of Economic Progress* (3rd ed.), Macmillan, London, 1957, pp. 188-9. The figures for 1900-12 are logarithmic interpolations between Clark's estimates for 1890 and 1913. For 1914-1923 the figures are interpolations of Clark's 1913-24 trend with year to year variations as in Sweden (which was also neutral during the war).

United Kingdom: 1700-1831 revised using N.F.R. Crafts, "British Economic Growth 1700-1831: A Review of the Evidence", *Economic History Review*, May 1983. His 1700-1801 estimates refer to England and Wales, and I adjusted them to a UK basis. This was done by assuming Scottish GDP per head to have been threequarters of that in England and Wales in 1801 and to have moved parallel to that in England and Wales from 1700 to 1801; it was further assumed that Irish output per head increased at half the rate which Crafts found for England and Wales for 1700-1801. 1801-31 growth shown by Crafts (p. 187) refers to Great Britain (i.e England, Wales and Scotland). His estimates were adjusted to a UK basis assuming Irish output per head of population in 1831 to have been half of that in Great Britain (hypothesis of P. Deane, "New Estimates of Gross National Product for the United Kingdom 1830-1914", *Review of Income and Wealth*, June 1968) and to have been stagnant from 1801 to 1831. Population estimates for 1700-1871 were revised using E.A. Wrigley and R.S. Schofield, *The Population History of England 1541-1871*, Arnold, London, 1981, p. 533-5.

United States: Figures up to 1929 from Maddison (1982). 1929-60 GDP from *The National Income and Product Accounts of the United States, 1929-82, Statistical Tables*, US Dept. of Commerce, September 1986, pp. 6, 7 for GNP, pp. 44-5 for income from abroad. 1960 onwards from OECD, *National Accounts*. Figures for years before 1960 exclude Alaska and Hawaii, which added .294 per cent to 1960 GDP (see *Survey of Current Business*, December 1980, p. 17). The figures were adjusted to exclude the impact of this geographic change.

Sources for Asian Countries

Bangladesh: 1900-1950 per capita GDP assumed to move as in India. 1950-66 from A. Maddison, *Class Structure and Economic Growth*, Allen and Unwin, London, 1971, p. 171. 1966-86 from World Bank, *World Tables*, (1988). 1986-87 from OECD Development Centre. The 1966-87 figures are for fiscal years.

China: 1933 to 1952 from D.W. Perkins, *China's Modern Economy in Historical Perspective*, Stanford, 1975, p. 117; 1914-18 – 1933 from the same source, except that we assume service output to move with population because Perkins' service output growth seems exaggerated. For 1900 – 1914-18 it was assumed that agricultural GDP per head grew at the same rate as for 1914/18-1933 as measured by Perkins, service output assumed to move parallel to population, traditional manufacturing to be stable and modern manufacturing to increase at the same rate Perkins shows for 1914-18 to 1933. 1933-38 movement as in Maddison (1985), p. 85. 1950-1973 calculated from A.G. Ashbrook's estimates for agriculture and industry in US Congress, Joint Economic Committee, *Chinese Economy Post-Mao* (Washington, D.C., 1978), Vol. 1, p. 231; assuming output in construction, transport and commerce to increase parallel to the average for agricultural and industrial product; and assuming government services and imputed income from dwellings to move parallel to population. Sector weights for 1970 from *Statistical Yearbook of China 1984*, p. 31 with a 10 per cent addition for government services and housing. 1973-86 from World Bank, *World Tables 1987*, Fourth edition, Washington, 1988. 1986-7 from US Joint Economic Committee, "China: Economic Policy and Performance in 1987", US Congress, April 1988, processed.

India: 1900-46 from A. Maddison, "Alternative Estimates of the Real Product of India, 1900-46", *Indian Economic and Social History Review*, 22, 2, 1985. 1946-50 from A. Maddison, 1971 *(Op. cit)*. All these figures refer to net domestic product and fiscal years. 1950-80, fiscal years, gross domestic product at 1970-1 market prices from *National Accounts Statistics, 1970-71–1984-5*, Central Statistical Organisation, Delhi, 1987, p. 158. 1980-87 from *Economic Survey 1987-88*, Ministry of Finance, Delhi.

Indonesia: 1900-1950 from A. Maddison "Dutch Income In and From Indonesia 1700-1938", *Modern Asian Studies*, 1989. 1950-66 from OECD Development Centre, 1966-86 from World Bank, *World Tables*, 1988. 1986-87 from OECD Development Centre. Official Indonesian national accounts date only from 1958. The previous year to year movements are shaky, but the OECD series we used is congruent with Muljatno "Perhitungan Pendapatan National Indonesia Untuk Tahun 1953 Dan 1954", *Ekonomi Dan Keuangan Indonesia*, March/April 1960, pp. 194, 206-7 for 1951-55 and the UN figures linking 1955 and 1958. The figures are not adjusted to exclude the impact of the acquisition of West Irian in 1962 and of East Timor in 1975.

Pakistan: As for Bangladesh. The 1966-87 figures are for fiscal years.

Philippines: 1900-50 derived by interpolation from figures for 1902, 1918, 1938, 1948 and 1961 in R.W. Hooley, "Long Term Growth of the Philippine Economy, 1902-1961", *The Philippine Economic Journal*, First Semester, 1968. 1950-87 supplied by National Statistical Coordination Board, Manila.

South Korea: 1913-38 average of expenditure and product estimates in T. Mizoguchi and M. Umemura, *Basic Economic Statistics of Former Japanese Colonies 1895-1938*, Toyo Keizai Shinposha, Tokyo, 1988, p. 238. 1938-40 commodity output derived from Sang-Chul Suh, *Growth and Structural Changes in the Korean Economy*, 1910-40, Cambridge, Mass., 1978, p. 171, and 1940-1953 commodity output from Kwang Suk Kim and M. Roemer, *Growth and Structural Transformation, Cambridge*, Mass., 1979, p. 35. For 1938-53 it was assumed that service output moved parallel to population, and sector weights for 1953 were taken from Kim and Roemer, p. 35. 1950-66 from A. Maddison, *Economic Progress and Policy in Developing Countries*, 1970. 1966-86 from World Bank, *World Tables*, 1988. 1986-87 from OECD Development Centre.

Taiwan: 1903-38 average of expenditure and product estimates in T. Mizoguchi and M. Umemura, *Basic Economic Statistics of Former Japanese Colonies 1895-1938*, Toyo Keizai Shinposha, Tokyo, 1988, p. 234. 1900 estimated by backward extrapolation of 1903-13 growth. 1938-51 from A. Maddison, *Economic Progress and Policy in Developing Countries*, Norton, New York, 1970, pp. 298-9. 1951 onwards from *National Income in Taiwan Area, The Republic of China*, Executive Yuan, December 1987.

Thailand: 1900-1950 derived from Sompop Manarungsan, "Economic Development of Thailand, 1850-1950", University of Groningen, Ph.D. thesis (his alternative procedure, using our population figures for 1950). 1950-85 from Oey Meesook and Associates, *The Political Economy of Poverty Equity and Growth: Thailand, 1850-1985*, Washington DC, 1988, processed. 1985-87 from Bank of Thailand.

Sources for Latin American Countries:

Argentina: 1900-1913 unpublished annual estimates supplied by ECLA/CONADE, Buenos Aires; these served as background for the quinquennial averages published in *El Desarollo Economico de la Argentina*, ECLA, Mexico, 1959, p. 15; 1913-83 from IEERAL, "Estadisticas de la evolucion economica de Argentina, 1913-84", *Estudios*, Buenos Aires, July-September, 1986. 1984-87 from ECLAC, *Balance Preliminar de la Economia Latinoamericana*, Santiago, 1987.

Brazil: 1900-20 indicators for industry, commerce, transport and communications from C.L.S. Haddad, *Crescimento do Produto Real no Brasil 1900-1947*, Vargas Foundation, Rio, 1978, p. 7 and his revised index for agriculture in P. Neuhaus, ed., *Economia Brasileira: Uma Visao Historica*, Campus, Rio, 1980, p. 24. 1920-47 for these sectors from R. Zerkowski and M.A. de Gusmao Veloso, "Seis decadas de economia brasileira atraves do PIB", *Revista Brasileira de Economia*, July-September, 1982. Finance and insurance assumed to move like transport and communication. 1947-80 for these sectors from M.A. de Gusmao Veloso, "Brazilian National Accounts 1947-85", IBGE, Rio, 1987, processed. For 1900-50 we used 1947 weights from Gusmao Veloso, and for 1950-87 the figures are at 1970 weights. Haddad, Zerkowski and Gusmao Veloso, and Gusmao Veloso 1947-80 all assumed that growth in "other services" (mainly government services and rental services from housing and other real estate) moves parallel to that in the sectors they cover. This exaggerates growth, so I assumed half of growth in "other services" to move like the aggregate for the covered sectors, the other half to increase parallel to population. 1980-85 GDP from Gusmao Veloso, 1985-87 from ECLAC, 1988.

Chile: 1913-29 derived by extrapolation from estimates for 1908-29 in M.A. Ballesteros and T.E. Davis, "The Growth of Output and Employment in Basic Sectors of the Chilean Economy, 1908-57", *Economic Development and Cultural Change*, Vol. 11, 1962/3. 1929-50 from ECLA, "Cuadros del producto interno bruto a precios del mercado en dollares de 1950", Santiago, 1962, processed. 1950-66 from ECLA, *Series Historicas del Crecimiento de America Latina*, Santiago, 1978. 1966-86 from World Bank, *World Tables*, 1988, 1986-87 from ECLAC 1988.

Colombia: 1913-29 from L.J. Zimmerman, *Arme en rijke landen*, The Hague, 1964. 1929-50 from ECLA (1978). 1950-85 from A. Urdinola and M. Carrizosa, *Poverty, Equity and Growth in Colombia*, processed, Bogota, 1985. 1985-87 from ECLAC, 1988.

Mexico: 1900-50 from INEGI, *Estadisticas Historicas de Mexico*, Tomo I, Mexico, 1985, Table 9.1. 1950-86 from Bank of Mexico, *Indicadores Economicos*. 1986-87 from ECLAC, 1988.

Peru: 1913-38 from C.A. Bolona Behr, "Tariff Policies in Peru, 1880-1980", Ph.D. thesis, Oxford University, 1981. 1929-50 link from per capita figure of Zimmerman (1964). 1950-85 from Richard Webb, *Poverty, Equity and Growth in Peru*, processed, Lima, 1987. 1985-87 from ECLAC, 1988.

USSR: 1900-13 derived from R.W. Goldsmith, "The Economic Growth of Tsarist Russia 1860-1913", *Economic Development and Cultural Change*, April 1961, pp. 450, and 463-4, giving agriculture a weight of 2 and industry 1 in 1913 as Goldsmith suggests. This gives very similar results to those derived from deflated expenditure by P. Gregory, *Russian National Income*, Cambridge, 1982, pp. 56-7, 1913-28 from A. Maddison, *Economic Growth in Japan and USSR*, Allen and Unwin, 1969, pp. 151-2. 1928-40 and 1945-50 from R. Moorsteen and R.P. Powell, *The Soviet Capital Stock 1928-1962*, Irwin, Illinois, 1966, p. 361. 1940-5 from *Narodnoe Khoziastvo 1984*, Moscow, 1985, p. 40. 1950-5 from *U.S.S.R.: Measures of Economic Growth and Development, 1950-80*, Joint Economic Committee, US Congress, 1982, pp. 62-64. 1955-65 from US Joint Economic Committee, *Allocation of Resources in the Soviet Union and China 1986*, US Congress 1987, p. 67. 1965-87 from US Joint Economic Committee, *Gorbachev's Economic Program: Problems Emerge*, US Congress, April 13, 1988, processed, p. 58. Annual interpolation 1950-80 derived from the 1982 source above combined with other sources for benchmark years.

Sources for other OECD Countries

Greece: 1913-29 real product in international units from C. Clark, *Conditions of Economic Progress*, 3rd Edition, Macmillan, London, 1957. 1929-38 GNP at factor cost from *Ekonomikos Tachidromos*, 22 May, 1954; 1938-50 from OEEC, *Europe and the World Economy*, Paris, 1960, p. 116. 1950 onwards from OECD, *National Accounts*, various issues.

Ireland: 1913-50 from A. Maddison, "Economic Policy and Performance in Europe 1913-70", in C.M. Cipolla, *Fontana Economic History of Europe*, Vol. 5 (2), London, 1976. 1950 onwards from OECD sources.

New Zealand: 1900-50 from C. Clark, *Op. cit.*, 1957 (with some interpolation), 1950-5 from World Bank, *World Tables*, 1983. 1955 onwards from OECD *National Accounts* adjusted to a calender year basis.

Portugal: 1900-1913 derived from N. Valerio, "The Role of Government in Portuguese Economic Growth 1851-1939", *Estudos de Economia*, Oct.-Dec., 1986, p. 68. 1913-38 from N. Valerio, "O Produto Nacional de Portugal entre 1913 e 1947: Uma Primeiro Approximacao", *Revista de Historia Economica e Social*, 1983, pp. 99-100. 1938-53 from OEEC, *Europe and The World Economy*, Paris, 1960. 1953-87 from OECD, *National Accounts*, various issues.

Spain: 1900-54 derived from J. Alcaide, « La renta nacional 1901-70: una revision urgente », in *Datos Basicos para la Historia Financiera Espanola 1850-1975*, Instituto de Estudios Fiscales, Madrid, 1976. 1954-87 from OECD *National Accounts*, various issues.

Turkey: 1923-50 estimates of GNP at constant prices supplied by Bent Hansen. 1950-87 from OECD *National Accounts*, various issues.

Sources for Eastern European Countries

Bulgaria, Czechoslovakia, East Germany, Hungary, Poland and *Rumania* up to 1950 from sources cited in A. Maddison, "Economic Policy and Performance in Europe 1913-1870", in C.M. Cipolla, ed., *The Fontana Economic History of Europe*, Vol. 5 (2), Collins, London, 1976. 1950-65 from T.P. Alton, "Economic Growth and Resource Allocation in Eastern Europe", *Reorientation and Commercial Relations of the Economies of Eastern Europe*, Joint Economic Committee, US Congress, August 1974, p. 270. 1965-82 from T.P. Alton, "East European GNPs: Origins of Product,

Final Uses, Rates of Growth and International Comparisons", in *East European Economies: Slow Growth in the 1980s*, Vol. 1, *Economic Peformance and Policy*, Joint Economic Committee, US Congress, October, 1985, pp. 109-10. 1982-87 from OECD Development Centre.

Yugoslavia: 1909/12-50 from I. Vinski, "National Product and Fixed Assets in the Territory of Yugoslavia 1909- 59", in P. Deane, ed., *Studies in Social and Financial Accounting, Income and Wealth*, Series IX, Bowes and Bowes, London, 1961. 1950-73 from World Bank, *World Tables*, 1984; 1973-87 from World Bank, *World Tables*, 1989.

Table B-1. GDP indices for 16 OECD countries, selected years, 1700-1912

1913 = 100.0

	Australia	Austria	Belgium	Canada	Denmark	Finland	France	Germany
1700								
1820					12.6	14.7		
1870	25.6	35.9	42.5	18.0	32.4	31.3	49.9	30.4
1900	66.9	73.4	77.5	45.3	66.2	69.1	80.8	68.4
1901	65.0	73.7	78.2	49.1	69.0	68.3	79.5	66.8
1902	65.9	76.6	79.8	53.4	70.6	66.9	78.2	68.4
1903	67.3	77.3	81.6	55.4	74.8	71.4	79.9	72.2
1904	70.4	78.5	83.7	56.3	76.4	74.1	80.5	75.1
1905	71.3	82.9	86.1	62.0	77.7	75.3	81.9	76.7
1906	78.0	86.1	87.9	68.6	79.9	78.3	83.4	79.0
1907	80.0	91.4	89.2	72.3	82.9	81.0	87.0	82.5
1908	78.3	91.8	90.1	69.1	85.5	81.9	86.5	83.9
1909	82.1	91.5	91.8	76.0	88.8	85.5	90.1	85.6
1910	88.2	92.8	94.2	82.8	91.5	87.4	84.6	88.7
1911	91.3	95.7	96.4	88.9	96.4	89.9	92.9	91.7
1912	95.1	100.5	98.7	95.7	96.4	94.9	100.6	95.7

	Italy	Japan	Netherlands	Norway	Sweden	Switzerland	United Kingdom	United States
1700							4.7	
1820					17.8		16.2	2.03
1870	53.5	35.2	38.1	40.6	39.8		44.6	17.3
1900	69.8	72.6	74.6	70.6	75.3	71.7*	82.3	60.4
1901	73.4	75.2	72.9	72.5	74.5	73.9*	82.3	67.2
1902	73.8	71.3	76.6	74.0	74.4	76.0*	84.4	67.9
1903	74.8	76.3	78.7	73.7	79.9	78.2*	83.5	71.2
1904	74.9	76.9	78.0	73.6	80.7	80.4*	84.0	70.3
1905	77.5	75.6	80.6	74.5	81.6	82.6*	86.5	75.5
1906	79.1	85.5	84.5	77.2	86.9	84.8*	89.4	84.2
1907	87.1	88.2	84.8	80.1	88.8	86.9*	91.1	85.5
1908	87.0	88.8	84.7	82.7	88.6	89.1*	87.4	78.5
1909	92.4	88.7	88.5	84.9	88.0	91.3*	89.4	88.1
1910	87.7	90.1	89.3	87.9	93.3	93.5*	92.2	89.0
1911	93.1	95.0	91.9	90.6	95.6	95.6*	94.9	91.9
1912	95.3	98.4	97.0	94.7	98.3	97.8*	96.3	96.2

* Interpolations, see country notes for rationale. These interpolations were required for Graph 1.

Table B-2. GDP indices for 16 OECD countries, 1913-49

1913 = 100.0

	Australia	Austria	Belgium	Canada	Denmark	Finland	France	Germany
1913	100.0	100.0	100.0	100.0	100.0	100.0	100.0	100.0
1914	94.4	83.5*	93.7*	93.5	106.3	95.6	92.9	85.2
1915	93.5	77.4*	92.5*	100.3	98.9	90.8	91.0	80.9
1916	97.1	76.5*	97.9*	110.2	103.1	92.0	95.6	81.7
1917	94.7	74.8*	84.1*	113.6	97.0	77.3	81.0	81.8
1918	95.0	73.3*	67.8*	106.9	93.8	67.0	63.9	82.0
1919	93.4	61.8*	79.9*	99.6	105.9	80.9	75.3	72.3
1920	97.0	66.4	92.5	99.0	110.9	90.5	87.1	78.6
1921	105.9	73.5	94.1	90.8	107.7	93.5	83.5	87.5
1922	110.5	80.1	103.3	104.1	118.6	103.4	98.5	95.2
1923	114.5	79.3	107.0	110.6	131.1	111.0	103.6	79.1
1924	120.5	88.5	110.5	111.7	131.5	113.9	116.6	92.6
1925	122.5	94.5	112.2	123.2	128.5	120.4	117.1	103.0
1926	123.2	96.1	116.0	130.1	136.0	125.0	120.2	105.9
1927	125.7	99.0	120.3	143.0	138.7	134.8	117.7	116.5
1928	123.4	103.6	126.6	155.7	143.4	143.9	125.9	121.6
1929	123.1	105.1	125.5	155.5	153.0	145.6	134.4	121.1
1930	118.1	102.2	124.3	150.3	162.1	143.9	130.5	119.4
1931	113.3	94.0	122.1	127.1	163.9	140.4	122.7	110.3
1932	117.6	84.3	116.6	118.0	159.6	139.8	114.7	102.0
1933	123.3	81.5	119.1	109.6	164.7	149.1	122.9	108.4
1934	127.0	82.2	118.1	121.2	169.7	166.0	121.7	118.3
1935	131.6	83.8	125.4	131.0	173.5	173.1	118.6	127.2
1936	137.1	86.3	126.3	138.1	177.8	184.8	123.1	138.4
1937	143.7	90.9	128.0	151.1	182.1	195.3	130.2	153.4
1938	145.2	102.5	125.1	155.0	186.5	205.4	129.7	169.1
1939	146.2	116.2	133.6*	164.3	195.4	196.6	139.0	182.7
1940	155.7	113.2	117.7*	186.9	168.0	186.4	114.7	184.0
1941	173.2	121.3	111.5*	213.0	151.4	192.5	90.7	195.7
1942	193.1	115.2	101.9*	250.7	154.8	193.1	81.3	198.4
1943	199.9	118.0	99.5*	262.0	171.9	215.3	77.2	202.3
1944	193.0	121.0	105.4*	271.9	189.9	215.4	65.2	207.5
1945	183.4	50.0	111.7*	263.5	175.6	202.9	70.7	145.3
1946	176.8	58.4	118.3*	260.8	203.0	219.4	107.5	83.0
1947	181.1	64.4	125.4*	272.3	214.4	224.5	116.5	101.9
1948	192.8	82.0	132.9	277.3	221.5	242.3	125.0	120.8
1949	205.4	97.5	138.3	283.3	231.5	257.0	142.0	140.7

* Interpolations. In Austria, the 1914-19 year to year movement was assumed to have the same pattern as in Germany (around Austrian 1913-20 trend). In Belgium, the 1914-19 year to year movement was assumed to have the same pattern as in France (around Belgian 1913-20 trend); the 1939-43 year to year Belgian movement was assumed to be as in the Netherlands, with logarithmic interpolation for the years 1943-47, i.e. after the liberation.

Table B-2 *(cont'd).* GDP indices for 16 OECD countries, 1913-49

1913 = 100.0

	Italy	Japan	Netherlands	Norway	Sweden	Switzerland	United Kingdom	United States
1913	100.0	100.0	100.0	100.0	100.0	100.0	100.0	100.0
1914	99.0	97.0	97.3	102.2	99.1	100.1*	101.0	92.3
1915	110.8	106.0	100.6	106.6	99.1	100.1*	109.1	94.9
1916	122.5	122.4	103.3	110.0	97.8	100.7*	111.5	108.0
1917	126.5	126.5	96.7	100.0	85.8	89.7*	112.5	105.3
1918	127.5	127.8	90.7	96.3	84.5	89.4*	113.2	114.8
1919	107.8	140.9	112.4	112.6	89.4	95.3*	100.9	115.8
1920	100.0	132.1	115.8	119.7	94.6	101.5*	94.8	114.7
1921	98.0	146.6	122.9	109.8	91.1	99.0*	87.1	112.1
1922	103.9	146.2	129.6	122.6	99.7	108.5*	91.6	118.3
1923	109.8	146.3	132.8	125.3	105.0	114.8*	94.5	133.9
1924	111.8	150.4	142.5	124.7	108.3	119.1	98.4	138.0
1925	119.6	156.6	148.5	132.4	112.3	127.8	103.2	141.2
1926	120.6	158.0	160.4	135.3	118.6	134.2	99.4	150.4
1927	117.6	160.3	167.1	140.5	122.3	141.4	107.4	151.9
1928	126.5	173.4	176.0	145.1	128.1	149.3	108.7	153.6
1929	130.4	178.8	177.4	158.6	135.9	154.5	111.9	163.0
1930	123.5	165.8	177.0	170.3	138.7	153.5	111.1	147.5
1931	122.5	167.2	166.2	157.1	133.7	147.1	105.4	135.2
1932	125.5	181.2	163.9	167.6	130.1	142.1	106.2	117.1
1933	125.5	199.0	163.6	171.6	132.6	149.2	109.3	114.7
1934	125.5	199.4	160.6	177.1	142.7	149.5	116.5	123.7
1935	137.3	204.9	166.6	184.7	151.8	148.9	121.0	133.6
1936	137.3	219.8	177.1	196.0	160.6	149.4	126.5	152.7
1937	146.1	230.3	187.2	203.0	168.2	156.5	130.9	160.2
1938	148.0	245.7	182.7	208.1	171.0	162.5	132.5	152.9
1939	158.8	284.4	195.1	218.0	182.8	162.3	133.8	165.0
1940	159.8	292.7	171.9	198.6	177.4	164.0	147.2	178.2
1941	157.8	296.7	162.8	203.4	180.4	162.9	160.6	209.6
1942	155.9	295.1	148.8	195.5	191.4	158.8	164.6	249.2
1943	141.2	299.3	145.2	191.6	199.9	157.4	168.2	294.6
1944	114.7	286.4	97.4	181.6	206.7	161.2	161.6	318.7
1945	89.8	143.2*	99.7	203.5	212.3	207.5	154.5	312.8
1946	117.6	155.6*	168.3	225.3	235.6	221.7	147.8	252.9
1947	138.2	168.0	194.8	251.1	241.4	248.4	145.6	245.6
1948	146.1	193.0	215.6	271.1	248.9	253.4	150.2	255.0
1949	156.9	205.9	234.6	276.4	258.0	246.5	155.8	255.2

* Interpolations, see country notes for rationale.

121

Table B-3. GDP indices for 16 OECD countries, 1950-87

1913 = 100.0

	Australia	Austria	Belgium	Canada	Denmark	Finland	France	Germany
1950	219.6	109.6	145.9	304.2	248.2	266.9	152.6	161.0
1951	229.0	117.1	154.2	321.5	246.4	289.6	162.0	177.8
1952	231.1	117.2	153.0	344.9	251.0	299.3	166.3	193.5
1953	238.3	122.3	157.9	361.0	265.5	301.4	171.1	209.5
1954	253.1	134.8	164.4	358.5	274.7	327.8	179.4	225.6
1955	267.0	149.7	172.2	392.0	273.7	344.5	189.7	252.8
1956	276.1	160.0	177.2	423.7	279.2	354.9	199.3	270.9
1957	281.7	169.8	180.5	436.0	291.3	371.6	211.3	286.1
1958	295.2	176.0	180.3	443.8	299.5	373.6	216.6	296.3
1959	313.4	181.0	186.0	461.8	320.0	395.8	222.8	318.2
1960	326.5	195.9	196.0	476.1	339.0	432.0	238.5	346.5
1961	334.0	206.3	205.8	490.7	360.6	465.0	251.7	362.6
1962	347.4	211.3	216.5	525.6	381.0	478.8	268.5	379.7
1963	371.2	219.9	225.9	552.8	383.5	494.5	282.8	390.2
1964	397.4	233.1	241.6	589.9	419.0	520.5	301.2	416.3
1965	415.5	239.8	250.2	629.0	438.1	548.0	315.6	439.1
1966	433.8	253.3	258.1	671.8	450.1	561.0	332.1	452.0
1967	455.9	261.0	268.1	691.4	465.5	573.3	347.7	451.5
1968	486.0	272.6	279.4	727.9	484.0	586.4	362.5	476.6
1969	521.9	289.7	298.0	767.3	514.6	642.6	387.8	512.1
1970	551.1	310.4	316.9	787.2	525.0	690.6	410.0	538.5
1971	581.3	326.2	328.5	832.6	539.0	705.1	432.2	554.1
1972	609.7	346.5	345.8	879.9	567.5	758.9	457.7	577.4
1973	635.9	363.4	366.3	947.8	588.1	809.9	482.3	604.5
1974	655.1	377.8	381.3	989.3	582.6	834.4	497.9	606.1
1975	670.6	376.4	375.6	1015.0	578.7	844.0	498.8	596.5
1976	688.9	393.6	396.5	1077.4	616.2	846.3	524.6	628.8
1977	700.9	410.8	398.4	1115.9	626.2	847.3	540.6	647.3
1978	721.7	412.9	409.3	1167.0	635.4	865.7	558.7	665.9
1979	745.8	432.4	418.0	1212.5	658.0	929.3	576.8	693.6
1980	763.0	445.4	436.0	1230.4	655.1	979.3	586.2	703.0
1981	782.1	444.7	430.1	1275.8	649.2	995.2	593.1	704.2
1982	786.5	449.6	436.7	1234.8	668.8	1031.3	608.2	699.6
1983	803.2	459.4	437.2	1274.2	685.7	1062.1	612.4	710.1
1984	845.5	465.7	446.5	1355.0	709.4	1096.6	620.9	729.6
1985	886.8	478.8	452.8	1412.1	739.2	1134.8	631.3	748.6
1986	915.4	486.8	463.1	1458.6	764.3	1162.3	644.6	767.3
1987	944.7	495.0	468.9	1513.3	758.6	1200.1	654.3	778.8

Table B-3 *(cont'd).* **GDP indices for 16 OECD countries, 1950-87**

1913 = 100.0

	Italy	Japan	Netherlands	Norway	Sweden	Switzerland	United Kingdom	United States
1950	169.6	227.1	243.0	291.5	271.6	258.1	160.8	277.0
1951	182.5	255.4	248.1	305.0	282.4	279.0	166.6	305.4
1952	190.6	285.0	253.1	315.9	286.4	281.3	166.2	317.2
1953	204.9	306.0	275.1	330.5	294.4	291.2	173.9	330.1
1954	212.4	323.3	293.8	346.9	306.8	307.6	180.5	325.6
1955	226.5	351.1	315.6	353.6	315.7	328.3	186.5	343.6
1956	237.1	377.5	327.2	372.1	327.7	350.1	189.4	350.4
1957	249.7	405.1	336.4	382.9	342.4	364.0	193.1	356.1
1958	261.8	428.7	335.4	379.4	344.1	356.3	193.4	353.8
1959	278.9	467.8	351.8	398.9	354.6	378.7	201.1	374.5
1960	296.5	529.2	381.4	421.8	373.4	405.2	213.3	381.5
1961	320.9	606.2	382.5	448.3	394.8	438.0	220.4	391.8
1962	340.8	649.0	408.7	460.9	417.1	459.0	222.8	412.6
1963	359.9	717.2	423.5	478.3	438.1	481.5	232.0	430.2
1964	370.0	811.9	458.6	502.3	479.0	506.8	224.0	455.5
1965	382.1	853.6	482.6	528.8	505.4	522.9	249.8	482.5
1966	404.9	942.8	495.8	548.9	520.1	535.7	254.5	507.1
1967	434.0	1 036.9	522.0	538.2	534.6	552.1	261.9	518.5
1968	462.4	1 171.6	555.5	596.4	561.0	571.9	272.7	540.2
1969	490.6	1 313.1	591.2	623.2	575.0	604.1	276.0	555.8
1970	516.6	1 436.6	624.9	635.7	612.8	642.7	282.3	555.3
1971	525.1	1 497.3	651.3	664.8	636.2	668.8	289.9	573.5
1972	541.9	1 622.8	672.9	699.1	634.9	690.3	296.3	602.9
1973	580.1	1 750.6	704.4	727.9	667.3	711.3	319.0	631.9
1974	604.1	1 729.3	732.3	765.7	688.7	721.7	316.0	627.3
1975	582.1	1 774.3	731.7	797.6	706.2	664.5	313.9	621.1
1976	616.3	1 859.2	769.1	851.9	713.7	659.7	325.7	651.5
1977	628.0	1 957.5	786.9	882.4	702.3	675.8	329.1	680.7
1978	644.9	2 057.3	806.3	922.5	714.6	678.6	340.9	715.8
1979	676.5	2 164.1	825.4	969.2	742.1	695.5	348.1	730.3
1980	702.9	2 260.3	832.5	1 010.0	754.4	727.5	340.8	730.3
1981	710.9	2 347.5	826.7	1 018.9	752.2	738.0	336.8	757.4
1982	712.7	2 414.1	815.0	1 022.3	758.2	729.7	340.5	738.7
1983	716.1	2 490.2	826.5	1 069.6	776.6	734.7	352.4	768.5
1984	741.3	2 615.1	852.6	1 131.1	807.3	747.5	359.6	822.4
1985	761.7	2 732.7	872.4	1 192.1	824.6	778.1	373.0	848.1
1986	782.6	2 799.4	893.0	1 244.1	834.1	798.8	383.8	873.3
1987	804.1	2 917.0	908.6	1 265.8	855.0	818.8	398.3	898.7

Table B-4. GDP indices for 9 Asian countries, 1900-87

1913 = 100.0

	Bangladesh	China	India	Indonesia	Pakistan	Philippines	South Korea	Taiwan	Thailand
1900	86.0	90.0	88.3	78.8	93.1	56.9	76.9[a]	78.9	80.8
1913	100.0	100.0	100.0	100.0	100.0	100.0	100.0	100.0	100.0
1929	108.6	120.9	109.9	155.1	115.0	151.5	160.2	180.5	131.0
1932	108.9	126.8	110.2	161.8	115.3	n.a.	167.9	214.4	n.a.
1938	115.8	126.8	114.9	177.2	124.2	179.3	258.6	272.0	169.5
1950	121.1	103.7	128.4	138.2	167.8	195.0	184.9	263.8	224.2
1951	122.8	117.3	131.7	145.9	162.3	204.0	170.7	282.6	240.1
1952	126.4	135.6	136.1	154.4	162.9	222.1	181.7	316.6	247.3
1953	128.2	141.9	144.7	163.1	178.5	239.3	234.4	345.9	274.9
1954	130.7	146.7	149.7	172.5	182.6	252.1	251.1	379.2	269.0
1955	123.8	159.4	155.4	182.3	186.8	272.0	265.9	409.8	292.6
1956	136.8	169.9	163.7	185.7	192.3	285.7	269.1	432.4	311.9
1957	133.9	179.2	162.3	189.3	200.7	298.4	290.9	464.3	304.0
1958	131.3	206.8	175.7	193.1	203.5	310.8	309.9	495.5	315.9
1959	138.3	193.0	179.6	193.9	205.7	298.7	324.8	533.5	334.5
1960	146.2	186.7	189.1	195.0	215.8	303.2	333.4	567.0	369.0
1961	154.5	157.2	197.0	206.2	228.9	320.2	348.4	606.0	388.5
1962	153.7	173.1	202.7	210.1	245.5	335.4	360.3	653.8	420.2
1963	170.0	191.0	215.1	205.4	260.9	358.8	393.3	715.0	455.4
1964	171.8	210.7	231.6	212.6	280.6	371.3	426.3	802.4	482.5
1965	180.2	230.0	222.3	214.9	293.1	390.8	457.4	891.8	516.6
1966	182.5	254.8	222.0	220.8	317.0	408.1	516.2	971.5	581.1
1967	178.5	248.7	240.6	221.7	328.9	429.0	539.2	1 075.1	619.0
1968	195.1	249.0	249.0	250.4	351.9	453.6	587.9	1 173.0	669.5
1969	197.8	271.7	264.9	271.0	374.7	475.4	664.6	1 277.5	720.1
1970	208.5	311.1	280.3	293.4	413.6	498.4	723.8	1 422.1	776.0
1971	197.0	330.0	286.8	310.5	414.8	526.9	795.5	1 603.9	812.3
1972	169.4	342.3	284.9	343.4	419.5	554.4	850.0	1 816.3	851.3
1973	177.2	382.9	295.6	383.5	449.0	601.4	974.7	2 050.0	931.6
1974	197.3	386.9	296.2	415.6	477.2	631.4	1 053.9	2 073.0	982.2
1975	207.3	418.9	325.9	436.6	500.4	672.9	1 112.8	2 172.5	1 052.2
1976	222.7	396.2	329.3	466.6	517.3	725.8	1 251.0	2 469.1	1 143.9
1977	226.5	427.5	356.2	506.4	538.5	770.4	1 385.2	2 715.7	1 226.4
1978	242.1	481.0	379.9	545.1	580.1	813.0	1 529.2	3 081.7	1 349.9
1979	252.3	514.0	361.6	581.5	612.6	863.7	1 636.2	3 333.1	1 431.7
1980	255.2	547.7	384.9	630.7	657.8	909.7	1 572.0	3 577.2	1 514.2
1981	270.9	572.6	408.7	679.8	699.7	944.6	1 686.8	3 796.7	1 609.5
1982	274.7	626.6	421.5	674.7	750.4	972.1	1 772.6	3 901.9	1 675.4
1983	284.2	692.4	454.8	696.3	798.4	981.0	1 948.4	4 202.2	1 773.2
1984	296.1	793.7	469.2	736.9	833.1	925.1	2 133.3	4 604.0	1 883.1
1985	307.4	891.2	491.5	755.5	908.1	888.4	2 255.7	4 802.2	1 958.4
1986	319.8	958.8	511.3	778.5	975.3	891.3	2 530.6	5 310.1	2 027.0
1987	328.2	1 049.0	518.9	805.0	1 026.9	936.8	2 811.5	5 905.1	2 160.6

a) Rough proxy, see note to Table 1.3.

Table B-5. GDP indices for 6 Latin American countries and USSR, 1900-87

1913 = 100.0

	Argentina	Brazil	Chile	Colombia	Mexico	Peru	USSR
1900	44.5	63.6	64.9[a]	58.6[a]	71.7[a]	64.0[a]	63.6
1913	100.0	100.0	100.0	100.0	100.0	100.0	100.0
1929	174.2	174.5	189.4	183.3	114.4	190.5	116.2
1932	150.3	183.9	139.1	190.7	94.3	141.4	124.2
1938	192.3	262.3	207.2	249.8	136.4	237.9	197.8
1950	294.3	452.0	326.7	388.7	259.9	278.8	264.6
1951	305.8	473.4	343.7	400.7	279.9	301.4	272.7
1952	290.2	501.6	355.8	426.0	291.1	320.4	288.8
1953	305.8	525.6	380.9	452.1	291.9	337.4	303.8
1954	318.4	560.4	383.5	483.5	321.2	359.2	318.3
1955	341.1	601.6	394.0	502.2	348.5	376.4	345.6
1956	350.5	619.2	396.9	522.4	372.2	392.6	373.4
1957	368.5	661.0	408.0	541.5	400.5	418.8	386.4
1958	391.1	721.0	427.7	555.1	421.8	416.6	414.9
1959	365.8	781.5	457.4	595.1	434.3	431.7	438.0
1960	394.4	846.2	480.6	620.4	469.6	484.6	454.5
1961	422.6	909.9	510.0	651.8	488.4	520.3	479.1
1962	415.8	965.3	533.5	687.2	510.7	563.8	496.2
1963	405.8	975.1	560.6	709.8	548.9	584.7	489.5
1964	447.6	1 008.0	584.5	753.7	607.1	622.9	543.3
1965	488.5	1 028.4	614.2	780.9	646.6	653.9	576.6
1966	491.8	1 092.8	657.3	822.5	686.4	709.1	604.4
1967	505.0	1 136.5	670.1	857.1	727.2	735.9	630.8
1968	526.5	1 237.9	698.2	909.6	780.0	738.4	667.8
1969	571.5	1 345.7	725.3	967.5	825.2	766.0	685.3
1970	602.1	1 477.8	733.4	1 032.8	879.5	810.9	737.4
1971	631.3	1 627.7	807.3	1 094.2	916.1	844.9	760.6
1972	651.0	1 802.9	808.9	1 178.1	993.9	869.2	769.0
1973	690.7	2 028.5	747.5	1 257.4	1 077.5	915.7	821.1
1974	735.5	2 187.5	710.6	1 329.7	1 143.3	1 000.5	848.4
1975	729.0	2 300.7	628.2	1 360.5	1 207.5	1 034.5	856.9
1976	727.2	2 516.6	652.7	1 425.0	1 258.7	1 054.9	894.0
1977	771.1	2 633.6	711.6	1 484.1	1 302.1	1 059.1	918.3
1978	737.2	2 764.8	775.9	1 610.0	1 409.4	1 062.1	946.0
1979	789.9	2 959.7	854.3	1 696.3	1 538.3	1 123.8	947.9
1980	801.1	3 220.4	924.9	1 765.9	1 666.5	1 174.2	956.0
1981	751.1	3 110.7	952.0	1 805.9	1 799.0	1 226.1	965.1
1982	708.7	3 139.1	822.6	1 823.0	1 789.2	1 229.2	991.4
1983	730.5	3 060.8	821.3	1 840.5	1 694.8	1 077.5	1 024.8
1984	745.2	3 234.8	855.6	1 897.2	1 757.2	1 128.8	1 038.8
1985	710.1	3 503.2	891.2	1 935.3	1 806.0	1 157.5	1 045.2
1986	752.8	3 790.7	916.4	2 034.1	1 738.2	1 250.1	1 088.0
1987	767.8	3 900.6	966.7	2 146.0	1 757.7	1 337.6	1 092.4

a) Rough proxy, see note Table 1.3.

Table B-6. GDP indices for 6 other OECD countries, 1900-87

1950 = 100.0

	Greece	Ireland	New Zealand	Portugal	Spain	Turkey
1900	n.a.		17.3	42.4	49.5	n.a.
1913	59.6	80.7[a]	29.9	52.9	66.8	47.1[b]
1929	101.4	80.6	53.7	58.1	97.3	52.1
1938	130.4	88.3	70.8	74.2	n.a.	85.6
1950	100.0	100.0	100.0	100.0	100.0	100.0
1965	264.3	143.9	160.6	197.1	238.3	233.4
1973	468.5	208.9	207.4	342.8	392.1	389.8
1980	593.0	282.2	213.1	428.0	452.9	521.5
1987	638.9	326.7	248.8	490.3	528.5	765.6

a) 1911.
b) Per capita product assumed equal to that of 1929.

Table B-7. GDP indices for Eastern Europe, 1913-87

1950 = 100.0

	Bulgaria	Czecho-slovakia	East Germany	Hungary	Poland	Rumania	Yugoslavia
1913	45.6	64.0		78.2			54.4[b]
1929	48.2	97.4		95.4	97.1		76.8
1938	72.0	95.8[a]		105.1	111.6		86.6
1950	100.0	100.0	100.0	100.0	100.0	100.0	100.0
1965	272.5	180.8	219.8	190.5	196.1	236.4	231.5
1973	393.2	236.6	279.7	248.3	294.8	377.1	358.1
1980	459.9	280.3	341.4	287.6	338.6	505.3	544.4
1982	486.6	278.8	351.4	293.6	307.6	521.9	557.3
1987	503.9	301.9	395.5	300.1	338.6	611.3	604.2

a) 1937.
b) 1909-12.

Appendix C

POPULATION, EMPLOYMENT AND EDUCATION

Table C-1. Population of OECD countries 1820-1987

Adjusted to present-day boundaries, 000s at mid-year

	Australia	Austria	Belgium	Canada	Denmark	Finland	France	Germany
1820	33[a]	3 189	3 546	657[a]	1 155	1 169	31 250	15 788
1870	1 620	4 520	5 096	3 736	1 888	1 754	38 440	24 870
1900	3 741	5 973	6 719	5 457	2 561	2 646	40 731	34 162
1913	4 821	6 767	7 666	7 852	2 983	3 027	41 690	40 825
1929	6 396	6 664	8 032	10 305	3 518	3 424	41 230	43 793
1938	6 904	6 755	8 374	11 452	3 777	3 656	41 960	46 376
1950	8 177	6 935	8 640	13 737	4 269	4 009	41 836	49 983
1965	11 648	7 271	9 464	19 678	4 757	4 564	48 758	58 619
1973	13 505	7 586	9 739	22 072	5 022	4 666	52 118	61 976
1980	14 695	7 549	9 847	24 070	5 125	4 780	53 880	61 566
1986	15 974	7 566	9 851	25 591	5 121	4 918	55 393	61 080
1987	16 196	7 562	9 862	25 922	5 108	4 952	55 685	60 858

	Italy[b]	Japan	Netherlands	Norway	Sweden	Switzerland	United Kingdom	United States
1820	19 510	28 900	2 344	970	2 585	1 829	19 746	9 656[a]
1870	27 238	34 437	3 607	1 735	4 169	2 664	29 185	40 061
1900	33 286	44 103	5 142	2 230	5 136	3 300	38 426	76 391
1913	36 137	51 672	6 164	2 447	5 639	3 864	42 622	97 606
1929	39 997	63 244	7 782	2 795	6 120	4 022	45 672	122 245
1938	43 004	71 879	8 685	2 936	6 310	4 192	47 494	130 476
1950	46 769	83 662	10 114	3 265	7 042	4 694	50 363	152 271
1965	51 526	97 950	12 295	3 723	7 734	5 943	54 350	194 303
1973	54 462	108 660	13 439	3 961	8 137	6 441	56 210	211 909
1980	56 157	116 800	14 150	4 087	8 311	6 385	56 314	227 757
1986	57 015	121 490	14 572	4 169	8 370	6 573	56 763	241 596
1987	57 094	122 897	14 616	4 180	8 366	6 593	56 687	244 171

a) Excludes indigenous population.
b) Present in area (de facto) population adjusted to include institutional population (see Maddison, 1982).
Sources: 1820-1950 generally from worksheets for Maddison (1982). 1965 onwards from OECD *Labour Force Statistics*. Sweden, 1820 to 1950 supplied by Olle Krantz. United Kingdom, 1820 and 1870 revised in line with Wrigley and Schofield (1981) - See source note for GDP.

Table C-2. Population in our 32 country sample

000s at mid-year

	16 OECD countries	9 Asian countries	6 Latin American countries	USSR	Total
1900	310 004	749 909	47 047	122 995	1 229 955
1913	361 782	813 589	59 477	158 371	1 393 219
1950	580 163	1 128 299	121 785	180 050	2 010 227
1973	639 903	1 855 931	228 332	249 800	2 973 966
1980	671 473	2 129 654	270 696	265 500	3 337 323
1986	696 052	2 355 576	309 252	280 250	3 641 130
1987	700 749	2 405 305	316 092	283 100	3 705 246

Source: Derived from Tables C-1, C-3, C-4 and C-6.

Table C-3. Population of Asian countries, 1820-1987

000s at mid-year

	Bangladesh	China	India[a]	Indonesia	Pakistan
1820		350 000	*209 000*	16 443	
1870		350 000	*253 000*	26 528	
1900	29 012	400 000	234 655	40 209	19 759
1913	31 786	430 000	251 826	48 150	20 007
1929	34 428	485 000	273 895	59 830	22 813
1938	39 718	527 600	309 737	68 409	26 645
1950	43 135	546 815	359 943	72 747	37 646
1965	60 482	715 185	485 000	101 308	54 192
1973	74 368	881 940	579 000	124 189	67 900
1980	88 678	981 235	679 000	146 360	83 840
1986	100 620	1 054 700	766 140	166 940	99 160
1987	102 961	1 069 608	787 930	170 744	101 611

	Philippines	South Korea[b]	Taiwan	Thailand
1820	2 176			4 665
1870	5 063			5 775
1900	7 324	8 772	2 858	7 320
1913	9 384	10 277	3 469	8 690
1929	12 837	13 397	4 493	12 059
1938	15 651	15 275	5 678	14 490
1950	20 062	20 557	7 882	19 442
1965	31 436	28 705	12 928	30 720
1973	39 701	34 103	15 427	39 303
1980	48 320	38 124	17 642	46 455
1986	55 000	41 569	19 357	52 090
1987	57 011	42 512	19 551	53 377

a) Figures for 1820-1870 refer to undivided India. Equivalent figures for 1900, 1913, 1929 and 1938 were 284 500, 303 700, 333 100 and 376 100 respectively. All Indian figures are for 1st October, and not mid-year.
b) Figures refer to South Korea. For Korea as a whole the figures for 1900, 1913, 1929 and 1938 were 13 219, 15 486, 20 187 and 23 017 respectively.

Sources:

Unless otherwise stated, the 1870-1913 figures are from A. Maddison, *Economic Progress and Policy in Developing Countries*, Norton, New York, 1970, and 1950-87 supplied by the OECD Development Centre.

Bangladesh: Prepartition (1941) population estimated at 41 966 thousand by K. Davis, *Population of India and Pakistan*, Princeton, 1951, p. 198 from 1941 census. For earlier years population assumed to move as in prepartition Bengal (plus native States and agencies) as given in the censuses from 1891 to 1941 (see M.W.M. Yeatts, *Census of India 1941*, vol. I, India, Part I Tables, Delhi, 1943, pp. 62-6).

China: 1820-1933 from D.H. Perkins, *Agricultural Development in China 1368-1968*, Aldine, Chicago, 1969, p. 16. 1950 onwards from *Statistical Yearbook of China*, State Statistical Bureau, People's Republic of China, Hong Kong, adjusted to a mid-year basis.

India: 1820 derived by interpolation of Irfan Habib's estimate of 200 million in 1800 (see "Population" in T. Raychaudhuri and I. Habib, *The Cambridge Economic History of India*, Cambridge, 1982, p. 167 and Moni Mukherjee's estimate for 1856. 1856-1929 from A. Maddison, *Class Structure and Economic Growth*, Norton, New York, 1971, pp. 164-5. For prepartition adjustment, see notes on Bangladesh and Pakistan. It should be noted that Burma was included in the Indian customs area until 1937. In order to derive trade per capita, Burmese population should be added to the Indian denominator. Burmese population in 1900, 1913 and 1929 was 10 174, 12 327 and 14 364 thousand respectively (see A. Hlaing, "Trends of Economic Growth and Income Distribution in Burma, 1870-1940", *Journal of the Burma Research Society*, 1964, p. 96).

Indonesia: 1820-1929 from A. Maddison, "Dutch Income In and From Indonesia", *Modern Asian Studies*, 1989.

Pakistan: Prepartition (1941) population estimated at 28 169 thousand by K. Davis, *op. cit.* p. 198. For earlier years, population assumed to move as in prepartition total for Punjab (province, states, etc.), Sind and North West Frontier Province as given for census years by M.W.M. Yeatts, *op. cit.*

Philippines: 1820-1938 from E. Kirsten, E.W. Buchholtz and W. Köllman, *Raum und Bevölkerung in der Weltgeschichte*, Ploetz, Wurzburg, 1956.

South Korea: 1900-1913 assumed to grow at same pace as Japan. 1913-40 growth for Korea as a whole from Sang-Chul Suh, *Growth and Structural Change in Korean Economy, 1910-1940*, Harvard, 1978, p. 41. 1940-53 movement from K.S. Kim and M. Roemer, *Growth and Structural Transformation*, Harvard, 1979, p. 35.

Taiwan: 1905-50 from S.P.S. Ho, *Economic Development of Taiwan, 1860-1970*, Yale, 1978, pp. 313-4 adjusted to a mid-year basis. 1965 onwards from *National Income in Taiwan Area, The Republic of China*, Executive Yuan, Taipei, December 1987, p. 26.

Thailand: 1820-1950 from Manarungsan, *op. cit.*

129

Table C-4.   Population of Latin America and USSR, 1820-1987

000s at mid-year

	Argentina	Brazil	Chile	Colombia	Mexico	Peru	USSR
1820	534	4507	885	1206	6587	1317	50392
1870	1796	9797	1943	2392	9219	2606	79354
1900	4693	17984	2974	3998	13607	3791	122995
1913	7653	23660	3491	5195	14971	4507	158371
1929	11592	32894	4306	7821	16875	5576	171500
1938	13724	39480	4915	8702	19828	6372	186500
1950	17150	51941	6091	11597	27376	7630	180050
1965	22283	80403	8510	18488	43500	11470	230900
1973	25195	99836	9899	22571	56481	14350	249800
1980	28237	118518	11104	25892	69655	17290	265500
1986	30977	137288	12253	28961	79563	20210	280250
1987	31500	140692	12485	29496	81163	20756	283100

Sources:

Argentina: 1820-1913 from *The Cambridge History of Latin America,* vol. III. p. 626 and vol. IV, p. 122; 1913-50 from IEERAL, *op. cit.* Thereafter from World Bank, *World Tables* (1988).

Brazil: 1820 from N.H. Leff, *Underdevelopment and Development in Brazil,* vol. I, Allen and Unwin, London, 1982, p. 241. 1870-1940, from *O Brasil em Numeros,* IBGE, Rio, 1960, p. 5. 1950-87 IBGE (Brazilian Statistical Office) estimates.

Chile: 1820-1913 from B.R. Mitchell, *International Historical Statistics: The Americas and Australasia,* Macmillan, London, 1983, p. 51. 1929-38 from ECLA (1962), 1950 onwards from World Bank (1983 and 1988).

Colombia: 1820-1938 from B.R. Mitchell, *op. cit.,* 1950 onwards as for Chile.

Mexico: 1820 to 1987 from A. Maddison, *The Political Economy of Poverty, Equity and Growth in Mexico,* forthcoming.

Peru: 1820-70, B.R. Mitchell, *op. cit.,* 1983. 1900-1938 interpolated from N. Sanchez Albornoz, "The Population of Latin America, 1850-1930", in L. Bethell, ed., *The Cambridge History of Latin America,* vol. IV, Cambridge, 1986, p. 122. 1950-85 from R. Webb, *The Political Economy of Poverty, Equity and Growth in Peru,* forthcoming. 1913 and 1929 interpolated between 1900 and 1938 between 1930 and 1950 figures. 1986 from OECD Development Centre.

USSR: 1820-1913 from B.R. Mitchell, *European Historical Statistics 1750-1970,* Macmillan, London, 1975, p. 65. Thereafter from *Narodnoe Khoziastvo SSSR,* Moscow, various issues.

Table C-5. Population of other OECD countries, 1820-1987

Adjusted to present boundaries, 000s at mid-year

	Greece	Ireland	New Zealand	Portugal	Spain	Turkey
1820		7 084[a]		3 420	12 958	
1870		5 419[a]	310	4 370	16 213	
1900		3 230[b]	815	5 451	18 594	
1913	5 425	3 110	1 060	6 001	20 330	13 000
1929	6 275	2 943	1 450	6 738	23 210	14 392
1938	7 061	2 937	1 600	7 569	25 398	17 211
1950	7 566	2 969	1 921	8 441	27 977	20 809
1965	8 551	2 876	2 635	8 511	32 085	31 391
1973	8 929	3 073	2 971	8 368	34 810	38 451
1980	9 642	3 401	3 144	9 289	37 424	44 737
1987	9 994	3 543	3 309	9 744	38 832	52 028

a) Prepartition population.
b) In 1900, the figure for the whole of Ireland was 4 483.
Sources: Greece 1913 and 1950 (population within present frontiers) from A. Maddison, "Economic Policy and Performance in Europe 1913-70", *Fontana Economic History of Europe*, vol. 5 (2), 1976, with interpolation for 1929 and 1938 from I. Svennilson and Associates, *Growth and Stagnation in the European Economy*, UN, Geneva, 1954, p. 237. 1950 onwards from OECD Development Centre. Ireland 1820-1900 from J.M. Goldstrom and L.A. Clarkson, *Irish Population, Economy and Society*, OUP, 1981, and B.R. Mitchell, *op. cit.*; 1913-50 as for Greece; thereafter from OECD. New Zealand 1870-1938 (including Maoris) from G.R. Hawke, *The Making of New Zealand*, Cambridge, 1985, pp. 11 and 20; thereafter from OECD sources. Portugal 1820 from A. Armengaud "Population in Europe 1700-1914", in C.M. Cipolla, ed., *Fontana Economic History of Europe*, vol. 3, London, 1973, p. 29; 1870-1950 from N. Valerio (1983) and (1986); 1965 onwards from OECD *National Accounts, 1960-1986*, vol. I, p. 150. Figures refer to the population of continental Portugal only. Spain 1820 from Armengaud (1973); 1870-1950 from *Espana: Anuario Estadistico 1977*, p. 49; 1965 onwards as for Portugal; figures exclude population of Spain's African territories. Turkey, 1913 derived from E. Kirsten, E.W. Buchholz and W. Köllmann, *Raum und Bevölkerung in der Weltgeschichte*, Ploetz, Wurzburg, 1956, vol. II, p. 247; 1929 and 1938 derived by interpolation from B.R. Mitchell, *International Historical Statistics: Africa and Asia*, Macmillan, London, 1982, p. 45; 1950 onwards from OECD *Labour Force Statistics*; estimates adjusted throughout to refer to population within present boundaries of Turkey.

Table C-6. Population of Eastern Europe, 1913-87

Adjusted to present boundaries, 000s at mid-year

	Bulgaria	Czecho-slovakia	East Germany	Hungary	Poland	Rumania	Yugoslavia
1813	4 794	13 245		7 840	26 710	12 527	13 591
1929	5 950	13 927		8 583	27 856	13 905	14 194
1950	7 251	12 389	18 388	9 338	24 824	16 311	16 346
1965	8 201	14 159	17 020	10 153	31 496	19 027	19 434
1973	8 621	14 560	16 980	10 426	33 363	20 828	20 963
1980	8 862	15 311	16 737	10 711	35 578	22 201	22 304
1982	8 917	15 370	16 732	10 706	36 227	22 465	22 630
1987	9 000	15 600	16 700	10 600	37 800	22 900	23 410

Sources: 1913-50 from A. Maddison, "Economic Policy and Performance in Europe 1913-70", *Fontana Economic History of Europe*, vol. 5 (2), 1976, p. 494; 1929, interpolated from Svennilson (1954), p. 237; 1965-82 from Alton *(op. cit.)*, p. 87; 1987 from INED, *Population et Sociétés*, September 1987. Yugoslavia 1950 onward from OECD Development Centre.

Table C-7. Employment in OECD countries, 1900-86

000s

	1900	1913	1950	1973	1986
Australia	1 477	2 006	3 459	5 838	7 016
Austria	2 675	3 122	3 215	3 160	3 226
Belgium	2 839	3 376	3 341	3 831	3 734
Canada	2 047	3 014	5 030	8 843	11 711
Denmark	1 080	1 277	1 978	2 426	2 662
Finland	1 158	1 323	1 959	2 194	2 458
France	20 241	21 013	19 092	21 158	21 269
Germany	13 842	17 303	21 164	26 849	25 702
Italy	14 915	16 349	18 536	22 708	24 819
Japan	24 252	25 751	35 683	52 590	58 530
Netherlands	1 911	2 330	3 625	4 779	5 328
Norway	877	984	1 428	1 654	2 086
Sweden	2 314	2 602	3 422	3 879	4 269
Switzerland	1 607	1 904	2 237	3 277	3 218
United Kingdom	16 472	18 566	22 400	25 076	24 542
United States	27 929	38 821	61 651	88 868	111 303

Sources: France, Germany, Japan, United Kingdom and United States 1950-80 from Maddison (1987). Otherwise from Maddison (1982) and OECD, *Labour Force Statistics,* except Italy where an upward adjustment was made for workers in the underground economy, and Japan 1900-13 from M. Umemura and Associates, *Estimates of Long Term Economic Statistics of Japan since 1868,* vol. 2, *Manpower,* Toyo Keizai Shinposha, Tokyo, 1988.

Table C-8. Hours worked per person per year in OECD countries and the USSR, 1900-86

000s

	1900	1913	1950	1973	1986
Australia	2 688	2 588	1 838	1 708	1 630
Austria	2 679	2 580	1 976	1 778	1 620
Belgium	2 707	2 605	2 283	1 872	1 411
Canada	2 707	2 605	1 967	1 788	1 704
Denmark	2 688	2 588	2 283	1 742	1 706
Finland	2 688	2 588	2 035	1 707	1 596
France	2 688	2 588	1 926	1 788	1 533
Germany	2 684	2 584	2 316	1 804	1 630
Italy	2 634	2 536	1 997	1 612	1 515[a]
Japan	2 688	2 588	2 289	2 213	2 129
Netherlands	2 707	2 605	2 208	1 825	1 645
Norway	2 688	2 588	2 101	1 721	1 531
Sweden	2 688	2 588	1 951	1 571	1 457
Switzerland	2 725	2 624	2 144	1 930	1 807
United Kingdom	2 725	2 624	1 958	1 688	1 511
United States	2 707	2 605	1 867	1 710	1 609
USSR	n.a.	n.a.	1 947	1 791	1 791

a) 1985.
Sources: OECD countries from sources cited in A. Maddison, *Phases of Capitalist Development,* OUP, 1982, and A. Maddison, *Journal of Economic Literature,* 1987. USSR from S. Rapawy, "Labour Force and Employment in the USSR", in Joint Economic Committee, *Gorbachev's Economic Plans,* US Congress, 1987, pp. 210-11.

Table C-9. **Employment in non-OECD countries, 1950-86**

000s

	1950	1973	1980	1986
Bangladesh	15 438	20 925	24 128	28 465
China	184 984	362 530	412 385	505 775
India	161 386	239 645	269 858	304 227
Indonesia	30 863	46 655	154 003	62 373
Pakistan	14 009	20 144	24 398	29 534
Philippines	8 525	14 195	16 832	19 563
South Korea	6 377	11 140	13 710	15 952
Taiwan	2 872	6 091	7 797	9 187
Thailand	10 119	18 576	22 215	25 913
Argentina	6 821	9 402	10 065	10 558
Brazil	17 657	33 164	43 091	54 524
Chile	2 256	2 896	3 317	3 563
Colombia	3 844	6 418	7 605	8 819
Mexico	8 563	15 044	19 402	23 167
Peru	2 788	4 464	5 489	6 611
USSR	85 246	128 278	140 468	145 972

Sources: Bangladesh, Indonesia, Pakistan and Philippines derived from benchmark estimates of ILO for labour force (reduced by 4 per cent for unemployment); see ILO, *1950-2025: Economically Active Population,* Geneva, 1985. China from *Statistical Yearbook of China,* various editions adjusted to a mid-year basis. India 1950-73 movement derived from B.H. Dholakia, *The Sources of Economic Growth in India,* Good Companions, Baroda, 1974, pp. 97 and 102; 1973-86 movement from ILO (1985) benchmarked on Dholakia. South Korea 1950 derived from 1960 activity rate as given by Kim and Roemer, p. 64 assuming 600 000 additional persons were in the armed forces; 1973 and 1980 from Kim and Park, *op. cit.,* p. 13. Taiwan 1950 derived by using 1956 activity rate given by S.P.S. Ho, *op. cit.,* pp. 312 and 326 and assuming 600 000 persons in the armed forces. 1973 onwards from *Statistical Yearbook of the Republic of China, 1987,* p. 22. Thailand from R.R. Corsel, *Labour Input and Patterns of Growth in Thai Agriculture,* M.A. Thesis, Groningen, 1986 processed, p. 26. Peru labour force from CEPAL, *Statistical Yearbook for Latin America 1987,* p. 646 (reduced by 4 per cent). Brazil and Mexico from Maddison (1989). Other Latin America from CEPAL sources. USSR from S. Rapawy, "Labour Force and Employment in the USSR", in Joint Economic Committee, *Gorbachev's Economic Plans,* vol. I, US Congress, November 1987, pp. 202-3 for civilian employment, armed forces from p. 194.

Table C-10. **Distribution of employment by sector 1950 and 1980: OECD countries**

Percentages

	1950			1980		
	Agriculture	Industry	Services	Agriculture	Industry	Services
Australia	15	36	49	6	31	63
Canada	22	36	42	6	28	66
United States	13	33	54	3	30	67
Austria	34	35	31	11	40	49
Belgium	10	47	43	3	33	64
Denmark	25	33	42	7	29	64
Finland	46	28	26	13	34	53
France	28	35	37	8	35	57
Germany	22	43	35	6	43	51
Italy	45	29	36	14	37	49
Netherlands	14	40	46	5	31	64
Norway	30	33	37	8	30	62
Sweden	20	41	39	6	32	62
Switzerland	17	46	37	7	40	53
United Kingdom	5	47	48	3	37	60
Japan	48	23	29	11	35	54
OECD average	25	36	39	7	34	59

Source: 1950 from Maddison (1980). 1980 from OECD, *Labour Force Statistics 1964-1984,* Paris, 1986.

Table C-11. **Distribution of employment by sector 1950 and 1980: developing countries**

Percentages

	1950			1980		
	Agriculture	Industry	Services	Agriculture	Industry	Services
Bangladesh	(77)	(7)	(16)	75	6	19
China	77[a]	7[a]	16[a]	74	14	12
India	72	10	18	70	13	17
Indonesia	75[b]	8[b]	17[b]	57	13	30
Pakistan	(77)	(7)	(16)	54	16	30
Philippines	71	9	20	51	16	33
South Korea	73	3	24	36	27	37
Taiwan	57[c]	16[c]	27[c]	22	38	40
Thailand	82	3	15	71	10	19
Arithmetic average	73	8	19	57	17	26
Argentina	25	31	44	13	34	53
Brazil	60	18	22	31	27	42
Chile	36	30	34	17	25	58
Colombia	57	18	25	34	24	42
Mexico	61	17	22	36	29	35
Peru	58	20	22	40	18	42
Arithmetic average	50	22	28	29	26	45
Developing country average	63	14	23	45	21	34

a) 1952.
b) 1960.
c) 1951.
Note: "Agriculture" includes agriculture, forestry and fisheries; "industry" includes mining, manufacturing, construction, gas, water and electricity; "services" covers the rest (including armed forces).
Sources: 1950 for Asian countries from A. Maddison, *Economic Progress and Policy in Developing Countries,* Norton, New York, 1970, p. 304, supplemented by *Yearbooks of Labour Statistics,* ILO, Geneva. China 1952 from T-C. Liu and K-C. Yeh, *The Economy of the Chinese Mainland: National Income and Economic Development 1933-1959,* Princeton, 1965, p. 69. 1950 for Latin America from ECLAC, *Statistical Yearbook for Latin America 1984,* Santiago. 1980 from World Bank, *World Development Report 1988,* except for Taiwan which is from *National Income in Taiwan Area, The Republic of China,* Executive Yuan, December 1987.

Table C-12. Average years of formal educational experience of population aged 15-64 in 1950 and 1980

	1950				1980			
	Total	Primary	Secondary	Higher	Total	Primary	Secondary	Higher
China[a]	2.13	1.98	0.14	0.01	4.50	3.40	1.07	0.03
India[b]	1.30	1.19	0.10	0.01	2.94	2.03	0.85	0.06
Korea	3.13	2.62	0.46	0.05	7.38	4.35	2.48	0.55
Taiwan	3.40	2.90	0.46	0.04	8.07	4.32	3.43	0.32
Argentina	4.60	4.15	0.42	0.03	7.22	5.00	1.74	0.47
Brazil	1.83	1.36	0.42	0.05	3.94	2.52	1.31	0.11
Chile	4.88	3.59	1.16	0.13	7.57	4.38	2.77	0.42
Colombia	3.61	2.95	0.56	0.10	5.15	3.47	1.52	0.16
Mexico	2.30	1.61	0.65	0.04	4.94	2.87	1.95	0.12
France	8.18	4.96	3.04	0.18	10.30	5.00	4.59	0.71
Germany	8.51	4.00	4.37	0.14	9.41	4.00	5.15	0.26
Japan	8.12	5.88	2.08	0.16	10.77	6.00	4.26	0.51
United Kingdom	9.40	6.00	3.27	0.13	10.66	6.00	4.31	0.35
United States	9.46	5.61	3.40	0.45	12.02	5.80	4.92	1.30

a) Population 12 years and over.
b) Population 10 years and over.

Sources: China extrapolated from data for 1964 and 1982 censuses, *Statistical Yearbook of China 1984,* State Statistical Bureau, People's Republic of China, Hong Kong, 1984, p. 87. India 1950 from M. Selowsky, "Education and Economic Growth: Some International Comparisons", Ph. D. thesis, University of Chicago, 1967, p. 61 except that I imputed 3 rather than 2 years education to "literates"; 1980 derived from *Census of India 1981, Series I, India,* Part II, *Special Report and Tables based on 5 per cent Sample Data,* pp. 192-5. Korea from K.S. Kim and J.K. Park, *Sources of Economic Growth in Korea: 1963-82,* K.D.I., Seoul, 1985, p. 18 with 1950 extrapolated from 1960 and 1980 census results. Taiwan, 1980 from *Statistical Yearbook of the Republic of China, 1987,* Executive Yuan, Taipei, pp. 16 et 17; 1950 extrapolated from 1957 figure in same source. Argentina 1950 extrapolated from 1947 figures given by UNESCO, *Statistics of Educational Attainment and Illiteracy, 1945-1974.* Paris, 1977, p. 75; 1980 census results derived from *Demographic Yearbook 1983,* UN, New York. Brazil 1950 from C.G. Langoni, *As Causas do Crescimento Economico do Brazil,* APEC, Rio, 1974; 1980 from *Censo Demografico,* IBGE, Rio. Chile 1950 and 1980 by extrapolation from 1952 and 1982 censuses, figures for population aged 15 and over from *XII Censo General de Poblacion y I de Vivienda, Tomo I, Resumen del Pais,* SNEC, Santiago, p. 188 (refers to 15 April 1952); *XV Censo Nacional de Poblacion y IV de Vivienda, Chile, Total Pais, Tomo I,* Santiago, 1987, p. 238 (refers to occupied population in April 1982 aged 15 and over). Colombia 1950 and 1980, derived by extrapolation from 1951 and 1985 censuses; Figures for population 15 and over from *Censo de Poblacion de Colombia 1951 Resumen,* DANE, Bogota, pp. 132-3 (refers to May 1951); *XV Censo Nacional de Poblacion y IV de Vivienda, Colombia, Vol. I,* DANE, Bogota 1986, p. 436 (refers to 1985). Mexico 1950 from Selowsky, *op. cit.*; 1980 from *X Censo General de Poblacion y Vivienda, 1980, Resumen General Abreviado,* Mexico, 1984, p. 51.

OECD countries by interpolation from 1973 and 1984 estimates of A. Maddison, "Growth and Slowdown in Advanced Capitalist Economies: Techniques of a Quantitative Assessment", *Journal of Economic Literature,* June 1987.

Appendix D

EXPORTS AND RELATED ITEMS

The figures in this appendix are not adjusted for changes in geographic boundaries.

Table D-1. Value of exports f.o.b.

$ milllion at current exchange rates

	1900	1913	1929	1950	1973	1986
Australia	223	382	592	1 668	9 559	22 622
Austria	393	561	308	326	5 283	22 508
Canada	173	421	1 141	3 020	26 437	90 193
Belgium	371	717	884	1 652	22 455	68 892
Denmark	76	171	433	665	6 248	21 243
Finland	38	78	162	390	3 836	16 356
France	793	1 328	1 965	3 082	36 635	124 948
Germany	1 120	2 454	3 212	1 993	67 563	243 327
Italy	258	485	783	1 206	22 223	97 811
Japan	102	315	969	825	37 017	210 757
Netherlands	227	413	800	1 413	23 496	79 435
Norway	46	105	199	390	4 725	18 230
Sweden	105	219	486	1 103	12 201	37 263
Switzerland	161	266	404	894	9 528	37 471
United Kingdom	1 416	2 555	3 550	6 325	29 637	106 989
United States	1 418	2 380	5 157	10 282	71 404	217 307
OECD	6 920	12 850	21 045	35 234	388 247	1 415 352
Bangladesh				(303)	358	880
China	132	299	660	550	5 876	31 148
India	367	786	1 177	1 145	2 917	9 352
Indonesia	104	270	582	800	3 211	14 824
Pakistan				(330)	955	3 384
Philippines	23	48	163	331	1 885	4 770
South Korea	5	15	159	23	3 225	34 715
Taiwan	7	26	125	73	4 483	39 789
Thailand	15	43	94	304	1 564	8 794
Total	653	1 487	2 965	3 538	24 474	147 656
Argentina	149	515	908	1 178	3 266	6 852
Brazil	182	317	462	1 359	6 199	22 393
Chile	61	149	283	281	1 231	4 222
Colombia	11	34	124	394	1 177	5 102
Mexico	75	150	285	532	2 261	16 237
Peru	22	43	117	193	1 112	2 509
Total	500	1 208	2 179	3 937	15 246	57 315
USSR	369	783	482	1 801	21 458	97 336
32 country total	8 442	16 328	26 671	44 510	49 425	1 717 659

Sources: OECD countries 1900-1929 from A. Maddison, "Growth and Fluctuation in the World Economy, 1870-1960", *Banca Nazionale del Lavoro Quarterly Review,* June 1962, W.A. Lewis, "The Rate of Growth World Trade 1830-1973", in S. Grassman and E. Lundberg, *The World Economic Order,* Macmillan, London, 1981, and League of Nations. 1950 onwards from IMF, *International Financial Statistics.* Non OECD countries 1900-1950 from W.A. Lewis (1981), Maddison (1970), *Statistical Abstract of Foreign Countries,* Dept. of Commerce and Labour, Washington DC, 1909, and Ho, *op. cit.* 1950 onwards from IMF, *International Financial Statistics* except for USSR which is from the UN *Monthly Bulletin of Statistics,* and Taiwan which is from the *Monthly Bulletin of Statistics,* Taipei.

Table D-2. **Volume of exports: OECD countries, 1900-86**

1913 = 100.0

	1900	1913	1929	1950	1973	1980	1986
Australia	58.2	100.0	111.9	158.7	582.0	755.8	990.2
Austria	72.2[a]	100.0	41.2	31.8	339.4	547.4	733.5
Canada	48.0	100.0	193.2	311.0	1 474.3	1 776.3	2 504.5
Belgium	53.9	100.0	107.2	111.8	875.7	1 081.1	1 351.4
Denmark	56.4	100.0	181.0	239.5	1 114.7	1 548.2	1 950.7
Finland	52.0	100.0	161.4	199.5	989.2	1 355.1	1 571.9
France	61.6	100.0	147.0	149.2	922.4	1 263.4	1 415.0
Germany	44.7	100.0	91.8	34.8	514.3	695.0	896.6
Italy	64.4	100.0	122.7	126.5	1 619.2	2 381.2	3 000.0
Japan	29.3	100.0	257.9	210.1	5 672.7	10 505.0	14 707.0
Netherlands	55.6	100.0	171.2	171.2	1 632.1	2 014.9	2 438.1
Norway	49.4	100.0	167.1	269.5	1 369.1	2 173.2	2 760.0
Sweden	54.0	100.0	156.1	275.9	1 297.7	1 441.9	1 946.6
Switzerland	63.3	100.0	100.7	113.2	676.0	877.9	1 062.3
United Kingdom	58.6	100.0	81.3	100.0	241.9	314.2	389.6
United States	72.8	100.0	158.2	224.6	912.0	1 341.2	1 140.0

a)   1900-13 values deflated by German export unit value.
Sources: 1900-1973 from Maddison (1982). Thereafter from UN, *Monthly Bulletin of Statistics,* and IMF *International Financial Statistics.*

Table D-3. Volume of exports: non OECD countries, 1900-86

1913 = 100.0

	1900	1913	1929	1950	1973	1980	1986
Bangladesh[a]	—	—	—	100.0	156.9	212.7	268.6
China	54.9	100.0	149.2	151.0	278.6	505.1	1 004.5
India	58.4	100.0	86.6	57.9	102.1	113.5	140.8
Indonesia	60.2	100.0	263.8	227.9	971.2	1 312.5	1 483.1
Pakistan[a]	—	—	—	100.0	225.6	360.4	526.2
Philippines	69.6	100.0	376.6	387.4	1 449.7	2 709.6	3 061.7
Korea	36.7	100.0	756.9	65.5	4 620.7	12 488.3	25 601.0
Taiwan	39.3	100.0	374.4	258.6	8 302.6	16 988.6	34 393.9
Thailand	53.3	100.0	129.4	232.2	623.4	1 304.2	2 003.3
Argentina	58.8	100.0	157.7	195.9	213.0	320.7	372.0
Brazil	95.8[b]	100.0	137.3	184.8	529.6	919.4	1 241.2
Chile	61.3	100.0	192.8	166.2	289.3	604.2	894.1
Colombia	37.6	100.0	303.8	417.0	985.9	1 257.0	2 111.9
Mexico	55.9	100.0	157.2	84.6	221.7	492.4	873.9
Peru	43.0	100.0	279.3	264.1	974.3	825.6	726.5
USSR	54.8	100.0	52.4	97.1	870.3	1 312.1	1 587.6

a) 1950 = 100.0.
b) 1901.
Sources:

Asia: 1950 onwards generally from IMF, *International Financial Statistics,* unless otherwise specified. Otherwise as follows:

Bangladesh: 1950-69 from *Reports of the Advisory/Panels for the Fourth Five Year Plan,* Islamabad, 1970, including exports to West Pakistan. 1969-73 assumed stagnant. 1973-86 from World Bank, *World Tables 1987,* Washington DC, 1988.

China: 1900-36 from Hsiao Liang-lin, *China's Foreign Trade Statistics 1864-1949,* Harvard, 1974, pp. 190-2 and 268-9. 1936-50 US dollar values deflated by world unit value index in A. Maddison, 1962. 1950-73 US dollar values deflated by US import unit value index. 1973-86 from World Bank, 1988.

India: 1900-20 rupee values of exports (Gurtoo) deflated by Mukherjee's price index, 1920-30 Gurtoo's export volume index. See D.N. Gurtoo, *India's Balance of Payments,* Chand, Delhi, 1961, pp. 20 and 112 and M. Mukherjee, *National Income of India: Trends and Structure,* Statistical Publishing Society, Calcutta, 1969, p. 94. 1930-50, from UN *Yearbook of International Trade Statistics,* New York, 1959.

Indonesia: 1900-40 Fisher index of B. van Ark, "Indonesian Export Growth", *Research Memo 189,* University of Groningen, May 1986. 1940-50, my own estimates. 1950-73 from World Bank, *World Tables,* Washington DC, 1984 (which refer to goods and services).

Pakistan: 1950-69 as for Bangladesh.

Philippines: 1900-29 derived from T.B. Birnberg and S.A. Resnick, *Colonial Development: An Econometric Study,* Yale, 1975. 1929-50 dollar value of exports deflated by the export unit value index for "third countries", in Maddison, 1962.

Korea: 1900-13 and 1938-50 dollar value of exports deflated by the export unit value index for third countries in Maddison (1962); 1913-38 from T. Mizoguchi, "Foreign Trade in Taiwan and Korea Under Japanese Rule", *Hitotsubashi Journal of Economics,* February 1974 (yen unit value index) and yen export value from *Annual Economic Review of Korea 1948,* Bank of Chosun, Seoul. 1950-65 from World Bank, *World Tables,* Washington DC, 1984.

Taiwan: 1900-40 volume index from S.P.S. Ho, *op. cit.,* pp. 380-4. 1951-86 from *National Income in Taiwan Area, the Republic of China,* Taipei, 1987, pp. 102-5. 1940-51 link obtained from export-GDP ratios (30 per cent in prewar and 13.8 per cent in 1951) and movement in GDP (1940 being 1.5 per cent higher than 1951).

Thailand: My own index estimated by export movements for rice, tin, teak and rubber as reported in Manarungsan (1989) and using weights given by in J.C. Ingram, *op. cit.*

Latin America: 1950 onwards generally from IMF, *International Financial Statistics,* and 1929-50 from ECLA, *America Latina: Relacion de Precios del Intercambio,* Santiago, 1976. Otherwise as follows:

Argentina: 1900-1913 derived from 1900-4 - 1910-4 figures given by C.F. Diaz Alejandro, *Essays on the Economic History of the Argentine Republic,* Yale 1970, p. 5. 1913-84 from IEERAL, *op. cit.,* pp. 114-5.

Brazil: 1901-29 from A. Villela and W. Suzigan, p. 362.

Chile: 1900-29 from Birnberg and Resnick, *op. cit.*

Colombia: 1900-29 dollar value of exports were deflated by the export unit value index for "third countries", in A. Maddison, "Growth and Fluctuation in the World Economy 1870-1960", *Banca Nazionale del Lavoro Quarterly Review,* June 1962. 1950-86 from ECLA, *Statistical Yearbook for Latin America.*

Mexico: 1900-1 to 1910-11 from *Comercio Exterior de Mexico 1877-1911,* El Colegio de Mexico, 1960, p. 165. 1910-11 assumed equal to 1913, 1910-11 to 1929 movement obtained by deflating export value by US import unit value.

Peru: 1900-1929 from S.J. Hunt, "Price and Quantum Estimates of Peruvian Exports, 1830-1962", *Discussion Paper No. 33,* Princeton University Program in Economic Development, January 1973, processed.

USSR: 1900-50 as for Colombia. 1950-63 from UN, *Yearbook of International Trade Statistics 1972-73,* and 1973-85 from UN, *Monthly Bulletin of Statistics.* 1963-73 from E.A. Hewett, "Foreign Economic Relations, in A. Bergson and H.S. Levine, *The Soviet Economy: Toward the Year 2000,* Allen and Unwin, London, 1983, p. 272, variant B.

Table D-4. **Exports at 1980 prices 1900-38**

$ million

	1900	1913	1929	1932	1938
Australia	1 696	2 915	3 262	4 303	4 483
Austria	2 307	3 195	1 317	739	0
Belgium	3 224	5 981	6 412	4 396	6 125
Canada	1 830	3 813	7 367	5 006	7 321
Denmark	619	1 097	1 986	2 385	2 027
Finland	543	1 044	1 685	2 270	1 929
France	5 657	9 184	13 500	7 898	8 357
Germany	12 404	27 750	25 475	15 152	15 818
Italy	2 101	3 262	4 002	2 319	2 280
Japan	364	1 242	3 203	3 248	7 307
Netherlands	2 040	3 670	6 283	4 573	5 138
Norway	421	853	1 425	1 462	1 989
Sweden	1 157	2 143	3 345	2 107	3 422
Switzerland	2 137	3 375	3 399	1 698	2 676
United Kingdom	20 545	35 059	28 503	17 775	20 089
United States	12 368	16 462	26 043	13 400	20 693
OECD total	69 431	121 045	137 207	88 731	109 654
Bangladesh	0	0	0	0	0
China	1 967	3 583	5 346	3 149	2 017
India	4 418	7 565	6 551	4 547	6 135
Indonesia	1 005	1 669	4 403	4 117	3 660
Pakistan	0	0	0	0	0
Philippines	147	212	798	723	957
South Korea	51	140	1 060	1 017	2 944
Taiwan	46	117	438	528	751
Thailand	266	499	646	779	876
Asia total	7 900	13 785	19 242	14 860	17 340
Argentina	1 471	2 501	3 944	3 447	2 422
Brazil	2 098[a]	2 190	3 007	2 430	4 685
Chile	473	773	1 490	429	1 323
Colombia	118	314	954	935	1 253
Mexico	1 768	3 162	4 971	2 908	2 485
Peru	203	472	1 318	927	1 389
Latin America total	6 131	9 412	15 684	11 076	13 557
USSR	3 193	5 826	2 989	4 466	2 366
32 country total	86 655	150 068	175 122	119 133	142 917

a) 1901.
Source: Tables D-1, D-2 and D-3.

Table D-5. Exports at 1980 prices 1950-86

$ million

	1950	1973	1980	1986
Australia	4 626	16 965	22 031	28 864
Austria	1 017	10 843	17 489	23 436
Belgium	6 686	52 372	64 656	80 821
Canada	11 859	56 218	67 734	95 502
Denmark	2 627	12 227	16 982	21 397
Finland	2 083	10 328	14 148	16 412
France	13 702	84 712	116 030	129 953
Germany	9 657	142 717	192 861	248 805
Italy	4 126	52 817	77 673	97 858
Japan	2 609	70 438	130 441	182 617
Netherlands	6 282	59 893	73 940	89 470
Norway	2 999	11 681	18 542	23 549
Sweden	5 914	27 815	30 906	41 724
Switzerland	3 821	22 817	29 632	35 856
United Kingdom	35 059	84 807	110 155	136 589
United States	36 973	150 132	220 786	193 678
OECD total	149 340	866 782	1 204 006	1 446 531
Bangladesh	356	559	758	957
China	5 411	9 983	18 099	35 994
India	4 380	7 724	8 586	10 651
Indonesia	3 804	16 212	21 909	24 757
Pakistan	726	1 639	2 618	3 822
Philippines	821	3 071	5 741	6 487
South Korea	92	6 477	17 505	35 885
Taiwan	302	9 682	19 811	40 108
Thailand	1 158	3 109	6 505	9 992
Asia total	17 050	58 456	101 532	168 653
Argentina	2 649	5 327	8 021	9 304
Brazil	4 047	11 597	20 132	27 178
Chile	1 285	2 236	4 671	6 912
Colombia	1 309	3 094	3 945	6 628
Mexico	2 675	7 010	15 570	27 633
Peru	1 247	4 600	3 898	3 430
Latin America total	13 212	33 864	56 237	75 085
USSR	5 657	50 708	76 449	92 503
32 country total	185 259	1 009 810	1 438 224	1 782 772

Table D-6. **Ratio of merchandise exports to GDP at current market prices**

Percentages

	1900	1913	1929	1950	1973	1986
Australia	22.2	18.3	15.1	22.0	13.7	13.5
Austria	10.1	8.2	18.1	12.6	19.0	24.0
Belgium	38.0	50.9	39.9	20.3	49.9	61.4
Canada	18.3	15.1	18.1	17.5	20.9	24.8
Denmark	20.7	26.9	26.7	21.3	21.9	25.8
Finland	19.7	25.2	24.0	16.6	20.5	23.2
France	12.5	13.9	13.3	10.6	14.4	17.3
Germany	13.5	17.5	15.3	8.5	19.7	27.3
Italy	10.1	12.0	10.4	7.0	12.5	16.3
Japan	8.3	12.3	13.0	4.7	8.9	10.8
Netherlands	31.8	38.2	30.7	26.9	37.3	45.3
Norway	16.4	22.7	18.4	18.2	24.4	26.5
Sweden	17.4	20.8	18.8	17.8	23.5	28.6
Switzerland	30.5	31.4	19.4	20.0	23.2	27.7
United Kingdom	14.9	20.9	15.6	14.4	16.4	19.5
United States	7.5	6.1	5.0	3.6	8.0	5.2
OECD average	18.2	21.2	18.9	15.1	20.9	24.8
Bangladesh			(7.8)	(6.5)	6.2	5.6
China			4.0	3.0	4.3	12.1
India			7.8	6.5	3.9	4.3
Indonesia			29.0	7.7[a]	18.7	19.7
Pakistan			(7.8)	(6.5)	15.1	10.3
Philippines			n.a.	9.5	17.6	15.5
South Korea			19.0	2.3	24.4	35.4
Taiwan			36.0	8.6	41.1	55.7
Thailand			16.1	18.4	14.7	21.0
Asian average			15.9	7.7	16.2	20.0
Argentina			26.7	8.4	8.6	8.7
Brazil			12.6	8.9	7.8	8.3
Chile			30.0	15.2	11.9	25.1
Colombia			21.0	9.8	11.4	15.6
Mexico			12.4	10.9	4.1	12.5
Peru			30.0	15.9	11.0	9.9
Latin American average			22.1	11.5	9.1	13.4

a) 1951.
Source: Exports from Table D-1, GDP generally from sources cited for Tables B-1, B-2 and B-3, World Bank (1980) and *National Accounts of OECD Countries,* various issues.

Table D-7. **Average ratio of exports f.o.b. to imports c.i.f., 1900-86**

Averages of annual ratios in period stated

	1900-13	1913-38	1950-73	1974-82	1983-86
Bangladesh	—	—	158.5[a]	32.8	36.4
China	77.5	79.0	103.1	98.2	81.7
India	141.2	133.4	75.1	74.9	68.9
Indonesia	148.6	175.0	123.4	173.3	115.3
Pakistan	—	—	51.3[a]	50.7	52.8
Philippines	98.3	118.6	90.5	58.2	79.8
South Korea	44.6	85.1	23.1[b]	80.5	99.1
Taiwan	118.8	129.5	79.2	104.1	145.0
Thailand	151.6	134.4	78.5	74.7	76.3
Arithmetic average	111.5	122.1	87.0	83.0	83.9
Argentina	129.3	124.5	104.2	117.2	179.7
Brazil	144.3	127.0	99.0	80.2	158.5
Chile	125.4	160.2	113.8	90.6	113.7
Colombia	82.1	116.2	97.7	91.2	94.1
Mexico	131.8	131.6	72.1	74.6	193.3
Peru	134.9	179.7	103.5	102.0	122.1
Arithmetic average	124.6	139.9	98.4	92.6	143.6
Developing country average	117.6	130.3	91.5	86.9	107.8

a) 1950-70.
b) Excludes 1950 and 1951.
Sources: 1950 onwards from UN, *Yearbooks of International Trade Statistics,* and IMF, *International Financial Statistics,* except Bangladesh and Pakistan 1950-70 which are from Planning Commission, *Reports of the Advisory Panels for the Fourth Five Year Plan 1970-75,* Islamabad, July 1970, p. 143. Earlier years from B.R. Mitchell, *International Historical Statistics: Africa and Asia,* Macmillan, London, 1982, and B.R. Mitchell, *International Historical Statistics: The Americas and Australasia,* Macmillan, London, 1983, except as follow:

Argentina: C.F. Diaz Alejandro, *Essays on the Economic history of the Argentine Republic,* Yale, 1970, pp. 461, 475-6.

Brazil: *O Brasil em Numeros,* IBGE, Rio, 1960, p. 84.

China: From Hsia Liang-lin, *China's Foreign Trade Statistics 1864-1949,* Harvard, 1974, pp. 268-9 adjusted to a c.i.f./f.o.b. basis, and excluding reexports (pp. 22-4).

Mexico: *La Economia Mexicana en Cifras,* Nacional Financeira, Mexico, 1966, pp. 243-4. 1913-38 imports adjusted upwards by 47.4 per cent for undercounting of border trade. This is the average adjustment factor apparently applied by the Bank of Mexico in revaluing 1950-53 imports for this purpose. The previous figures for 1950-53 are in *50 Anos de Revolucion Mexicana en Cifras,* Nacional Financeira, Mexico, p. 140.

Thailand: J.C. Ingram, *Economic Change in Thailand 1850-1970,* Stanford, 1971, pp. 333-4 (including trade in precious metals).

Table D-8. Carrying capacity of world merchant shipping, 1800-1950

	Sail and barge	Steam or motor	Carrying capacity in terms of steam	Index of carrying power	Index of world trade
	Million tons			1913 = 100.0	
1800	4.0	0.0	1.00	2.3	2.8
1850	11.4	0.8	3.65	8.5	9.8
1900	6.5	22.4	24.03	56.2	59.1
1913	4.2	41.7	42.75	100.0	100.0
1950	0.0	84.6	84.60	197.9	159.0

Sources: First two columns 1800-50 from C. Day, *A History of Commerce*, New York, 1921. 1900-50, supplied by Lloyds Register of Shipping, London; 1913 is an interpolation of Lloyds figures for 1910 and 1920. The conversion coefficient of sail to steam tonnage (4 sail = 1 steam) is used by Day and allows for greater speed and regularity. There should be some upgrading for the impact of the Suez Canal on both sail and steam journeys after 1869. The canal cut the distance from London to Bombay by 41 per cent, to Madras 35 per cent, Calcutta 32 per cent, Singapore 29 per cent, and Hong Kong 26 per cent (see L.C.A. Knowles, *The Economic Development of the British Overseas Empire*, London, 1928. Similarly the opening of the Panama canal after 1900 increased carrying capacity. Volume of world exports is taken from Maddison (1962) for 1900-50 and for earlier years from Maddison (1982).

Table D-9. Exchange rates 1900-73
US cents per unit of national currency

	1900	1913	1938	1950	1973
China[a]	75.00	73.00	21.00		50.27
India	32.24	32.44	36.63	20.87	12.92
Indonesia	40.20	40.20	55.01	13.23	0.2410
South Korea	n.a.	50.66	28.50	2.00[b]	0.2511
Philippines	47.40	50.00	50.00	49.62	14.79
Taiwan	50.66	50.66	28.50	9.76	2.62
Thailand	29.05	37.43	44.05	4.48[b]	4.84
Argentina	98.29	98.29	32.60	6.25[b]	1.07
Brazil	19.26	32.36	5.84	5.44	0.0002
Chile	34.06	19.77	4.00	1.67	0.0009
Colombia	120.90	113.80	55.95	51.28	0.42
Mexico	48.50	48.12	22.15	11.56	8.00
Peru	48.66	47.70	22.42	6.69	2.58
USSR	51.51	51.51	18.87	25.00	135.00
France	19.30	19.30	2.88	0.2857	22.45[c]
Germany	23.82	23.82	40.16	23.81	37.42
Japan	50.66	50.66	28.50	0.2778	0.3687
United Kingdom	486.60	486.60	489.00	280.00	245.22
United States	100.00	100.00	100.00	100.00	100.00

a) China had several kinds of silver coinage. The Haekwan tael (the rate shown here) was the main unit of account in prewar years.
b) Free rate.
c) New francs = 100 old francs.
Sources: 1913-38 generally from US Federal Reserve System, *Banking and Monetary Statistics,* various issues. 1950 and 1973 generally from IMF, *International Monetary Statistics,* various issues. 1900 for countries outside the gold standard, China from Hsiao, *op. cit.* Thailand from Ingram, *op. cit.* Brazil from *Annuaire statistique du Brésil,* Rio, 1917, p. 243. Chile, 1900-13 from *Anuario Estadistico,* vol. VI, *Hacienda, Ano 1916,* Santiago, 1917, p. 5. Colombia implicit exchange rate derived from Mitchell, *op. cit.* Mexico from Maddison (1990). Peru from Thorp and Bertram, *op. cit.*

Table D-10. Total international reserves of OECD countries, 1950-87

$ billion end year position

	1950	1970	1973	1987
Australia	1.5	1.7	6.2	12.6
Austria	0.1	1.8	4.3	17.8
Belgium	0.8	2.8	8.1	26.0
Canada	1.8	4.7	7.3	16.3
Denmark	0.1	0.5	1.5	10.9
Finland	0.1	0.5	0.7	7.4
France	0.8	5.0	15.6	70.6
Germany	0.2	13.6	41.5	125.6
Italy	0.6	5.4	12.2	62.6
Japan	0.6	4.8	13.7	92.8
Netherlands	0.5	3.2	10.4	37.4
Norway	0.1	0.8	1.6	15.0
Sweden	0.3	0.8	2.9	11.1
Switzerland	1.6	5.1	14.3	67.5
United Kingdom	3.4	2.8	7.9	50.7
United States	24.3	14.5	33.7	164.5
Total	36.9	67.9	182.0	788.8

Source: IMF, *International Financial statistics.* The figures include SDRs and IMF positions as well as gold and foreign exchange. The IMF shows foreign currency reserves in SDRs, and gold in ounces. Both are converted to dollars here at end year rates. 1950 and 1970 gold holdings were valued at $35 an ounce, 1973 at $112.25 and 1987 at $486.24 respectively (London price).

Table D-11. **Capital flows from DAC countries to developing countries, 1950-87**

	Official development assistance	Other flows	Total flow	World export unit value index	Total flow in 1980 prices
	$ million	$ million	$ million		$ million
1950-55 average	1 953	1 547	3 500	23.7	14 768
1956	3 172	3 071	6 243	24.0	26 013
1957	3 632	4 005	7 637	24.3	31 428
1958	4 169	3 136	7 305	23.5	31 085
1959	4 058	3 099	7 157	23.4	30 585
1960	4 676	3 439	8 115	23.6	34 386
1961	5 244	4 005	9 249	23.7	39 025
1962	5 554	2 883	8 437	23.5	35 902
1963	5 752	2 820	8 572	23.9	35 866
1964	5 924	3 721	9 645	24.3	39 691
1965	6 489	3 831	10 320	24.6	41 951
1966	6 459	3 931	10 390	25.2	41 230
1967	6 358	5 083	11 441	25.3	45 221
1968	6 914	6 511	13 425	25.1	53 486
1969	6 889	6 890	13 779	25.9	53 201
1970	6 949	8 999	15 948	27.1	58 849
1971	7 551	9 849	17 400	28.6	60 839
1972	9 201	10 999	20 200	31.3	64 537
1973	9 097	13 303	22 400	38.5	58 182
1974	11 613	10 887	22 500	53.4	42 135
1975	13 846	30 964	44 810	58.2	76 993
1976	13 953	32 719	46 672	58.9	79 239
1977	15 733	36 126	51 859	64.1	80 903
1978	19 993	50 987	70 980	70.5	100 681
1979	22 820	52 581	75 401	83.5	90 301
1980	27 267	48 089	75 356	100.0	75 356
1981	25 540	65 850	91 390	99.0	92 313
1982	27 731	56 334	84 065	95.4	88 119
1983	27 590	42 610	70 200	90.4	77 655
1984	28 738	56 106	84 844	88.6	95 761
1985	29 429	15 734	45 163	87.2	51 792
1986	36 663	38 895	75 558	92.2	81 950
1987	42 531	28 443	61 097	98.4	62 090

Source: First column from *Twenty Five Years of Development Cooperation: A Review,* OECD, Paris 1985, p. 334, *The Flow of Financial Resources to Countries in Course of Economic Development 1956-1959,* OEEC, Paris, 1961, *Resources for the Developing World,* OECD, Paris, 1969, *Development Cooperation,* successive reports for 1972, 1982, 1986 and 1988, OECD Paris, 1972, 1982, 1987 and 1988. World export unit value index from IMF *International Financial Statistics.* The figures in the second column are intended to be as comprehensive as the first, but liberalisation of capital movements means that some types of short term capital are not fully recorded. Hence it is not possible to make a detailed reconciliation between capital flow and debt statistics.

WHERE TO OBTAIN OECD PUBLICATIONS
OÙ OBTENIR LES PUBLICATIONS DE L'OCDE

ARGENTINA – ARGENTINE
Carlos Hirsch S.R.L.,
Galería Guemes, Florida 165, 4° Piso,
1333 Buenos Aires
Tel. 30.7122, 331.1787 y 331.2391
Telegram.: Hirsch-Baires

AUSTRALIA – AUSTRALIE
D.A. Book (Aust.) Pty. Ltd.
11-13 Station Street (P.O. Box 163)
Mitcham, Vic. 3132   Tel. (03) 873 4411
Telex: AA37911 DA BOOK   Telefax: (03)873.5679

AUSTRIA – AUTRICHE
OECD Publications and Information Centre,
4 Simrockstrasse,
5300 Bonn (Germany)   Tel. (0228) 21.60.45
Telex: 8 86300 Bonn   Telefax: (0228)26.11.04
Gerold & Co., Graben 31, Wien 1   Tel. (1)533.50.14

BELGIUM – BELGIQUE
Jean de Lannoy, Avenue du Roi 202
B-1060 Bruxelles   Tel. (02) 538.51.69/538.08.41
Telex: 63220

CANADA
Renouf Publishing Company Ltd
1294 Algoma Road, Ottawa, Ont. K1B 3W8
Tel: (613) 741-4333
Telex: 053-4783   Telefax: (613)741.5439
Stores:
61 Sparks St., Ottawa, Ont. K1P 5R1
Tel: (613) 238-8985
211 rue Yonge St., Toronto, Ont. M5B 1M4
Tel: (416) 363-3171
Federal Publications Inc.,
165 University Avenue,
Toronto, ON M5H 3B9   Tel. (416)581-1552
Telefax: (416)581.1743
Les Publications Fédérales
1185 rue de l'Université
Montréal, PQ H3B 1R7   Tel.(514)954.1633
Les Éditions la Liberté Inc.,
3020 Chemin Sainte-Foy,
Sainte-Foy, P.Q. G1X 3V6,   Tel. (418)658-3763
Telefax: (418)658.3763

DENMARK – DANEMARK
Munksgaard Export and Subscription Service
35, Nørre Søgade, P.O. Box 2212148
DK-1016 København K   Tel. (45 1)12.85.70
Telex: 19431 MUNKS DK   Telefax: (45 1)12.93.87

FINLAND – FINLANDE
Akateeminen Kirjakauppa,
Keskuskatu 1, P.O. Box 128
00100 Helsinki   Tel. (358 0)12141
Telex: 125080   Telefax: (358 0)121.4441

FRANCE
OCDE/OECD
Mail Orders/Commandes par correspondance :
2, rue André-Pascal,
75775 Paris Cedex 16   Tel. (1) 45.24.82.00
Bookshop/Librairie : 33, rue Octave-Feuillet
75016 Paris
Tel. (1) 45.24.81.67 et/ou (1) 45.24.81.81
Telex: 620 160 OCDE   Telefax: (33-1)45.24.85.00
Librairie de l'Université,
12a, rue Nazareth,
13602 Aix-en-Provence   Tel. 42.26.18.08

GERMANY – ALLEMAGNE
OECD Publications and Information Centre,
4 Simrockstrasse,
5300 Bonn   Tel. (0228) 21.60.45
Telex: 8 86300 Bonn   Telefax: (0228)26.11.04

GREECE – GRÈCE
Librairie Kauffmann,
28, rue du Stade, 105 64 Athens   Tel. 322.21.60
Telex: 218187 LIKA Gr

HONG KONG
Government Information Services,
Publications (Sales) Office,
Information Services Department
No. 1, Battery Path, Central
Tel.(5)23.31.91   Telex: 802.61190

ICELAND – ISLANDE
Mál Mog Menning
Laugavegi 18, Pósthólf 392
121 Reykjavik   Tel. 15199/24240

INDIA – INDE
Oxford Book and Stationery Co.,
Scindia House,
New Delhi 110001   Tel. 331.5896/5308
Telex: 31 61990 AM IN   Telefax: (11) 332.5993
17 Park St., Calcutta 700016   Tel. 240832

INDONESIA – INDONÉSIE
Pdii-Lipi, P.O. Box 3065/JKT.
Jakarta   Tel. 583467
Telex: 73 45875

IRELAND – IRLANDE
TDC Publishers - Library Suppliers,
12 North Frederick Street,
Dublin 1   Tel. 744835-749677
Telex: 33530TDCP EI Telefax: 748416

ITALY – ITALIE
Libreria Commissionaria Sansoni,
Via Benedetto Fortini 120/10,
Casella Post. 552
50125 Firenze   Tel. (055)645415
Telex: 570466   Telefax: (39.55)641257
Via Bartolini 29, 20155 Milano   Tel. 365083
La diffusione delle pubblicazioni OCSE viene assicurata
dalle principali librerie ed anche da :
Editrice e Libreria Herder,
Piazza Montecitoro 120, 00186 Roma
Tel. 6794628   Telex: NATEL I 621427
Libreria Hœpli,
Via Hœpli 5, 20121 Milano   Tel. 865446
Telex:31.33.95   Telefax: (39.2)805.2886
Libreria Scientifica
Dott. Lucio de Biasio "Aeiou"
Via Meravigli 16, 20123 Milano   Tel. 807679
Telefax: 800175

JAPAN – JAPON
OECD Publications and Information Centre,
Landic Akasaka Building, 2-3-4 Akasaka,
Minato-ku, Tokyo 107   Tel. 586.2016
Telefax: (81.3) 584.7929

KOREA – CORÉE
Kyobo Book Centre Co. Ltd.
P.O.Box 1658, Kwang Hwa Moon
Seoul   Tel. (REP) 730.78.91
Telefax: 735.0030

MALAYSIA/SINGAPORE – MALAISIE/SINGAPOUR
University of Malaya Co-operative Bookshop Ltd.,
P.O. Box 1127, Jalan Pantai Baru 59100
Kuala Lumpur, Malaysia/Malaisie
Tel. 756.5000/756.5425   Telefax: 757.3661
Information Publications Pte Ltd
Pei-Fu Industrial Building,
24 New Industrial Road No. 02-06
Singapore/Singapour 1953   Tel. 283.1786/283.1798
Telefax: 284.8875

NETHERLANDS – PAYS-BAS
SDU Uitgeverij
Christoffel Plantijnstraat 2
Postbus 20014
2500 EA's-Gravenhage   Tel. (070)78.99.11
Voor bestellingen: Tel. (070)78.98.80
Telex: 32486 stdru   Telefax: (070)47.63.51

NEW ZEALAND – NOUVELLE-ZÉLANDE
Government Printing Office Bookshops:
Auckland: Retail Bookshop, 25 Rutland Street,
Mail Orders, 85 Beach Road
Private Bag C.P.O.
Hamilton: Retail: Ward Street,
Mail Orders, P.O. Box 857
Wellington: Retail, Mulgrave Street, (Head Office)
Telex: COVPRNT NZ 31370   Telefax: (04)734943
Cubacade World Trade Centre,
Mail Orders, Private Bag
Christchurch: Retail, 159 Hereford Street,
Mail Orders, Private Bag
Dunedin: Retail, Princes Street,
Mail Orders, P.O. Box 1104

NORWAY – NORVÈGE
Narvesen Info Center – NIC,
Bertrand Narvesens vei 2,
P.O.B. 6125 Etterstad, 0602 Oslo 6
Tel. (02)67.83.10/(02)68.40.20
Telex: 79668 NIC N   Telefax: (47 2)68.53.47

PAKISTAN
Mirza Book Agency
65 Shahrah Quaid-E-Azam, Lahore 3   Tel. 66839
Telegram: "Knowledge"

PORTUGAL
Livraria Portugal, Rua do Carmo 70-74,
1117 Lisboa Codex   Tel. 347.49.82/3/4/5

SINGAPORE/MALAYSIA – SINGAPOUR/MALAISIE
See "Malaysia/Singapore". Voir «Malaisie/Singapour»

SPAIN – ESPAGNE
Mundi-Prensa Libros, S.A.,
Castelló 37, Apartado 1223,
Madrid-28001   Tel. 431.33.99
Telex: 49370 MPLI   Telefax: 275.39.98
Libreria Bosch, Ronda Universidad 11,
Barcelona 7   Tel. 317.53.08/317.53.58

SWEDEN – SUÈDE
Fritzes Fackboksföretaget
Box 16356, S 103 27 STH,
Regeringsgatan 12,
DS Stockholm   Tel. (08)23.89.00
Telex: 12387   Telefax: (08)20.50.21
Subscription Agency/Abonnements:
Wennergren-Williams AB,
Box 30004, S104 25 Stockholm   Tel. (08)54.12.00
Telex: 19937   Telefax: (08)50.82.86

SWITZERLAND – SUISSE
OECD Publications and Information Centre,
4 Simrockstrasse,
5300 Bonn (Germany)   Tel. (0228) 21.60.45
Telex: 8 86300 Bonn   Telefax: (0228)26.11.04
Librairie Payot,
6 rue Grenus, 1211 Genève 11   Tel. (022)731.89.50
Telex: 28356
Maditec S.A.
Ch. des Palettes 4
1020 – Renens/Lausanne   Tel. (021)635.08.65
Telefax: (021)635.07.80
United Nations Bookshop/Librairie des Nations-Unies
Palais des Nations, 1211 – Geneva 10
Tel. (022)734.60.11 (ext. 48.72)
Telex: 289696 (Attn: Sales)   Telefax: (022)733.98.79

TAIWAN – FORMOSE
Good Faith Worldwide Int'l Co., Ltd.
9th floor, No. 118, Sec.2, Chung Hsiao E. Road
Taipei   Tel. 391.7396/391.7397
Telefax: 394.9176

THAILAND – THAILANDE
Suksit Siam Co., Ltd., 1715 Rama IV Rd.,
Samyam, Bangkok 5   Tel. 2511630

TURKEY – TURQUIE
Kültur Yayinlari Is-Türk Ltd. Sti.
Atatürk Bulvari No. 191/Kat. 21
Kavaklidere/Ankara   Tel. 25.07.60
Dolmabahce Cad. No. 29
Besiktas/Istanbul   Tel. 160.71.88
Telex: 43482B

UNITED KINGDOM – ROYAUME-UNI
H.M. Stationery Office   (01)873-8483
Postal orders only:
P.O.B. 276, London SW8 5DT
Telephone orders: (01) 873-9090, or
Personal callers:
49 High Holborn, London WC1V 6HB
Telex:297138   Telefax: 873.8463
Branches at: Belfast, Birmingham, Bristol, Edinburgh,
Manchester

UNITED STATES – ÉTATS-UNIS
OECD Publications and Information Centre,
2001 L Street, N.W., Suite 700,
Washington, D.C. 20036-4095   Tel. (202)785.6323
Telex:440245 WASHINGTON D.C.
Telefax: (202)785.0350

VENEZUELA
Libreria del Este,
Avda F. Miranda 52, Aptdo. 60337,
Edificio Galipan, Caracas 106
Tel. 951.1705/951.2307/951.1297
Telegram: Libreste Caracas

YUGOSLAVIA – YOUGOSLAVIE
Jugoslovenska Knjiga, Knez Mihajlova 2,
P.O.B. 36, Beograd   Tel. 621.992
Telex: 12466 jk bgd

Orders and inquiries from countries where Distributors
have not yet been appointed should be sent to: OECD,
Publications Service, 2, rue André-Pascal, 75775 PARIS
CEDEX 16.

Les commandes provenant de pays où l'OCDE n'a pas
encore désigné de distributeur devraient être adressées à :
OCDE, Service des Publications. 2, rue André-Pascal,
75775 PARIS CEDEX 16.

72547-6-1989

WITHDRAWN
FROM STOCK
QMUL LIBRARY

OECD PUBLICATIONS, 2,rue André-Pascal, 75775 PARIS CEDEX 16 - No.44869 1989
PRINTED IN FRANCE
(41 89 05 1) ISBN 92-64-13274-0

DEVELOPMENT CENTRE STUDIES

IN   RY

DEVELOPMENT CENTRE
OF THE ORGANISATION FOR ECONOMIC CO-OPERATION AND DEVELOPMENT

Pursuant to article 1 of the Convention signed in Paris on 14th December 1960, and which came into force on 30th September 1961, the Organisation for Economic Co-operation and Development (OECD) shall promote policies designed:

- to achieve the highest sustainable economic growth and employment and a rising standard of living in Member countries, while maintaining financial stability, and thus to contribute to the development of the world economy;
- to contribute to sound economic expansion in Member as well as non-member countries in the process of economic development; and
- to contribute to the expansion of world trade on a multilateral, non-discriminatory basis in accordance with international obligations.

The original Member countries of the OECD are Austria, Belgium, Canada, Denmark, France, the Federal Republic of Germany, Greece, Iceland, Ireland, Italy, Luxembourg, the Netherlands, Norway, Portugal, Spain, Sweden, Switzerland, Turkey, the United Kingdom and the United States. The following countries acceded subsequently through accession at the dates indicated hereafter: Japan (28th April 1964), Finland (28th January 1969), Australia (7th June 1971) and New Zealand (29th May 1973).

The Socialist Federal Republic of Yugoslavia takes part in some of the work of the OECD (agreement of 28th October 1961).

Publié en français sous le titre:

L'ÉCONOMIE MONDIALE
AU 20ᵉ SIÈCLE

*
* *

This study, designed to link all five topics of the Development Centre's 1987-89 research programme, was written while the author was a consultant to the Centre.

Also available

ONE WORLD OR SEVERAL? Edited by Louis Emmerij (1989)
(41 89 04 1) ISBN 92-64-13249-X   320 pages   £19.50   US$34.00   FF160.00   DM66.00

* * *

"Development Centre Studies"

FINANCIAL POLICIES AND DEVELOPMENT by Jacques J. Polak (1989)
(41 89 01 1) ISBN 92-64-13187-6   234 pages   £17.00   US$29.50   FF140.00   DM58.00

DEVELOPING COUNTRIES DEBT: THE BUDGETARY AND TRANSFER
PROBLEM by Helmut Reisen and Axel Van Trotsenburg (1988)
(41 88 01 1) ISBN 92-64-13053-5   196 pages   £14.00   US$26.40   FF120.00   DM52.00

RECYCLING JAPAN'S SURPLUSES FOR DEVELOPING COUNTRIES by
T. Ozawa (1989)
(41 88 05 1) ISBN 92-64-13177-9   114 pages   £11.00   US$19.00   FF90.00   DM37.00

TWO CRISES: LATIN AMERICA AND ASIA. 1929-38 AND 1973-83 by Angus
Maddison (1985)
(41 85 03 1) ISBN 92-64-12771-2   106 pages   £7.00   US$14.00   FF70.00   DM31.00

"Development Centre Seminars"

THE IMPACT OF DEVELOPMENT PROJECTS ON POVERTY. Seminar organised
jointly by the OECD Development Centre and the Inter-American Development Bank
(1989)
(41 88 07 1) ISBN 92-64-13162-0   100 pages   £9.00   US$16.50   FF75.00   DM33.00

DEVELOPMENT POLICIES AND THE CRISIS OF THE 1980s edited by Louis
Emmerij (1987)
(41 87 03 1) ISBN 92-64-12992-8   178 pages   £11.00   US$23.00   FF110.00   DM47.00

LATIN AMERICA, THE CARIBBEAN AND THE OECD. A Dialogue on
Economic Reality and Policy Options edited by Angus Maddison (1986)
(41 86 07 1) ISBN 92-64-12887-5   166 pages   £11.00   US$22.00   FF110.00   DM49.00

Prices charged at the OECD Bookshop.

*THE OECD CATALOGUE OF PUBLICATIONS and supplements will be sent free of charge
on request addressed either to OECD Publications Service,
2, rue André-Pascal, 75775 PARIS CEDEX 16, or to the OECD Distributor in your country.*